Catholic Germany from the Reformation to the Enlightenment

Catholic Germany from the Reformation to the Enlightenment

MARC R. FORSTER

First published 2007 by
PALGRAVE MACMILLAN
Houndmills, Basingstoke, Hampshire RG21 6XS and
175 Fifth Avenue, New York, N.Y. 10010
Companies and representatives throughout the world

PALGRAVE MACMILLAN is the global academic imprint of the Palgrave Macmillan division of St. Martin's Press, LLC and of Palgrave Macmillan Ltd. Macmillan® is a registered trademark in the United States, United Kingdom and other countries. Palgrave is a registered trademark in the European Union and other countries.

ISBN-13: 978–0–333–69837–2 hardback
ISBN-10: 0–333–69837–1 hardback
ISBN-13: 978–0–333–69838–9 paperback
ISBN-10: 0–333–69838–X paperback

This book is printed on paper suitable for recycling and made from fully managed and sustained forest sources. Logging, pulping and manufacturing processes are expected to conform to the environmental regulations of the country of origin.

A catalogue record for this book is available from the British Library.

A catalog record for this book is available from the Library of Congress.

10   9   8   7   6   5   4   3   2   1
16   15   14   13   12   11   10   09   08   07

Printed and bound in Great Britain by
Antony Rowe Ltd, Chippenham and Eastbourne

For Tina

Contents

Acknowledgments

Support for this project came from the National Endowment for the Humanities, the Guggenheim Foundation, and the R.F. Johnson Faculty Development Fund and the Dean of the Faculty Office at Connecticut College. The staffs of the Generallandesarchiv in Karlsruhe and the Hauptstaatsarchiv in Stuttgart continue to be generous with their time and expertise. The staff of the Connecticut College library, particularly the Interlibrary Loan office, has been wonderfully efficient in finding obscure books and articles.

Every book benefits from the comments, criticisms, and suggestions of colleagues. I would like to particularly thank Thomas A. Brady Jr., Jay Goodale, Benjamin J. Kaplan, David Martin Luebke, H.C. Erik Midelfort, Steven Ozment, James Printy, David Sabean, Laura A. Smoller, Peter Wallace, Wolfgang Zimmermann, and the anonymous readers at Palgrave Macmillan. My colleagues at Connecticut College have also provided important support, especially Geoffrey Atherton, Roger Brooks, David Canton, Leo Garafalo, Fred Paxton, Catherine McNicol Stock, Stuart Vyse, and Lisa Wilson. This book owes much to Anita Allen, Deborah Bensko, Gina Foster, and Nancy Lewandowski. My students have read and commented on many sections of this book over the last 5 years and have made it a better and more accessible book.

Special thanks go to my aunt and uncle, Gisela and Horst Cyriax, who keep both my German and my thinking in good order. Everything I write benefits immeasurably from the suggestions and editing of my parents, Elborg and Robert Forster. Thanks to Sara and Jenny Forster for (usually) listening patiently to their father's anecdotes about German peasants and Catholic religious practices.

This book is dedicated to Tina, who has supported, in many different ways, my study of German Catholicism since the 1980s. Far more importantly, she has been an indispensable part of my whole life for over 25 years.

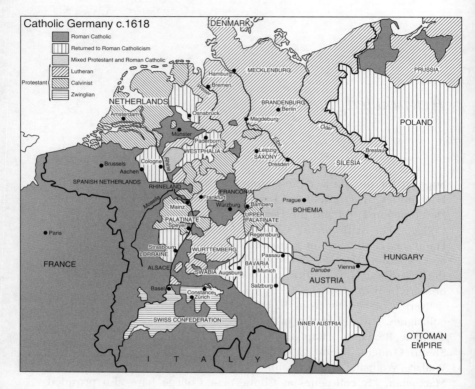

Catholic Germany c.1618

Roman Catholic
Returned to Roman Catholicism
Mixed Protestant and Roman Catholic
Lutheran
Protestant { Calvinist
Zwinglian

DENMARK

NETHERLANDS
Amsterdam
Hamburg
Bremen
MECKLENBURG
BRANDENBURG
Berlin
Magdeburg
PRUSSIA
POLAND
Osnabruck
Munster
Paderborn
WESTPHALIA
Leipzig
SAXONY
Dresden
Breslau
SILESIA
Brussels
Cologne
Aachen
SPANISH NETHERLANDS
RHINELAND
Frankfurt
FRANCONIA
Mainz
Wurzburg
Bamberg
Prague
BOHEMIA
Paris
PALATINATE
Speyer
UPPER
PALATINATE
Regensburg
FRANCE
Strasbourg
LORRAINE
ALSACE
WURTTEMBERG
SWABIA Augsburg
Passau
BAVARIA
Munich
Salzburg
Danube
Vienna
HUNGARY
AUSTRIA
Basel
Constance
Zurich
SWISS CONFEDERATION
INNER AUSTRIA
OTTOMAN
EMPIRE
I T A L Y

Adapted from Hajo Holborn, *A History of Modern Germany: vol. 1, The Reformation,* new edition (Princeton: Princeton University Press, 1982).

Introduction

This is a history of Catholicism in the German-speaking lands in the early modern period. Between the Protestant Reformation and the French Revolution, German Catholicism evolved in important, even dramatic, ways. Most significantly, Germans living in the portion of the Holy Roman Empire who did not become Protestant – about one-third of the population – developed a strong sense of Catholic identity by the seventeenth century. This confessionalization of Catholic Germans paralleled developments in Protestant regions and led to a hardening of religious divisions and the rise of distinct confessional cultures, each with its own lifestyle, traditions, beliefs, and practices.

This study focuses on religious developments, particularly the practices, beliefs, and religiosity of the population as a whole. To understand this religious culture, it is essential to analyze the developments and changes in the institutions and personnel of the Catholic Church in Germany. Thus, the history of German Catholicism is also – although not primarily – a history of the Catholic Church. It is also, in a sense, a history of Catholic Germany, for as confessional boundaries solidified, especially in the century after the Thirty Years' War, society, politics, and religion interacted in clearly defined Catholic regions of the Empire.

Catholic Germany was neglected in the traditional history of Germany in the early modern period, which focused on the rise of Protestant Prussia as the future unifying state of Germany. In the past 20 years, however, historians have developed an appreciation for the Holy Roman Empire, in which Catholic regions played an important, even central, role.[1] Although the Protestant Reformation weakened the ties between the Empire and the Catholic Church, the *Reich* retained some of its Catholic character until its dissolution. The Habsburgs, the leading Catholic princely dynasty of the Empire, were emperors and the rulers of several important Catholic territories. The Catholic ecclesiastical territories, along with the Imperial Cities and the Free Imperial Knights, were some of the strongest supporters of the unique political system of the Empire. A better understanding of the social and religious culture of Catholic Germany is vital for our understanding of the Empire as a whole.

German Catholicism is also somewhat of a poor stepchild in the history of European Catholicism. The fact that Germany is the land of Luther and the homeland of Protestantism has caused many mainstream historians to overlook the presence of Catholics in Germany. German Catholic Church historians certainly researched the history of German Catholicism, but, unlike the work of (mostly Protestant) Reformation scholars, their studies have had a limited reception among English-speaking historians.[2] General studies of European Catholicism, such as the influential works of Jean Delumeau and John Bossy, generally pass over German developments, focusing on Spain, France, and Italy.[3] However, conditions in Germany offer useful comparative and conceptual frameworks for students of early modern Catholicism, for example, in understanding the importance of confessional frontiers, or examining the development of Baroque religiosity as the interplay of tradition and innovation in Catholic practice.

This study will examine developments in the German-speaking Catholic territories of the Holy Roman Empire, ranging from Westphalia in the north to Lake Constance in the south and from the Rhineland in the west to Austria in the east.[4] It is informed by a wide variety of local and regional studies, with a slight bias in favor of the territories in the Rhineland and southwestern Germany. The more detailed discussion of these regions is partly the result of my own scholarly expertise and is also a consequence of the importance of this part of Germany for the creation of Catholic religiosity in the early modern period.

The focus here is on the institutions of the German Catholic Church and on the religious culture of the wider population, and as a result, some important aspects of Catholic culture cannot be discussed in detail. These areas include literature, artistic fields, and philosophical developments. Furthermore although I have tried to integrate the history of German Catholicism into the wider histories of Germany and European Catholicism, I have not delved into detailed comparisons of religious and cultural developments across confessional lines. This is perhaps unfortunate, since, as historians of the Enlightenment in particular have begun to show, influences flowed back and forth between Protestant and Catholic Germany, despite the hardening of confessional boundaries. Obviously, no study can, or should, attempt to be a total history of a region or culture, and I have attempted to restrict myself to the religious and institutional developments within German Catholicism.

The Development of Catholic Identity – Chronology

In 1500, almost all Germans were undifferentiated Christians. By 1700, an "invisible boundary" between the confessions – Lutheran, Reformed, and Catholic – divided Germans and Germany.[5] Each confession developed its own confessional culture, based not only on theological positions and ecclesiastical institutions but also on traditions of popular piety and religious practice. The development of Catholic confessional identity is the central theme of this book.

There are a number of ways to examine the development of confessional identity between 1500 and 1800. Looking at this "confessionalization" chronologically, one can identify important turning points and several stages in the process. Obviously, German Catholics were forced to react to the Protestant Reformation, and Catholic leaders and theologians began to articulate what was distinctive about Catholicism in the first half of the sixteenth century. This effort was tentative and characterized by a rather unoriginal defense of traditional religious practice, theology, and institutions. It was the survival of Catholic institutions, particularly the ecclesiastical principalities, through the Reformation era that was probably the most important for the later development of German Catholicism. These structures gave Catholicism a diverse set of institutions to build on, institutions that were socially and politically imbedded in the Empire and at the regional and local levels.

The Council of Trent gave further impetus to the development of Catholic identity in the period between the 1560s and 1620s. The decrees of the Council received a lukewarm reception among many Germans, but the work of the Jesuits, papal nuncios, and a new generation of priests, many trained in Rome, remade Catholicism in important ways. Of great importance was the transformation of the clergy, which became (almost) uniformly celibate, increasingly well educated, and much more tied into trends in international Catholicism. Some clergymen of this kind became bishops, abbots, and high episcopal officials, where they sought to move beyond reform of the clergy and bring about a top-down transformation of popular religion, aiming to make popular practice more austere, disciplined, and regular. Tridentine reform along these lines was difficult to implement and moved very slowly and was always limited and channeled by local conditions.

The Thirty Years' War (1618–1648) was another important turning point. Some German Catholic leaders hoped for a restoration of pre-Reformation institutions and a conversion of significant Protestant regions to Catholicism in the aftermath of Catholic victories in the 1620s, which culminated in the Edict of Restitution (1629). As the war dragged on through the 1630s and 1640s, however, much of the Catholic elite came to reject the militant position, which was often linked to the work of the Jesuits and, by implication at least, to the more aggressive among the Tridentine reformers. Meanwhile, the social and demographic crisis precipitated by the war led to an outburst of religious fervor characterized not only by an enthusiasm for pilgrimage and processional piety but also, more darkly, by widespread witch-hunting. The foundations of a politically less confrontational Catholicism and of the dynamic popular religiosity that became Baroque Catholicism can both be found in these last decades of the war.

Between 1650 and the middle of the eighteenth century, German Catholics of all social classes participated in creating and sustaining Baroque Catholicism. This was a religious synthesis that incorporated the high culture of Baroque literature and architecture and the more popular aspects of a highly developed and diverse religious practice. Baroque Catholicism was a religion of pilgrimages and processions, confraternities and rural missions, frequent services, and a dense liturgical year. It was a dynamic synthesis, with a constantly shifting mix of devotional practices, and it was often highly regional and even local in its practice and institutions. This religious localism fit well with the particularism of the Holy Roman Empire, although there were always important groups such as the Jesuits and the Capuchins that linked German Catholics to broader developments within Catholicism.

The presentation of Baroque Catholicism, its characteristics and the institutions – the Imperial Church, monasteries and convents, the new orders – that supported it, is the centerpiece of this book. This synthesis started to come apart in the middle of the eighteenth century. The Enlightenment, even in its moderate German Catholic incarnation, criticized many of the popular religious practices that were so important in Baroque Catholicism, particularly pilgrimages, processions, and confraternities. Furthermore, the enlightened attack on the Jesuits and the monasteries undermined institutions that supported the great variety of Catholic devotions. The move to (once again) "reform" Catholicism, most famously exemplified by the Josephine reforms in Austria, also reflected a move away from traditional religious practices among elements of the Catholic elite, particular among middle-class men in cities and in the growing state bureaucracies. These various interrelated secularizing tendencies led to the closing of monasteries and convents in Austria and other states, the elimination of many church holidays and saints' days in the last decades of the 1700s, and, finally, the secularization of the ecclesiastical principalities in the Napoleonic period. The Baroque Catholicism that had dominated Catholic Germany for a century or more was gone, though many of its practices and much of its culture remained alive and vibrant in the countryside and experienced yet another revival starting in the 1820s and 1830s.

Confessionalization and Reform from Above

Historians have often felt most comfortable conceptualizing the development of confessional identity from a top-down perspective. This is the focus of much of the scholarship organized around the "confessionalization thesis," most often associated with Heinz Schilling and Wolfgang Reinhard.[6] The confessionalization thesis emphasizes the parallel programs of Protestant and Catholic leaders, found in both church and state institutions, to enforce religious unity. Princes and officials considered religious conformity essential for political unity, and church leaders turned to secular officials in order to effectively fight heresy and heterodox practices, and for support in disciplining disobedient clergymen. Historians of confessionalization also highlight efforts of the ruling elite to promote and enforce greater social discipline among the population, emphasizing restrictions on sexuality, "magical" practices, and forms of popular sociability and religious culture. Confessionalization in this formulation led to the internalization of religious identity by most people, while also pushing German Catholics (as well as Protestants) into the modern world.

Confessionalization is a modern concept and a modern word. When sixteenth- and seventeenth-century Catholic leaders spoke about the program they were involved in, they spoke about reform, *Reformatio*. The Catholic Church had regularly experienced waves of reform, but the reform inspired by the Council of Trent (1545–1563) was particularly powerful and provided many clergymen and devout princes with a blueprint for religious policy into the eighteenth century. Tridentine reformers operated from a traditional, hierarchical perspective, believing that an improvement in the moral behavior and educational level of the clergy would lead inevitably to a wider reform of the laity. Reformers had considerable faith in bureaucratic methods, for example resorting to the extensive use of visitations, new clerical councils, and parish registers. The Jesuits, certainly the most effective and consistent Tridentine reformers in Germany, also believed in creating an elite of devout laypeople, who, through their personal example, would help create a better world.

Reform from above evolved over the course of the early modern period. Reformers, for example, focused on reforming the clergy before the Thirty Years' War, then turned to direct missionary work among the rural population in the later seventeenth century. Tridentine reform was also a worldwide movement, actively supported by the Papacy. The influence of the Jesuits, the important role of papal nuncios, often Italian cardinals based in German cities such as Cologne, Vienna, and Graz, and the education of German priests in the *Collegium Germanicum* in Rome demonstrate some of the ways in which reform in German Catholicism was imbedded in international developments.

Reform ordinances, visitation reports, administrative records, judicial proceedings, council minutes, sermons, and devotional literature – the sources historians of early modern religion most frequently use – tend to lead scholars to overestimate the programs of the ruling classes. Confessionalization and Tridentine reform were, in a sense, doomed to failure, for their goals were unrealistically ambitious. Recent studies have examined the reception of these reforms and have shown that they achieved ambiguous results. Catholic Germany was not really fruitful ground for many reform projects. Cathedral chapters, collegiate chapters, exempt monasteries, military orders, and other institutions resisted Tridentine reforms aimed at centralizing Church administration under papal and episcopal leadership. At the local level, town councils and rural communal structures supported reforms selectively and the traditional benefice system placed financial constraints on many changes. There were only a couple of well-administered Catholic states – Bavaria and Austria – where close cooperation between church and state authorities could affect significant reforms and most German Catholics lived in lightly administered ecclesiastical principalities in western and southern Germany.

Resistance, Negotiation, Accommodation

Catholic identity nevertheless owed much to the programs coming from the Church and the Catholic elite. But the strength of Catholic identity also depended on the willing participation of the wider population in the practices of Baroque Catholicism. People did not go on pilgrimages and processions, join confraternities, or participate in frequent services because they were told to do so by their priest but because these practices had important functions in their lives and because they had often organized them through communal structures.

People actively resisted many reforms, for example efforts to abolish traditional practices like the blessings of fields and livestock. Disciplinary measures, such as the criminalization of premarital sexual activity, were very difficult to implement in the face of massive passive resistance. Despite repeated ordinances, sermons from the pulpit, and direct intervention by local officials, Catholic peasants continued to put on dances on Sunday afternoons throughout the early modern period.

Catholic religious practice developed most often out of a process of negotiation between Church authorities and the people in the parishes, with parish priests often serving as intermediaries. Thus, rural people depended on sacramentals – blessed candles, holy water, and other objects – for rituals aimed at protecting the fertility of fields and livestock, but the Church insisted that priests control their use within carefully proscribed bounds. The Catholic Church supported and encouraged pilgrimage piety and the cult of the saints but, by the late seventeenth century, often found itself attempting to limit the number of shrines credited by the people with miraculous powers. There was an ongoing negotiation around the nature of confraternities, understood as tools for increasing devotion by the Church, but often used to circumvent parochial obligations by city dwellers in particular. Even the role of the parish priest required constant negotiation. There was a certain clericalization of Catholicism, as a celibate priesthood became a marker of Catholic identity and as people came to accept the indispensable role of the priest in most Catholic rituals, particularly the sacraments. At the same time, parishioners never conceded to the priest's unlimited authority in the parish and managed much of parish life themselves.

Despite its hierarchical structure and the strengthening of episcopal authority promulgated by the Council of Trent, town councils and rural communes maintained communal control over much of local religious life. This communalism had especially deep roots in western and southern Germany, but was important across Germany. Communal leaders interfered in the hiring and firing of priests, participated in the management of parish finances, and frequently took the lead in organizing local devotional life. Communalism was one aspect of the tendency for the Catholic Church to accommodate popular demands in a many areas. Disciplinary measures were often limited in Catholic regions, compared to what happened in neighboring Protestant regions, as was the attack on popular magic. The inclination of the Catholic leadership to accommodate popular needs reflects a respect for long-standing practices and a desire to gain the high ground of tradition against the Protestant competition.

The German Church and Baroque Catholicism

Catholic identity, then, was primarily the result of a loyalty to the practices and beliefs of Baroque Catholicism. For most people, it was a religious and cultural identity, not the political-confessional loyalty that captured the Catholic elite in the early seventeenth century, only to fade after 1648. The central chapters of this book, Chapters 4 and 5, explain the nature of Baroque Catholicism. This means outlining not only the characteristic religious practices but also the institutions that provided the context in which Baroque Catholicism evolved.

The Imperial Church, the *Reichskirche*, was one of the peculiar institutions of the Holy Roman Empire. Historians have often employed the term quite loosely, but it most usefully designates the Catholic institutions, especially the prince-bishoprics, the military orders, and the collegiate chapters, where clergymen exercised a mix of secular and ecclesiastical authority. At the heart of the Imperial Church were the cathedral chapters, where noblemen elected their peers to episcopal sees and made them princes of the Empire. The Imperial Church was always a place for the sons and daughters of noble families to pursue a political career and live a lifestyle appropriate to their rank; it was only occasionally a place for an aristocrat with a religious calling.

Other institutions of the German Church, particularly the large and sometimes very wealthy Benedictine and Cistercian monastic houses, had some of the characteristics of the noble chapters. But most monks and nuns were from middle class, not noble families, with a considerable sprinkling of sons of propertied peasant families by the eighteenth century. Abbots and abbesses often exercised secular authority, especially in the fragmented regions of western and southern Germany, and were always managers of large estates. The houses of the mendicant orders, particularly the large number of convents, were less powerful and wealthy but were omnipresent and influential in cities and towns.

These institutions played an important role in local Catholicism as patrons of rural parishes, builders of churches, supporters of local shrines, and as preachers and pastors in the parishes. Mendicants, espe-cially the Capuchins, often served important pastoral functions in urban and rural parishes, as did the Jesuits in the bigger cities such as Munich, Vienna, and Cologne. Monks frequently served as parish priests after the Thirty Years' War, bringing the devotional traditions of their orders to the wider population. Particularly after 1650, monasteries, collegiate chap-ters, military orders, and sometimes even convents became centers of local or regional devotions.

All these institutions had exemptions and privileges, which they used to limit the authority of episcopal authorities. This meant of course that they tenaciously fought bishops' efforts to inspect monastic houses and col-legiate chapters and discipline monks and canons. Powerful monasteries, like the Cistercians at Salem on Lake Constance or the Benedictines of St Blasien in the Black Forest, also hindered efforts of bishops to oversee conditions in the parishes under their control, creating a sort of mini-bishopric in the region around each monastery. This defense of privilege and exemption was most pronounced and most effective when exercised by the cathedral chapters, where the sons of noble families could draw on family connections to supplement the extensive traditional rights of these institutions.

The Imperial Church and the other institutions of the German Church had the effect of restraining, sometimes to the point of gridlock, the ability of nuncios, reform-minded bishops, and the Jesuits to affect exten-sive changes in the structures of German Catholicism. Thus, it was very difficult to adjust the benefice system, based as it was on the incorporation of many parishes into monasteries, convents, and chapters, to support a more active pastorate. Restraints on episcopal judicial authority made it difficult to discipline disobedient or even incompetent priests, not to mention corrupt monks or nuns. Less concretely, but of great important to the culture of German Catholicism, the variety of institutions contrib-uted to the localism of Catholicism. Monasteries dominated the sacral landscape in southern Germany, building new monastic complexes in high Baroque style. Cathedral chapters defended not just their rights and privileges but also the liturgical traditions of their region and expressed an almost reflexive resistance to signs of Roman centralization.

The institutions of the German Church provided a context conducive to the development of a diverse, dynamic, and localized Baroque Catholicism. This religious synthesis developed out of a number of ten-sions within Catholicism, all of which were part of the history of western Christianity. One was a tension between communal and individual practices. If the popularity of pilgrimage and processions seems to indicate a widespread preference for communal practices, the growth in frequent confession and communion shows a trend toward individual piety. In fact, both modes coexisted, without great conflict, at pilgrimage shrines, which welcomed both communal processions and individual pilgrims. The Jesuits themselves certainly promoted an active, intense individual piety among literate townspeople and also organized rural missions that had the character of a mass religious revival. The Catholic Church's willingness to accommodate the communal religion of much of the population, while maintaining its effort to individualize religious practice, served it well.

There was also a tension between the tendency to constantly elaborate and diversify religious practice and the institutional penchant to organize and regulate. In a sense, this tension was typical of the period and Baroque culture more generally, which sought to systematize while celebrating the variety and diversity of human experience. Within German Catholicism, this tension expressed itself at the local level through the creation of new shrines, the organization of new processions, and the funding and practice of new devotions. The popular demand for more church services, more masses, more sermons, and more prayer meetings certainly indicates the strength of Catholic identity, but for some priests and episcopal officials, it also seemed to be a sign of a disorganized or overly diffuse piety, if not outright pagan superstition.

Both the mundane practices of daily and weekly services and the more extraordinary experiences of pilgrimage and the great feasts of the liturgical year became more elaborate in the century after 1650. Yet there was also a tension here, as the extraordinary could, and often did, overwhelm the more routine aspects of religious life. Baroque Catholicism, despite its tendency to highlight the dramatic, never chose between the two extremes. Indeed, the construction of highly dramatic Baroque and Rococo churches and chapels demonstrates an effort to contain the extraordinary within the everyday. It appears that people from all social classes experienced their religion as both routine and extraordinary, and this combination became a characteristic of Catholic culture that distinguished it from Lutheran Protestantism, which after 1650 seemed imbedded in a routine orthodoxy.

German Catholicism was conditioned by the institutional, political, and constitutional context of the Holy Roman Empire. It was profoundly affected by the existence of Protestantism and by the religious conflicts caused by the coexistence of multiple confessions within Germany. But

Catholic identity developed out of the religious experience of the population as much as it did out of these structural factors. To understand German Catholicism, it is essential to understand the characteristics of this experience, of Baroque Catholicism as a diverse religious synthesis that met the needs and aspirations of a wide portion of the population.

Chapter 1: Catholic Germany before Trent

The Protestant Reformation was obviously the most important develop-ment in the religious history of Germany in the sixteenth century. Historians of all sympathies have, in retrospect, recognized the centrality of Martin Luther's movement; secular rulers, the hierarchy of the Catholic Church, even town and village leaders, knew it at the time. For a time, especially in the tumultuous decade after Luther posted his 95 Theses on the church door in Wittenberg, it looked as if the evangelical movement would sweep all before it. Ultimately, however, Catholicism in Germany survived the Protestant onslaught and remained an important force in German culture and history.

The story of German Catholicism in the first half of the sixteenth century is, then, primarily a story of crisis. At times, in fact, it appeared that Catholicism as a set of practices and beliefs sanctioned and supported by the institutions and personnel of the Roman Catholic Church would not endure in Germany. Some leaders of Catholic institutions, including bishops, abbots, and abbesses and many individual monks, nuns, and parish priests, sympathized with or converted to the Protestant cause. The defection of large portions of the clergy left the Catholic leaders with little ability to resist either the theological challenges of Protestantism or the steady conversion of German princes and nobles to the new religion. By mid-century, Protestantism was well established in about two-thirds of the German-speaking lands, and even in nominally Catholic territories, an understaffed Catholic Church coexisted with both Protestant sympathizing believers and religiously indifferent Catholics.

Yet this story of crisis was also a story of survival. For sixteenth-century German Catholicism had many underestimated strengths, including the way its institutions were imbedded in the structure of the Holy Roman Empire, its links to powerful ruling families such as the Habsburgs and the

Wittelsbachs, and the deep traditions of popular piety in many (mostly rural) communities. An analysis of these strengths means evaluating the character of pre-Reformation Christianity in Germany, searching for the origins of Catholic resilience, as well as looking for the difficulties that led to the rise of Protestantism.

Although it is the contention of this book that German Catholicism had many particular characteristics that require that it be understood on its own, it should not be forgotten that German Catholics were part of the wider world of Roman Catholicism. Germans had a healthy skepticism about the Papacy, and one of the early appeals of Protestantism was its strong anti-Roman and anti-Italian tone with its call to Germans to throw of the financial and juridical tyranny of the papacy.[1] In the long run, however, institutional and cultural ties with other Catholics, and especially with Rome, were also a source of strength for German Catholicism. The resources and personnel of the Church, most dramatically in the persons of the Jesuits, played an important role in the survival and eventual revival of Catholicism in sixteenth-century Germany.

A final strength of German Catholicism was its diversity. Far from monolithic, medieval Christianity in Germany, as elsewhere in Europe, had developed in many different ways.[2] This diversity was part of the "imbeddedness" of Catholicism, especially in the long-settled regions of western and southern Germany. Here centuries of Christian evolution could be read in the landscape itself, in the churches, shrines, pilgrimage routes, and holy sites frequented by believers.[3] The diversity of the late medieval religious experience, as evidenced for example by the wide range of liturgical practices, also meant that Protestant attacks were not equally effective everywhere in Germany. What could be persuasively identified in one place as a liturgical abuse might not exist in another place, or might in a third place be considered a time-honored and popular local practice. Although this religious diversity helped Catholicism survive, it would also come to distress Catholic reformers as much as it did Protestants and pre-Reformation Church reformers.

On the Eve of the Reformation

Distinctive institutions, an ongoing movement for church reform, and an intense and diverse popular religious life all characterized German Catholicism on the eve of the Reformation.[4] Each of these aspects remained important in post-Reformation and post-Tridentine Catholicism.

The most significant institutional characteristic of German Catholicism was the secular role played by all bishops and many monastic institutions. Germany was the home of a number of distinctive Catholic institutions. The *Hochstift*, or prince-bishopric, was found across Germany and set the tone for the whole Imperial Church (*Reichskirche*). The *Hochstifte* varied in size and importance, but all were governed by aristocratic bishops elected by equally aristocratic cathedral chapters.[5] It is perhaps a cliché to say that almost every sixteenth-century bishop paid more attention to his duty as a secular prince than his position as spiritual leader of a diocese. Yet by all measures, the cliché is true. Few bishops were consecrated as priests, they tended to maintain appropriately princely or aristocratic courts, many lived with women and fathered children, and, when necessary, some resigned to marry and carry on the family name. Bishops could be efficient and dedicated princes, but they generally left the ecclesiastical administration of their dioceses to middle-class suffragan bishops and other officials.

The whole range of monastic institutions – great Benedictine and Cistercian abbeys for men and women, mendicant houses, collegiate chapters – could be found in Germany, along with other, more peculiar institutions, such as the commanderies of the military orders of Teutonic Knights and Knights of St John.[6] Many monastic institutions possessed secular lordships and extensive ecclesiastical privileges, most gained over the course of the Middle Ages from weak and financially strapped Emperors. Together with the prince-bishoprics, these institutions constituted the Imperial Church, and, like the bishops, their leaders feared secularization at the hands of the princes. Church leaders understood that these institutions could only survive in the particular incubator of the Empire. Loyalty to the Empire meant support for the imperial reform movement of the 1490s, close ties with the imperial knights and other smaller imperial estates, and growing ties to the Habsburgs. These traditions would remain important until the end of the Old Empire in 1806.

A shared loyalty to the Empire did not mean unity. Conflicts between bishops and other Church institutions, particularly the monasteries, were endemic. Long legal and political battles raged over monastic privileges, episcopal legal jurisdiction, patronage of rural parishes, and, of course, financial issues. On the surface, the German Church looked liked a ubiquitous and very powerful institution. In practice, however, it was fragmented and divided, incapable of any unified action at the national level and usually quite divided at the local level as well.

Princes, town councils, and village communities were as intensely involved in religious life as were the institutions of the Catholic Church. Princes saw it as their sacred duty to ensure the salvation of their subjects; they and their officials also sought to reduce ecclesiastical jurisdiction, gain control of church property, and control appointments to clerical positions.[7] The Dukes of Bavaria, despite a reputation for loyalty to the Church and the Pope, began in the fifteenth century a determined campaign to create just such a state church in their lands.[8] Similar developments can be found across Germany, well before the Protestant Reformation accelerated the process.

Town councils also felt it was their duty to promote the spiritual well-being of the community, while seeking to expand their authority at the same time.[9] Councils in imperial cities were particularly successful in gaining control of the local church. In the early decades of the sixteenth century, the city council of Nuremberg exercised oversight over the property and even the internal discipline of the city's eight monasteries and convents and controlled most ecclesiastical appointments in the city.[10] At Strasbourg, an episcopal see, the city council faced a larger and more self-assured clerical establishment, with five collegiate chapters, nine monasteries, eight convents, and nine parishes. Yet even here, the council increased its control of the local church in the decades around 1500, gaining control of the hospital, and the right to appoint many of the parish priests.[11] Despite these tendencies, however, the clergy in Strasbourg and most other cities maintained legal and financial privileges – tax immunities, the right to sell wine and beer, and exemption from military duties – that brought them into regular conflict with their neighbors.

Village communities shared this desire to control as many local religious institutions as possible. Peter Blickle and his students, in a series of influential books and articles, have demonstrated the existence of a strong "communal church" in pre-Reformation Germany.[12] Focusing on southwest Germany and Switzerland, Blickle demonstrates that villagers, led by communal officials, sought to control appointments of parish priests, demanded the right to depose priests, and frequently refused to give the tithe to priests who were not fulfilling their pastoral duties.[13] Rosi Fuhrmann's study of southwest Germany shows how communes achieved considerable control over religious life by investing their own resources in new religious foundations, mostly endowments for chaplains, altars, and additional masses. The communes then controlled these resources, hired priests for the positions or to fulfill the particular duties that came with the endowment.[14] This research emphasizes the ecclesio-political role that communes acquired, that is their ability to gain legal control over resources and appointments.

Fuhrmann, however, recognizes that villagers had a further motivation, "to create their own access to transcendence."[15] Villagers, like towns-people, wanted to control and discipline the clergy, but they also organized pilgrimages and processions, endowed masses and positions for preachers, and founded confraternities.[16] Their efforts were aimed in the first place at providing more religious activities beyond those provided in the parish. Furthermore, peasants and townspeople also sought to gain access to religious power, be it in services, at shrines, or through prayer, incantation or otherwise, without necessarily involving a clergyman.

The communal church has been most clearly identified in Switzerland and southwest Germany. There were strong communal elements in other parts of Germany as well, for example, in Westphalia.[17] Here, some parishes were strongly controlled by communes, while neighboring parishes were classic examples of the noble proprietary church, where noble families determined clerical appointments and used and exploited parish property with little or no interference from episcopal officials. In fact, the communal church (in cities and towns) and the aristocratic proprietary church were not contradictory concepts, but rather complementary aspects of two key characteristics of late medieval religion: religious life was profoundly local and it was primarily organized by the laity.

The Reform Movement

The movement to reform the Catholic Church began before Luther's arrival on the scene, in Germany as elsewhere in Europe.[18] The most vocal reformers were the humanists, led by Erasmus and his followers, such as Johannes Reuchlin and Ulrich von Hutten. The humanists pressed for a more personal devotion and a return to the virtues of early Christianity and criticized both the "superstitions" of popular religion and the Church's willingness to exploit them financially. The humanists also specialized in savage attacks on the failings of the clergy, particularly monks. These attacks focused on the three basic "abuses": absenteeism, pluralism, and concubinage. The first two were real problems at all levels of the clergy, while the last was of particular concern to the educated elite, who saw it as a marker of the hypocrisy of the clergy.

Reform movements could be found in all the major Catholic monastic orders. In Germany, by the 1520s, over 90 Benedictine houses were affiliated with the Bursfelder Congregation, a movement to enforce a stricter observance of monastic rules. Several different types of "Augustinian eremites of strict observance" could be found in Germany, including at the Augustinian house in Wittenberg where Martin Luther was a monk. Observant Franciscans took over many houses in German cities as well. This widespread effort to return to the original spirit and rules of each order had great appeal and remained an important tradition within German Catholicism. Not surprisingly, resistance within orders, financial difficulties, and opposition from bishops all limited its impact.

The Carthusians of Cologne provide a telling example of the place of observant monasticism in the German Church.[19] The Carthusians always claimed that their order did not need reform because it had never been corrupted. The Cologne Carthusians were influential within the city of Cologne, where they had ties with many important families, with local humanists, and with the humanists' archenemies in the theological faculty at the university. The Cologne Carthusians promoted observant movements within the order and published books promoting the mystical traditions that were so important within the house and in the lower Rhine and Flemish regions. Yet these writings, in Latin, reached only a small audience. Finally, the very conditions that gave the Carthusians great prestige – the strict rules of the order, which emphasized silence, a rigorous liturgical practice, and strict moral discipline – also meant that the small community of monks had little public presence in the city. The Cologne Carthusians are evidence of the strong Catholicism in Cologne, but in the decades around 1500, they could do little to reform the Church generally.

The aristocratic bishops and cathedral canons rarely supported reform measures. The reforming goal of making bishops "apostolic directors of renewal" did not fit well with the duties and background of the German episcopate.[20] The secular powers of the bishops and the nature of the imperial church as a *Versorgungsinstitut* for noblemen, that is a place where noblemen and women could live a lifestyle appropriate to their rank, tended to make pluralism and absenteeism common among German bishops and canons.[21] German bishops were often well educated, usually in law, and they were frequently diligent secular rulers. Few, however, were active in the pastoral aspects of their position.[22] Finally the structure of German dioceses, where monastic institutions were usually quite independent of episcopal authority and where cathedral chapters had considerable power to block a bishop's policies, undermined the efforts of reformist bishops.

Church reformers were correct when they complained that the secular clergy of the early sixteenth century was poorly educated and that absenteeism and pluralism were endemic. Despite the mocking attacks of the humanists, the inadequacies of the secular clergy were not simply or primarily the consequence of priests' laziness, greed, or lax morality. The structure of the benefice system explains many of the problems. Benefices were a form of property, funded by tithes paid by parishioners and property owned by the parish. In theory, benefices were supposed to support the priests who provided the basic pastoral services, particularly the sacraments. In practice, the situation was often quite different.

By the early sixteenth century, many benefices in Germany were incorporated parishes. This meant that monasteries, collegiate chapters, hospitals, universities, and other ecclesiastical institutions controlled benefices and received their income.[23] These institutions then hired a priest to fulfill the duties of a pastor, paying him a portion of the parish income. Needless to say, this system siphoned money away from parishes for the benefit of often distant institutions. The University of Freiburg, for example, held incorporated parishes scattered across the Austrian territories of southwest Germany and the University of Ingolstadt received new incorporated parishes in the years around 1500.[24] The holders of incorporated parishes often paid the vicars badly, which meant that only poorly trained "mercenary priests" were willing to serve such parishes.[25]

The benefice system was further undermined by the wide disparity of incomes priests earned. Some parishes were well enough endowed to allow the benefice holder to hire a substitute and live a more comfortable life in a town or city. Such benefices tended to be those most coveted by priests, or even priestly dynasties, pursuing careers in Church administration or seeking to provide for family members.[26] Other benefices were so poor that priests were forced to hold two or more in order to earn a living wage. In Alsace, parish priests often held several *beneficia simplex*, that is benefices without requirements of pastoral services, and also pressed their parishioners for fees for baptisms, marriages, and funerals in order to supplement meager incomes.[27]

This complex of issues, which Francis Rapp has labeled "the deterioration of the benefice system," had important effects on religious life.[28] Certainly influential elements among German clergymen, especially those who benefited from the incorporation of parishes, were reluctant to support reform measures aimed at limiting or eradicating pluralism and absenteeism. At the same time, those priests who lived on poor benefices or who served as substitutes and vicars for the clerical elite gave the clergy as a whole a bad name. Much of the anticlericalism of the early Reformation movement focused on the greed, impoverishment, and poor quality of the parish clergy.

Concubinage occupied an important place in the late medieval reforming program; it also occupies a central place in historical scholarship about the origins of the Reformation and even in the modern image of the late medieval clergy. A significant percentage of German priests did live with women, most of them in long-standing marriage-like relationships. Priest often paid "fines" to bishops that made this relationship legal under canon law. The incidence of concubinage appears to have varied by region, with somewhat higher rates in Switzerland and the southwest than elsewhere. Furthermore, the number of Catholic priests living with women probably increased during the sixteenth century, as a result of doctrinal confusion and disciplinary laxness.[29]

The social meaning of concubinage is hard to determine. Certainly, church reformers (and Protestants of course) pointed to the failure to enforce celibacy as a sign of clerical hypocrisy, as well as an indication of the Church's unwillingness to enforce its own rules. Local studies demonstrate that the rural population generally did not object to concubinage per se, as long as priests obeyed village sexual taboos.[30] After all, a priest living a stable family life with wife/concubine and children was not a threat as a sexual predator, one of the classic images of the priest in this and all periods.[31] Indeed, concubinage was less frequent in towns than in the countryside, but town dwellers were more likely to criticize a lack of chastity.

Another side of the reform movement was a catechetical tradition that emphasized lay obedience to the clergy. Fifteenth-century works such as Werner Rolevinck's manual for confessors told peasants to obey priests, regardless of their personal qualities.[32] Other catechists reminded the laity to attend services, attend the whole mass and sermon, and pay the tithe. As Robert Bast has emphasized, this late medieval focus on obedience was buttressed by a regular appeal, in catechism, sermons, and other penitential writings, to the Ten Commandments. This tradition would become part of the disciplinary tendency within post-Tridentine Catholicism as well.[33]

Late medieval church reform was, in Germany as elsewhere, a fairly unrealistic program. The structures of the German Church, especially the secular role of bishops and monastic institutions, and the extensive lay control of the benefice system made meaningful reforms very difficult, if not impossible. As Euan Cameron argues, "By 1500 the call for the reform of the priesthood had become not a newly recognized urgent problem, but a well-worn literary cliché."[34]

Religious Practice

The basic outlines of late medieval religious practice are now well known.[35] There was a core of "churchliness" to this practice, as the Church and its clergy were essential for much of popular religion.[36] People of all social classes attended weekly church services, especially to witness the elevation of the host, even if they did not always stay for the whole service. They also partook of the sacraments regularly, confessing and taking communion annually as required, and in some places somewhat more often. The sacraments of baptism and marriage, which served as important rites of passage for individuals, families, and communities, were especially important, and people expected priests to officiate at funerals.[37] The liturgical year, with its focus on the cycle of holidays leading up to Easter, organized time for people in villages and towns. Finally, priests regularly dispensed "sacramentals," such as blessed candles and water, or left the church to bless buildings, crops, and livestock.

Religious practice was generally local in its focus. Laypeople founded confraternities, organized in towns by trade or craft, heard extra masses, and paid for the funerals and prayers for deceased members. Parishes organized frequent processions. Some, like the Corpus Christi procession, were fairly recent innovations that supported the cult of the Eucharist. Others marked traditional holidays, such as the feast of the parish patron, which was also the occasion for the annual parish festival, attended by people from all the surrounding parishes. Most parishes also held a procession around the boundaries of the parish, the classic assertion of the primacy of local religion.

Much of popular religion was active, participatory, and diverse. Mystery plays, for example, were popular during Easter. In south Germany on Palm Sunday, a statue of Jesus on a donkey, the *Palmesel*, was drawn through villages to the church. On Good Friday, a representation of Christ's tomb was set up from which the church's crucifix was then raised on Easter Sunday. Villagers and townspeople participated in these spectacles, sometimes as actors and always as active spectators. New practices, such as praying the Rosary, were in vogue, as were far older Christian traditions, such as the worship of relics.

Pilgrimage piety was an even more dramatic version of the active character of religious practice. Many new shrines were founded in the decades around 1500, most of them as the result of popular sponsorship. The vast majority of pilgrimage destinations created in this period were Marian shrines, found in greatest numbers in southern Germany. In Bavaria, older shrines, mostly dedicated to local saints, continued to attract pilgrims as well. As Philip Soergel states, "The late medieval flowering of lay piety in Bavaria was expressed largely through the simultaneous popularity of these various cults."[38] Pilgrimage was a varied practice. Pilgrims went to local shrines and to regional centers journeying in groups of various sizes and as individuals.

Sermons were increasingly popular as well, especially in cities and towns. Many German cities and towns funded new preacherships, including 42 towns in the Duchy of Württemberg alone. People came from long distances to hear the most popular preachers, like Geiler von Kaisersberg, the cathedral preacher in Strasbourg in the decades around 1500. These sermons were mocked by humanists like Erasmus as superficial theatrical performances, but this "enthusiasm for the spoken word" was surely also an element of the diverse and active religiosity of the age.[39]

Preachers like Geiler and the Augustinian Johannes von Staupitz in Nuremberg, considered themselves part of a movement to reform Christianity and the Church.[40] Both published their sermons widely, in German and Latin, aiming at a literate audience of both clergy and laypeople. Staupitz's sermons encouraged people to abstain from sin while emphasizing God's mercy. Geiler's tone could be more judgmental and threatening, warning his listeners of God's wrath if they did not improve their behavior. Geiler also sometimes attacked the Strasbourg City Council for failing to care properly for the welfare of the poor. In retrospect, it is clear that this preaching tradition fed directly into the work of Martin Luther and the early evangelical preachers. It should not be forgotten, however, that the Jesuits and other Catholic preachers of the mid- and later sixteenth century also came out of a preaching tradition that aimed at improving lay religious practice.

Berndt Hamm has argued that late medieval piety in Germany was intense and active and also increasingly centered on particular themes. Hamm analyzes what he calls the "theology of piety," the devotional writings and images of the fourteenth to sixteenth centuries that were aimed at a wide audience of clergy and laity. These works "reveal relatively few principle themes and terms – always associated with a central figure such as Christ and Mary – [that] were treated with astounding multiplicity, repetition, and variability."[41] This theology of piety both reflected and encouraged a variety of devotional practices organized around these themes, such as the sacraments of confession and the Eucharist, an attachment to indulgences, and pilgrimages to Marian shrines. Hamm argues that the late medieval emphasis on the Passion, mercy, and trust was a forerunner of important aspects of Protestant theology. As we shall see, many of these themes were also important in post-Tridentine Catholic piety.

These essential characteristics of religious practice in the period before the Reformation – its churchliness, localism, diversity, and active character – were challenged but not destroyed by the crisis of the Protestant Reformation. This flourishing religious life also coexisted with a powerful strain of popular anticlericalism, which focused on the greed, economic power, and legal privileges of the clergy. This anticlericalism was an important force in the "evangelical movement" of the 1520s, and, like the structures of religious practice, it would remain part of the experience of German Catholicism throughout the early modern period.

The Impact of the Reformation

The Protestant Reformation began in the early 1520s as a powerful evangelical movement.[42] Widespread religious fervor characterized by a hope for a spiritual revival created by a new knowledge of and dedication to the Gospel spread from cities and towns into the countryside. This evangelical movement, although initially driven forward by the force of Martin Luther's theological insights, drew on many and varied theological traditions. As the movement rapidly spread through printed works, sermons, and word of mouth, its message about salvation and religious practice became increasingly diffuse and complex. In its view of the clergy, however, the evangelical movement exhibited two strong and consistent tendencies. The first attitude was a powerful anticlericalism, focused on the notion that priests and monks (in particular) had led the laity astray from true religion. This view easily dovetailed with the popular view that the clergy exploited its spiritual power for financial and personal gain. The second attitude was that laypeople should take charge of their own religious life and their own salvation by engaging the Gospel directly.

Salvation by faith meant that a layperson could achieve salvation without the intervention of the clergy. Furthermore, the Word, as Robert Scribner emphasizes "was seen not just as a way to salvation, but as a guide for life in this world."

Those men and women who held positions within the Roman Catholic Church had to engage this evangelical movement whether they wanted to or not. Few bishops or abbots supported Luther or the wider evangelical movement in the 1520s. As we have seen, most bishops had little or no interest in theological matters and thus found Luther's ideas and the anticlericalism of the evangelical movement both mystifying and threatening. Even in later years, when individual bishops converted to Protestantism, the Catholic hierarchy as a whole remained very loyal to the Church. An important consequence of this loyalty for the future of German Catholicism was the preservation, in the ecclesiastical territories of western and southern Germany, of important "intact Catholic communities."[43]

The clergy, especially priests and monks living in urban settings, were often the leaders of the evangelical movement. Over three-quarters of leading evangelical preachers studied in one sample were former Catholic clergymen.[44] Large numbers of monks from the mendicant orders left their monasteries in the 1520s and often reappeared as Protestant pastors. Nuns, however, were less likely to abandon their convents, partly because of their attachment to a (relatively) independent communal life and partly because even Protestant authorities recognized that convents had a certain social utility.[45] Rural priests were also much less likely than their urban counterparts to embrace the evangelical movement. Few of the more than 100 priests investigated by city officials in the region around Ulm in 1531 supported Protestant reforms, and rural priests in Saxony in the 1530s and 1540s were usually blissfully ignorant of Lutheran doctrine.[46]

In the 1520s, the Reformation had real popular appeal and threatened to destroy German Catholicism in a wave of religious revival. All social groups in cities and towns responded positively to the evangelical appeal, although wealthy patricians were perhaps underrepresented. Peasants, as studies of the "communal Reformation" have shown, also supported aspects of the evangelical movement in the early 1520s.[47] Yet the evangelical movement was short lived. Peasant support for Protestantism was greatly undermined by the defeat and savage repression of the extensive rural uprising of 1525 known as the Peasants' War. Luther's widely publicized treatise *Against the Robbing and Murdering Peasants*, in which he urged the princes to crush the revolt, identified him as an enemy of the peasants and an ally of the elites who feared social revolution. In the eyes of the public, the pamphlet superseded his earlier *Admonition to Peace*, which blamed the nobles and princes for the revolt.[48] By the 1530s, then, the evangelical movement was no longer a mass movement, at least in the countryside. In the long run, as Robert Scribner reminds us, most Protestants were in fact "involuntary Protestants, created by the princes' confessional choices."[49]

Protestantism, even after the early heady days of the evangelical movement had passed, challenged German Catholicism in two ways. First, Luther's theological positions forced the Catholic theologians to respond to the new religious ideas, a process that moved slowly until the Council of Trent outlined the official Church response. Secondly, the German Church was faced with a political and institutional crisis as princes and magistrates began to create new Protestant territorial churches. Both challenges undermined the confidence of the clergy at all levels, but the second one led, by mid-century, to a serious shortage of priests, considerable confusion about Catholic beliefs and practices, and a partial collapse of popular Catholicism, even in places little affected by Protestantism.

The Lutheran Reformation advanced steadily between the 1520s and the Schmalkaldic War of 1546–1547.[50] Lutheran princes and magistrates gained a voice in Imperial politics with their protest at the Diet of Speyer of 1529, developed some theological unity with the Confession of Augsburg (1530), and created a military alliance (the Schmalkaldic League) in 1531. By the 1550s, some kind of "Protestantism" was the official religion of most of the Imperial cities, all the lay principalities of northern Germany and many in the south, with the notable exceptions of Bavaria and Austria. Most north German bishoprics and ecclesiastical territories had either been absorbed or were threatened by Protestant princes, and monasteries and convents faced secularization. Catholicism was on the defensive politically and institutionally and appeared to be surviving only in the ecclesiastical territories of the west and south.

The 1540s and 1550s were a period of political turmoil in Germany, during which the Catholic party experienced a revival. Archbishop-Elector Herman of Cologne was foiled in his attempt to convert to Protestantism and make the electorate into a hereditary principality. With Spanish support, Herman was removed and replaced by a Wittlesbach prince. Charles V's victory in the Schmalkaldic War (1546–1547) and his imposition of a religious compromise – the Augsburg Interim – seemed to signal a Catholic victory.

At the Imperial Diet of Augsburg in 1548, Charles V promulgated the "Interim," a provisional religious settlement pending a unifying council. The Interim was a bit more than "a thinly veiled reformulation of the old faith," as Holborn calls it.[51] Based partly on the views of moderate Catholic theologians like Johannes Gropper and Julius Pflug, the Interim made concessions to Lutheran sensibilities by agreeing to the importance of justification by faith and accepting communion in both kinds as well as clerical marriage.[52] Some Catholic practices were particularly noxious to Protestants, like indulgences, and were purposely left unmentioned. On the other hand, the decree required the full restoration of the Catholic Mass and ordered the clergy to provide all seven sacraments. Not surprisingly, the Interim faced opposition from both Catholics and Protestants.

In some ways, the Interim provided a more difficult problem for Catholic princes, magistrates, and clergymen, than for Protestants. Committed Lutherans could, and did, oppose the Interim as a blatant attempt to restore Catholicism. Catholic leaders found themselves having to choose between support for Charles V, who had been vital for the political survival of German Catholicism, and the papacy, which condemned the Interim. Indeed, for many Catholics, this was the first real religious choice they had ever been forced to make; after all, depending on where one lived, remaining Catholic had not necessarily required a conscious choice.[53]

At the local level, the decree had confusing implications. In some places, it ratified existing practices, like the taking of communion in both kinds, while in other places it seemed to undermine traditional practice. Some priests certainly embraced the right of clerical marriage, while others resented the devaluation of celibacy. More generally, the Interim increased uncertainty about what constituted official and approved practice and enhanced regional and local variations within Catholicism. This trend probably would not have had much effect on popular practice, which had always been local and diverse, if it had not coincided with a crisis within the German Catholic elite.

The Catholic Response to the Reformation

Catholic leaders in Germany responded to Luther's challenge in the obvious way, by reaffirming their commitment to tradition. Walter Ziegler has argued, perhaps somewhat provocatively, that a conservative stance came naturally to the rulers of Catholic territories. "Their adherence to tradition meant, fundamentally, that they had no decision to make, and in fact they did not make one."[54] Ziegler further points out that the commitment to tradition was a double-edged sword. The appeal to tradition could be very effective, and everyone, from Protestant reformers to rebellious peasants, employed it. On the other hand, it was the evangelical movement, and later the Protestant princes, that took the initiative in religious and political affairs. "Traditions," as Ziegler points out, "are of course not called upon to act."[55]

It is, however, an oversimplification to say that German Catholic leaders did not react at all to the Lutheran attack. Catholic theologians, led by Johannes Eck, a professor in Ingolstadt in Bavaria, immediately responded to Luther's ideas. At the 1521 *Reichstag* in Worms, the emperor and the imperial estates confirmed the earlier Papal Bulls and condemned Luther's ideas, declaring him an outlaw. The Edict was impossible to enforce without the cooperation of princes and magistrates, but it was not universally rejected. Bavaria and Cologne provide two examples of Catholic rulers moving quickly to suppress the evangelical movement.

The Edict of Worms was promulgated and published immediately in Bavaria. The ruling Wittelsbach dukes, the brothers Ludwig and Wilhelm, met in 1522 and agreed to move aggressively against Luther's supporters in their territories.[56] The dukes considered the new religious ideas above all a threat to social order since (they said) Luther's supporters were turning the people against the clergy. Bavarian officials later claimed that their early and firm anti-Lutheran policies spared Bavaria from peasant rebellion in 1525. In 1522, the Bavarian dukes pressured the Archbishop of Salzburg to hold a "reform synod," the first of six such synods in the Salzburg Province between 1522 and 1576.[57] The Bavarians also worked in the 1520s to create and maintain a Catholic alliance with the Habsburgs. The anti-Lutheran policies of the Bavarian state did not prevent the development of a Protestant movement in Bavaria, but they made it much more difficult for such a movement to gain supporters.

What caused the Bavarian state to embrace such a consistent Catholic policy, and why did the wider population generally support it? In the 1520s, traditional ties to both the Papacy and the Emperor made a pro-Catholic policy the easy choice. Indeed, the Bavarian support of Catholicism was the same one provided by all the major territories in the 1520s and 1530s.[58] Over the course of the sixteenth century, such political calculations were reinforced by other factors. Religious traditions, especially the dense network of pilgrimage shrines and the strong support for the cult of saints, were another, often underestimated, source of Catholic loyalty.[59] At the same time, Bavaria had few cities and towns that could become centers of Protestantism. The countryside remained solidly Catholic and Bavaria got an early start as the bulwark of Catholicism.

The city of Cologne never experienced an organized Lutheran movement. As in Bavaria, local authorities, in this case the ruling council of this Free Imperial City, moved quickly and aggressively against the new heresy.[60] The theologians of the University of Cologne began the anti-Lutheran movement in 1519 when they became the first institution to condemn Luther's theological writings. In November 1520, Luther's works were openly burned in the courtyard of the cathedral in the presence of representatives of the cathedral chapter and the university. The city council then organized a fairly effective system of censorship, while proceeding severely against those suspected of Lutheran sympathies. A number of influential men were forced to leave the city and on September 28, 1529, two outspoken Protestants, Peter Fliesteden and Adolf Clarenbach, were publicly executed.[61]

Such policies left little space for Protestants of any kind in Cologne. Franz Bosbach, following the arguments of Robert Scribner, insists that there was no "clerical-theological space" for even the early evangelical movement.[62] Scribner emphasizes that the links between the University and the city's elite, as well as the importance of vigorous Catholic religious traditions like the *devotio moderna* in the city, strengthened popular and elite loyalty to the Catholic Church.

Gerald Chaix also argues that "the structures of religious life in Cologne hardly left any room for heretical movements."[63] All classes in the city participated in a vibrant religious life supported by a dense network of institutions. With 19 parishes and 11 monastic houses, Cologne resembled an Italian more than a German city.[64] "Holy Cologne" was a center of the veneration of the saints, focused on the relics of St Ursula and the Three Kings. These cults led to the creation of confraternities, which in turn involved a large number of laypeople in an active religious life.

Cologne's self-image as the citadel of Catholicism owed much to the commitment of the Cologne elite to the Church. This engagement was maintained in the first place by the close personal and family ties between the University and the leading families of the city. The *Kölner* had many family ties with the clergy, whom they also praised for their pastoral engagement and incorruptible lifestyle. Furthermore, Cologne was an important printing center, and the religious books published there allowed the literate classes to participate in the dynamic spirituality of the lower Rhine region in the decades around 1500. Laypeople were active in the most important of these spiritual movements, the *devotio moderna*, which was strongly supported by religious orders such as the Carthusians.[65]

There were also a variety of political and economic reasons why the ruling elite of Cologne supported Catholicism.[66] Close economic ties to the Spanish Netherlands encouraged the city to avoid antagonizing the Habsburgs. Moreover, Cologne needed the Emperor's support in its traditional conflict with the Archbishop-Elector. Internal political considerations also inclined the city's rulers to Catholicism. Like ruling groups across Germany, the Cologne elite had become more socially and politically exclusive in the decades leading up to the Reformation. By the 1520s, the leading families were particularly conservative, having lived through several serious artisan uprisings in this most populous of German cities. Unlike magistrates in many other cities, however, the Cologne *Rat* never faced an organized evangelical movement and could thus stand by its initial inclination to see the old Church as a bulwark against dangerous innovation and possible social unrest.

The response of Catholic leaders in Bavaria and Cologne was remarkably forceful and consistent. More typical was the response of the Franconian prince-bishops.[67] Some, like Bishop Konrad von Thüngen of Würzburg, moved fairly decisively against Lutherans, especially after the Peasants' War, which justified linking Luther's supporters with social and political rebellion. Von Thüngen expelled all Lutheran preachers from Würzburg and other towns within his own secular territory. Like the Bavarian dukes, he published and enforced Papal and Imperial edicts against Luther and Lutherans. As in Cologne, there was little intellectual space for Lutherans in the city of Würzburg. The episcopal court maintained close ties with strongly Catholic theologians, such as Johannes Eck, and with Catholic humanist circles around Erasmus and Cochleus. Episcopal officials kept a close eye on both the Augustinian and the Franciscan convents in the city, which in other cities often provided Protestant leaders, and they made sure the cathedral preachership was firmly in Catholic hands. Yet these policies were almost purely defensive. The cathedral chapter, solidly Catholic unlike many other chapters, opposed any real reforms of the clergy, the bishop's authority was not recognized in areas outside his secular control, and the countryside was apparently left to its own devices.

The policies of the Bishops of Bamberg demonstrate another kind of response to the Reformation.[68] Bishop Weigand von Redwitz, who ruled from 1522 to 1556, supported the Catholic party at all Imperial diets, but his policies in religious matters were indecisive. Before 1525, episcopal officials did nothing to discourage Luther's supporters, and although the Peasants' War discredited the evangelical movement among the elite, the Church's official response consisted exclusively of warnings and complaints about the state of Catholicism. Throughout the 1530s and 1540s, the bishop expressed skepticism about the Council of Trent and waited for a general council to settle the religious division, while at the diocesan level he concentrated on defending his principality from invasion and other threats to its territorial integrity.

Von Redwitz countered the Lutheran threat "primarily with the administrative methods of spiritual and secular bureaucracy."[69] Some of the administrators who led this effort were not clearly loyal to Catholicism, for example the influential Christoph von Henneberg, who was elected dean of the cathedral in the 1540s and was called by his enemies a "crypto-Lutheran." Although there were some zealous anti-Protestants in the episcopal administration, like the Vicar General Dr Paul Neidecker (served 1529–1565), the bishopric suffered from a real shortage of clerical leadership. Even Neidecker could not effectively promote reform of the clergy, since he lived openly with a concubine. Meanwhile, instability and confusion characterized the religious situation in the countryside. In some places, particularly in regions bordering on Lutheran territories or in villages dominated by Lutheran noblemen, there began to develop "a flourishing church life of a Lutheran stamp" by the 1550s.[70] More often, religious life remained basically Catholic, but rural priests took positions between the religious camps, offering, for example, communion in both kinds as part of a Catholic mass, or using Lutheran hymns during services. Faced with a shortage of priests and fearing that some peasants might choose to emigrate if pressed on religious matters, Catholic officials could not prevent the countryside from becoming a sort of free choice zone.

This religious instability was even more pronounced in Westphalia.[71] If the Franconian hierarchy remained firmly in the Catholic camp, by the 1540s, there were openly Lutheran canons and even bishops in the cathedral cities of Paderborn, Münster, and Osnabrück. A schematic ecclesiastical and political history of the city, prince-bishopric, and diocese of Osnabrück between 1521 and 1555 provides a fine example of this instability:

1521–1542: Steady growth of evangelical/Lutheran community in the city of Osnabrück. Bishops, cathedral chapter, and Osnabrück city council tolerate this community.

1520s/1530s: Evangelical preachers active in Osnabrück and other towns. Only the most aggressively anticlerical preachers removed from posts.

1532: Election of Franz von Waldeck as bishop. His family has close ties with Hessen, a leading Protestant principality.

1535–1543: Under popular pressure, the city council in Osnabrück moves from toleration to open support of Lutheranism in the city.

1542/1543: Bishop von Waldeck and Osnabrück city council together officially introduce Protestantism in the city, issuing a church ordinance (*Kirchenordnung*) influenced by Bugenhagen's Lübeck ordinance.

1543: Prince/Bishop von Waldeck orders Protestant services in countryside as well.

1547: The cathedral chapter, supported by the victorious Charles V, orders rural parishes to reestablish Catholic services.

1548: Von Waldeck withdraws Protestant church ordinance. Interim officially instituted later that year.

By the 1550s, these developments led to a variety of local accommodations. In the towns, most people were Lutheran, but they tolerated a sizeable Catholic clerical establishment, especially in Osnabrück. Country people may not have noticed all the twists and turns of the political situation, particularly since the rural clergy was left in place through the changes. Both clerical marriage and communion in both kinds received popular support, and both practices were widespread and tolerated by the weak episcopal administration. In the long run, confessional coexistence developed in the city of Osnabrück, while a variety of religious practices prevailed in the countryside.

Conditions in the other Westphalian prince-bishoprics of Münster and Paderborn were somewhat less confused, if in some ways more dramatic.[72] Münster was profoundly affected by the experience of the radical Anabaptist Kingdom (1533–1534). An extended siege of the city by Protestant and Catholic armies led by the Prince-Bishop ended with increasingly bizarre and apocalyptic behavior within the city and a very bloody repression when the city fell. After 1535, Lutherans never gained political power in Münster, but the bishop and the city council tolerated an important Lutheran community. In the countryside, the clergy continued to provide a variety of religious services. A 1549 visitation of part of the Diocese of Paderborn, for example, reported mixed results. On the one hand, villages under the Bishop's secular power had maintained "a generally intact old Church substance."[73] On the other hand, a variety of conditions prevailed in other places, especially where noble families had

introduced Lutheran pastors and practices into the parishes they controlled.[74] Across Westphalia, then, there was no clear division between
Catholic and Lutheran practices and beliefs, and as a result, the confessional identities of both individuals and communities remained unclear
as well.

The period between the 1520s and the 1570s was a time of indecision
and uncertainty for much of the Catholic clergy; it was a period of
religious confusion for laypeople as well, as their pastors changed some
practices and neglected others. Church historians have tended to present
the problems within German Catholicism in the first half of the sixteenth
century as a full-blown crisis, the result of the practical difficulties caused
by the Protestant Reformation, exacerbated by the moral failings of the
clergy. Yet important aspects of this situation can be traced to the ways in
which many Catholics, especially within the Church hierarchy, responded
to the rise of Protestantism.[75] Many leading German Catholics came out
of the humanist/reformist tradition exemplified by Erasmus and agreed
with Protestant critics that the Church needed major reforms. They also
tended to sympathize with a number of Lutheran theological positions,
especially on clerical marriage and communion in both kinds. What came
to be called "mixed religious forms" were in fact alternate forms of
Catholicism promoted by respected and powerful theologians, humanists, and bishops within the Church.

By the 1540s, a lasting compromise between Protestant and Catholic
theologians was probably not possible, as the ultimate collapse of the
Regensburg Colloquy of 1541, which began with an earnest effort at
compromise on major theological issues, demonstrates.[76] Yet the major
theological innovation of the Colloquy, the doctrine of "double justification," had considerable staying power. "Double justification" held that
"man was justified before God *both* by an alien imputed righteousness, as
the Lutherans maintained, and an inherent righteousness partly of his
own creation, as the medieval church had traditionally taught."[77] Most
decisively, the commitment of Charles V and many leading churchmen to
an ecumenical council that would heal the religious division of Germany
kept the moderate Catholic stance alive in Germany.

The *Kelchbewegung* ("chalice movement") was a particularly widespread
strand of this moderate or reformist Catholicism. Especially influential in
Lower Bavaria and Upper Austria, where it was dominated by the minor
nobility, proponents demanded that the laity receive the wine as well as
the bread during the celebration of the Eucharist.[78] This movement
looked dangerously Protestant to its opponents, especially since its

supporters often expressed a preference for clerical marriage as well, but its most powerful supporters also favored active church reforms, beginning with visitations and reform of the clergy. In the 1550s and 1560s, the Dukes of Bavaria successfully petitioned the Papacy for a special dispensation to allow the laity to receive the chalice, and the Habsburg emperors fairly consistently argued that the lay chalice and clerical marriage were compatible with orthodox Catholicism.

The *Kelchbewegung* became politically significant in Bavaria in the decade after 1555, when it was linked with noble opposition to the consolidation of ducal power. In much of Catholic Germany, moderate Catholicism was an elite stance. R.J.W. Evans has argued that a kind of orthodox humanism dominated the culture of the elite of the Habsburg lands in the sixteenth century, leading in religious issues to a sophisticated toleration of all Christians.[79] Bishops and abbots could take similar views, even as they defended their rights and privileges against Protestant incursions. Humanist toleration could easily blend with local and regional loyalties and a typically German dislike of papal (or "romanist") absolutism to strengthen a moderate Catholic position. Marquard von Hattstein, Bishop of Speyer from 1560 to 1581, associated regularly with Protestants, lived the life of a Renaissance prince, and admonished his clergy to avoid religious confrontations, but also reformed the finances of his little principality and advocated reforms of the clergy.[80] Marquard was not unusual among the German episcopate of the middle of the sixteenth century.

If the German Catholic elite often favored a kind of moderate, reformist Catholicism, the population of Catholic territories practiced a more rough and ready religious toleration. In religiously mixed areas, Protestant and Catholic peasants mingled fairly easily in the middle of the sixteenth century, especially since confessional identities, even of the clergy, were often unclear.[81] Furthermore, as John Bossy has argued, there was wide popular support in all of Germany for a communally organized religion that served as a mechanism to keep the communal peace.[82] Following this argument, the widespread adoption in Catholic regions of the lay chalice indicates a preference for church services that reinforce communal solidarity and sociability. Furthermore, clerical marriage (together with the lay chalice) undermined the special status of the clergy and integrated the priest more closely into the community.[83] All studies of rural religion in the mid-sixteenth century emphasize the communal and local nature of religious practice and ecclesiastical organization. This local focus tended to lead to a practical toleration of religious division, as it did in religiously divided cities such as Augsburg.

In this context, Catholic theologians only slowly evolved a more aggressive stance against Luther and Lutheranism. The earliest and perhaps best-known opponent of Luther was Johannes Eck (1486–1543).[84] Professor at the University of Ingolstadt and Cathedral Canon in Eichstätt, Eck developed a solid reputation as a learned humanist. In his early theological works, Eck emphasized the centrality of free will in the human quest for salvation, a focus that led him to early clashes with Luther. In 1519, Eck debated both Luther and Karlstadt at the Leipzig disputation. Blessed with an excellent memory and well trained in the skills of academic disputation, Eck flaunted his formal superiority over his opponents, but failed to gain the sympathy of audiences. His writings seem to have been similarly received. In his extensive writings, Eck aggressively defended the authority of the Church, vigorously rejected Luther's critique of the sacrament of penance, and brought considerable clarity to the theological divisions within Christendom. Eck probably exerted the most influence when he served on the commission that drew up the papal bull *Exsurge Domine*, which condemned Luther's works. Yet in the 1520s, neither his doctrinal clarity nor his early willingness to paint Luther as a dangerous heretic nor his unbending insistence on the authority of the papacy and the Church was popular in Germany.[85]

Eck was unusual in his early and consistent opposition to Luther. Johann Fabri, who served in a number of important clerical positions in southwest Germany until his death in 1541, is more representative of the mainstream of the educated Catholic elite.[86] Fabri was a personal friend of Erasmus and traveled in the same humanist circles as many leading evangelical leaders of the 1520s, such men as Zwingli, Rhenanus, Capito, and others. Writing in 1520, he expressed political, but not theological, differences with Luther.

I like Luther's writings very much; most of what he has written is correct. I am however displeased that he publicizes so widely teachings that are too difficult for uneducated people to digest. Even supposing (*Setzen wir den Fall*) that Luther is correct in everything he has written, it would not do to rashly lay these complicated matters before the wider public. If even St. Paul often delayed proclaiming the truth of scripture out of consideration for the weaknesses and varied abilities of the crowd, is it not even more necessary in our times to overlook things that cannot be changed without overthrowing public order – or to heal this dangerously sick world in another way?   A deeply rooted abuse can never be corrected by such impetuosity. Luther's doctrine of inner penance may indeed speak to some educated people; for the uneducated it exercises a destructive influence, which may destroy all piety. Uneducated people do not have the necessary judgment to understand the strange, new, and often contradictory teachings of the violently forward-looking Wittenberger.[87]

Behind an apparent sympathy for Luther's ideas, Fabri expresses almost all the ideas that characterized the works of Catholic thinkers down to the 1550s and even beyond. Luther and other Protestants, he suggests, are dangerous innovators who mislead the common people and threaten public order. They have no respect for tradition and authority and, in a critique that Catholic writers loved to repeat, their ideas are inconsistent and frequently contradictory. Needless to say, this kind of attack was highly elitist in content, as it was in form, since most of these works were published as extended Latin treatises. Fabri's massive masterwork, the *Malleus in haerisim Lutheranam* (*The Hammer against the Lutheran Heresy*), first published in 1522, was, as even his admiring biographer concedes, hardly read at all![88]

Although Catholic writers produced theological defenses of the Catholic mass, the sacrament of penance and so on, most of their works were attacks on Luther rather than defenses of Catholic practices and beliefs. Those writers who aimed at a more popular audience could lampoon Luther mercilessly. Johann Cochleus published "The Seven-headed Luther" in 1529, which, in response to Lutheran attacks on the "seven-headed Papal beast," accused Luther of inconsistency for having "as many messages as he had heads."[89] Robert Scribner argues that Thomas Murner's illustrated *Great Lutheran Fool* of 1522 "stands alone as the showpiece of Catholic counter-propaganda."[90] Murner's use of visual images, verse, and carnival themes to satirize Luther and his followers as thoughtless threats to social order was exceptional in the 1520s and would remain so until the last decades of the century.

Nevertheless, writers like Murner and Cochleus, began a trend toward increasingly polemic writings, most of which picked up the themes expressed by Fabri in his 1520 letter. Johann Hoffmeister, prior of the Augustian house in Colmar in Alsace, provides a good example of the increasingly strident tone among Catholic intellectuals in the 1530s and 1540s.[91] Hoffmeister's writings were apparently widely read among the Catholic clergy, especially his *Loci communes,* a sort of handbook of the theological disputes of the time, first published in 1547 and regularly republished in the second half of the sixteenth century.[92] Hoffmeister, like most other Catholic writers, read and studied the works of his Protestant opponents, writing for example a study of the Augsburg Confession whose main point was that Lutheran doctrine was riddled with inconsistencies. In other works, Hoffmeister expanded on this theme, attacking the notion that the Bible was so clear that any believer could read and understand it. Here he argues once again that "if the Holy Scripture is so clear, then one must ask oneself why the Lutherans, Zwinglians, and Anabaptists all interpret it so differently, and why the Lutherans argue over the correct understanding."[93] This position led, of course, to a strong defense of the authority of the Catholic Church and an assertion of the importance of tradition in reaching an understanding of "correct" doctrine. Hoffmeister's polemical writings and his sermons (in Munich, Ulm, Colmar, Dillingen, and elsewhere) illustrate the growing distrust, even among humanist-minded Catholic intellectuals, of Protestantism. This distrust, reinforced of course by the political and military conflicts around the Schmalkaldic War, contributed to the failure of the various attempts at religious reconciliation, including the Interim. The increasing strident tone of intellectuals like Hoffmeister and Fabri indicates a weakening of the moderate German Catholic position, aimed at reforming the Church without committing to a militant form of Catholicism promoted from Rome.[94] This tendency, however, remained important in the German Church into the eighteenth century.

Catholicism at Mid-century

A sense of crisis pervades the writings of Catholic leaders at mid-century. Papal nuncios tended to paint particularly grim pictures of conditions in Germany. In a detailed description of conditions in the Westphalian bishoprics, the nuncio to the imperial court blamed the abuses of the clergy for the problems of the Church.[95] In the first place, he wrote, one bishop held three sees, which was just the most egregious example of the pluralism that was rampant among the upper clergy. Cathedral canons lived like knights, Protestants could be found in ecclesiastical territories and even in cathedral chapters, and no effort was being made, through visitations or synods, to correct the abuses of the clergy.

Other, perhaps closer, observers bemoaned the consequences of clerical failings for religious practice. Peter Canisius, the leading German Jesuit, wrote to Rome in 1550 about conditions in Ingolstadt in Bavaria.

One should not search for any religious ardor among the Germans these days; Catholic services have declined so far that on feast days only a cold sermon [a sermon without the mass] is held. Only the name of Lent ("the forty day fast") remains, since in fact no one fasts anymore. O it happens very rarely that they go to church, or that they attend mass, or that they allow themselves to be gratified by the old church. And here I am talking about Catholics or about people who are still Catholics in name![96]

Canisius points to a number of interconnected problems for German Catholicism, which can all be traced to the impact of the Reformation. The evangelical movement profoundly unsettled the Catholic clergy. In the early years of the Reformation, many priests, especially in cities and towns, joined the new movement. In the next decades, those social groups that had provided much of the parish clergy, the urban artisan and merchant groups, generally embraced Protestantism as well. These conditions led to an acute shortage of clergymen in most parts of Catholic Germany. With few new priests being trained, episcopal officials were reluctant to remove even the most criminal of priests, not to mention the large number of priests with concubines, poor education, or even those with a drinking problem. The problems of the clergy in turn contributed to the partial collapse of popular religion, despite widespread loyalty to Catholic practice.

Canisius' lament applies above all to cities and towns, where, with a few exceptions such as Cologne, the neglect of services was clearly more severe than in the countryside. However, Catholic villagers failed to attend church services as well. In Westphalia and Franconia, on the middle Rhine and in parts of the southwest, in Austria, Alsace, and Switzerland, Protestant and Catholic territories existed side by side and religious uncertainty reigned. Traditional patterns of religious life collapsed when, for example, Protestant authorities outlawed a pilgrimage or abolished a parish festival. Pilgrimage, once a ubiquitous aspect of popular religion, went into severe decline, even in Bavaria.[97] Shrines, especially those that depended on pilgrims from beyond the local area, fell into disuse. Processional piety also declined, as did confraternities. A lack of clerical leadership was a factor in the decline of popular participation in traditional practices; the uncertainty caused by frequent changes in official religious policy was another factor, even where a dedicated clergy was in place.

The notion that German Catholicism was in crisis in the middle of the sixteenth century is, of course, commonplace. We should be careful not to overstate the case, as have many Church historians intent on demonstrating an almost miraculous renewal of Catholicism set in motion by the Council of Trent.[98] The reserves of strength outlined at the beginning of this chapter did not disappear with the Reformation, nor, apparently, did the popular commitment to Christianity in general. Local religion, closely linked to the cycles of agricultural life, embedded in the history and landscape of the community, remained vital, if not vibrant.

The institutions of Catholicism in Germany were certainly shaken badly by the Reformation, as was the confidence of the clergy. Two developments went a long way to repair these problems. The first was the Peace of Augsburg of 1555, which created the political and constitutional stability necessary for the renewal of Catholic life. Secondly, by the 1550s, the Council of Trent began to provide guidelines for official Catholic doctrine and practice, which, while ending any chance of agreement with Protestants, also provided a definitive position about these issues that had not existed for decades. The tone in Catholic Germany would gradually shift in the second half of the sixteenth century from a sense of crisis to a sense of confidence.

Chapter 2: The Counter-Reformation Episode: 1570s–1620s

Between 1550 and the Thirty Years' War, the leaders of the Catholic Church worked to revive and reinvigorate Catholicism in Germany. Developments in Germany were, of course, part of a European, indeed worldwide, Catholic expansion and revival. However, certain tensions within Catholicism limited the impact of this revival in Germany. One was the ongoing friction between the aims of the universal church, organized hierarchically and often autocratically, and the local church, generally organized more communally. This problem was compounded by the tendency of the Catholic elite to view the religious culture of the wider population with considerable condescension. As a result, efforts at reviving Catholicism often focused on "cleansing" popular religious practice of "abuses" and "superstitions," a program that could antagonize and even alienate villagers and townspeople. This kind of "reform from above" dominated Catholicism in the late sixteenth century and gave lower priority to the effort to revive popular religious practice. Reform from above, following the program of the Council of Trent, also meant strengthening the institutions and administration of the Catholic Church. Most importantly, it focused on putting a celibate, educated, and disciplined clergy in the parishes.

German Catholicism in the period between the Peace of Augsburg and the Thirty Years' War experienced all the trends that affected Catholicism in the rest of Europe. These included a strongly anti-Protestant *Counter-Reformation*, a *church reform* inspired and accelerated by the Council of Trent, but drawing on older reform traditions as well, and a period of close church–state cooperation – *confessionalization* – aimed at enforcing religious unity.[1] It should come as no surprise that in the land of Luther, Catholic leaders tended to focus on Counter-Reformation measures. The almost apocalyptic language of crisis that prevailed in educated Catholic circles at mid-century was only slowly replaced by a more confident tone later in the century. Even the most aggressive Catholic leaders continued to act as if the population were on the verge of converting to Protestantism and their church in imminent danger of collapse.

The Counter-Reformation as Anti-Protestantism

The Peace of Augsburg was vital in restoring a measure of security and stability to Catholicism in Germany. By enshrining in imperial law the *jus reformandi*, the right of the rulers to establish the confession of their choice (either the Lutheran Augsburg Confession or Roman Catholicism), the treaty did much to prevent the takeover of weaker Catholic territories, especially the prince-bishoprics, by powerful Protestant princes. In theory, the treaty also prevented princes from intervening in the internal affairs of neighboring territories in order to protect co-religionists. Although the impact of such rules varied across Germany according to the local balance of power, in the sixteenth century, the Peace of Augsburg tended to protect Catholic territories from aggressive Protestant neighbors.

The most difficult negotiations at Augsburg centered on the Catholic demand for a *reservatio ecclesiastica*, the Ecclesiastical Reservation. This clause stated that any ecclesiastical prince who converted to Protestantism would have to resign his position and that only a Catholic could be elected his successor. The aim of the Reservation was to keep the ecclesiastical principalities Catholic by preventing bishops and abbots from converting to Lutheranism and turning their territories into hereditary secular states. The Protestant party at Augsburg refused to ratify the *reservatio* but did agree to tolerate its inclusion in the Peace as an imperial decree. At the same time, King Ferdinand made a secret agreement with the Protestants, the so-called *declaratio Ferdinandea*, which protected existing Protestant communities within ecclesiastical territories.

The Ecclesiastical Reservation gave Catholic leaders a measure of security. Significantly, Ferdinand had demonstrated the Habsburg commitment to the Catholic cause by promulgating the Reservation, and other Catholic princes, particularly the Bavarian dukes, had supported him. The Reservation made it more difficult for Protestant princes to absorb ecclesiastical territories and made it possible for Catholic princes to begin a process of territorial consolidation that stabilized ecclesiastical territories and secured their independent status.[2] On the other hand, the

Protestants did not officially accept this clause and it would remain a cause for conflict over the next 60 years. Finally, the protection given to Lutheran communities by the *declaratio Ferdinandea* hindered efforts to strengthen Catholicism within ecclesiastical territories.

The Reservation strengthened, and in a sense restored, the links between the Catholic Church and the Empire, despite the constitutional fact that after 1555 the Holy Roman Empire was no longer exclusively Catholic. The Peace of Augsburg also openly protected the institutions of the Imperial Church and reaffirmed their Roman Catholic character. Catholic institutions remained embedded in the fabric of the Empire, protected by the Habsburg Emperor. This afforded Catholicism further security. The German Church could, and did, draw on this traditional identification with the Empire into the eighteenth century.

Germany experienced a period of peace and religious coexistence between 1555 and the mid-1580s. The Peace of Augsburg was partly responsible for this period of lowered tensions, in part by turning religious conflicts into legal and constitutional disputes. This process, in turn, tended to cover over religious differences at the local level. In this period, Germany was also left alone by its powerful neighbors; France was preoccupied with its own civil wars and Spain with the rebellion in the Netherlands.[3] This period of relative peace allowed both Protestant and Catholic princes to begin the process of consolidating religious loyalty in their territories.

H.R. Schmidt has outlined the stages of the "Catholic counteroffensive" of the later sixteenth century as follows:

1. Removal ("purging") of evangelical officials, town councilors, and guilds.
2. Oaths of obedience to Tridentine decrees from officials, teachers, and "Graduierten" (school graduates).
3. Expulsion of evangelical preachers and teachers.
4. Admission of approved Catholic priests only.
5. Confiscation of evangelical books and prohibition against attending Protestant religious services outside the territory.
6. Visitations with the purpose of recatholicizing the population.
7. Expulsion of notorious Protestants.[4]

The pace of this process varied widely across the German-speaking lands; we have seen aspects of it in places such as Bavaria and Cologne even before mid-century (Chapter 1). In other places, for example in the

Diocese of Paderborn in Westphalia or in Bamberg, such measures only began after 1600. The varied impact of the anti-Protestant program can be demonstrated with several examples.

Julius Echter von Mespelbrunn (Bishop of Würzburg, 1573–1617) served as a model bishop in the sixteenth century; he remains the classic example of Counter-Reformation prelate for modern scholars as well. Renowned for his energy (he was 29 when he was elected) and for the aggressiveness of his policies, von Mespelbrunn exploited the advantages of his position as a prince-bishop who held both secular and spiritual power.[5] Like his predecessors in Würzburg and his episcopal colleagues across Germany, he devoted much of his attention to his princely duties. The first decade of his rule was spent consolidating political control of his principality, using methods common among early modern princes. Von Mespelbrunn reduced the principality's debts, issued a series of new laws and ordinances, rebuilt his palaces, and built numerous new secular buildings, including fortresses and castles. He expanded the size of the territorial administration, hiring new non-noble bureaucrats, especially for the central ruling council and the clerical council. Finally he attempted to expand his territory by purchasing, absorbing, or conquering bordering lands, as when he seized the Princely Abbey of Fulda from its staunchly Catholic abbot, Balthasar von Dernbach.[6]

The bishop expanded this policy of political consolidation with the founding and endowment in the late 1570s of a huge hospital in Würzburg, modestly calling it the *Juliusspital*, followed by the founding of several more hospitals in his territory. In the 1580s, the University was founded (1582) and expanded; it had close links to the Jesuit College, which had been in place since 1567. Von Mespelbrunn conceived of these foundations as vital instruments for advancing both his major projects, namely the strengthening of his secular principality and the revitalization of Catholicism in his diocese. These new institutions were funded by contributions from the clergy and especially by the assignment of monastic endowments from orders and houses the bishop considered less than appropriately "active."

Von Mespelbrunn only began to seek a "complete solution to the religious question in the territory" around 1585, after almost 10 years as prince-bishop.[7] As Walter Ziegler argues, the delay in beginning an aggressive Counter-Reformation had been partly the consequence of the bishop's desire to build up his secular power as a weapon for the enforcement of confessional policies. Von Mespelbrunn's hesitation was also a response to the opposition aroused by an aggressive anti-Protestant program.

Powerful neighbors, like Saxony, invoked the *reservatio Ferdinandea* to protect Protestant subjects of the bishop from forced conversion. Among Catholics, a general lack of interest in assertive religious policies among clerical leaders in Würzburg greatly slowed the bishop's endeavors.

By 1585, though, von Mespelbrunn had most of the necessary tools in place for the "*conversio*" of his lands. From this point on, the Counter-Reformation in Würzburg followed the steps outlined above. The Clerical Council in Würzburg organized visitations of rural districts by teams of Jesuits and local clergymen, complete with sermons, church services, processions, and confessions. These visits identified the willingness of the population to submit to Catholic norms, with a particular focus on their attitude toward the reception of communion in one kind. Those unwilling to accept and participate in Catholic services were first warned, then punished, and, if they remained "stubborn," expelled from the territory. Von Mespelbrunn claimed complete success, stating in 1590 that over 100,000 of his subjects had returned to the Catholic fold. Officials and clergymen (including Jesuits) in the towns and villages were less sanguine and reported considerable Protestant resistance.[8] It is known that most of the bishop's subjects accommodated themselves to the new confessional setting; around 700–800 left the territory and settled in neighboring Lutheran towns such as Kitzingen and Schweinfurt.

Officials and priests in Würzburg worked to support and stabilize this forceful policy by founding new parishes, building and restoring churches, and encouraging pilgrimage piety and the veneration of the saints. The most dramatic result of these efforts can be found in the revival of the great shrine of the Holy Blood at Walldürn.[9] This revival was set in motion when in 1589 the local priest published a new history of the shrine, which had been almost moribund since about 1525. The number of pilgrims who came to Walldürn grew dramatically in the first decades of the seventeenth century after the Jesuits and the Capuchins began to actively promote the site. Although the most spectacular outburst of Baroque piety at Walldürn only came after the Thirty Years' War, the earlier success of the shrine attests to the positive reception of at least some of the Counter-Reformation measures of the late sixteenth century.

The policies of Julius Echter von Mespelbrunn in the 1580s and 1590s almost look like a stereotype of the Counter-Reformation. Organized by a forceful bishop and spearheaded by the Jesuits, the Catholics instituted "a confessional policy aimed at recatholicization, religious unity, the construction of a strong state, and the intensification of domination."[10] By 1600, there was no religious confusion in the Prince-Bishopric of

Würzburg, the principle of *cuius regio, eius religio* was strongly enforced, and Catholicism was no longer on the defensive.

Other bishops faced more effective restraints on aggressive anti-Protestant policies, and many were also less inclined to focus their energies on converting Protestants. Like von Mespelbrunn in Würzburg, Eberhard von Dienheim, Bishop of Speyer in the 1580s and 1590s, maintained close ties with the Jesuits and considered himself a church reformer.[11] Von Dienheim also brought middle-class officials into his service, sent visitations into the 30 or so parishes of his tiny principality, and demanded better work from the clergy. The Bishop of Speyer, however, could not ignore his powerful neighbor, the Elector of the Palatinate, one of the leading Protestant princes of late-sixteenth-century Germany, when he acted to enforce Catholic uniformity in the countryside.

The limits on the Counter-Reformation in this period are illustrated by the attempt to convert the sizeable Protestant population of five villages on the edge of the Prince-Bishopric Speyer. In this little corner of Germany, we find self-assured villagers defending their local traditions, some of which were broadly Protestant, against efforts to institute standardized Catholic practices. Bishops, church officials, and local priests found it difficult to impose their will on such people, especially when powerful Protestant states were willing to protect the villagers.

The Bishop of Speyer's officials administered these villages, although they were nominally under the secular lordship of the *Ritterstift*, or Knightly Chapter, in Bruchsal. The Knightly Chapter was one of those peculiar institutions of the Imperial Church; an ecclesiastical institution, the chapter admitted noble Catholic canons, most of whom lived aristocratic lifestyles supported by the incomes from the villages under their rule. Not surprisingly, the canons had little interest in religious conditions in the parishes.

An episcopal visitation conducted in the early 1580s revealed that there were apparently many Protestants in the Knightly Chapter's villages. As a result, Catholic authorities moved to institute the early stages of a Counter-Reformation. First, they established legal authority over ecclesiastical affairs, followed by an attempt to remove Protestant officials and ministers. After installing Catholic priests in the parishes, there followed an effort to persuade or convert the population to the benefits of Catholicism. The Jesuits played an important role at this stage, especially since well-trained parish clergy were not always available. A more coercive stage, such as it occurred in Würzburg, never took place. No restrictions were successfully placed on the Protestant inhabitants, and no effort was made to evict non-Catholics.

What Catholic officials in Speyer labeled "Protestantism" on the part of the peasants was mostly a long-standing commitment to communion in both kinds. The inhabitants of the village of Landshausen reported on one "evangelical preacher":

> He preached the Gospel and distributed the holy sacrament in both kinds, in bread and wine, to each person as Christ ordered and instituted the holy sacrament of communion. We in Landshausen liked him very much.[12]

Villagers in fact often expressed a general distaste for all official forms of Christianity imposed from outside the community. The village council of Odenheim complained in 1604 that "a while ago they were forced to hear a Lutheran pastor preach and had to accept that religion, as a result they are completely against both the Lutheran and the Catholic religion."[13] They also had no love for Calvinists. "They were quite shocked," a Catholic priest reported of the villagers of Landshausen, "when I warned them that they should protect their chalice and whatever else of value in their church [from the iconoclastic Calvinists]."[14]

Until the 1580s, religious practice in these villages had been the kind of mix of Catholic and Lutheran that was common in much of Germany. Married pastors distributed communion in both kinds in churches that kept their late medieval altars and decorations. The pastors generally accommodated themselves to local conditions. Michael Erb, priest between 1574 and 1581, claimed he "secretly" said mass before his parishioners arrived in church on Sundays. He was married and gave communion in both kinds. The villagers stated that "he got along well with the peasants and did not ask them to convert to Papism."[15]

Catholic priests were installed in these villages in the 1580s and 1590s, and some of them valiantly attempted to convert the villagers. Peter Herrodt, priest in Landshausen in 1588–1589, diligently tried to persuade his parishioners to attend mass, preached about Catholic beliefs and against Protestant practices, and tried to teach the Catholic catechism.[16] The villagers were hostile to his efforts. The Jesuits supported the priests by sending a mission to Landshausen in 1600, preaching and teaching the catechism.[17]

The inhabitants of these villages actively resisted these attempts to enforce Catholic practices. First, they appealed to the Elector Palatine in an effort to get Protestant clergymen installed. When this ultimately failed, they simply ignored the priests and went to neighboring villages for Protestant services. Within the villages they prevented priests from placing restrictions on baptisms, marriages, and funerals. In 1609, the villagers openly refused to pay fines, the imperial tax, and the small tithe; moreover, they resolved to remove a Catholic priest and institute their own church ordinance.[18] Palatine officials also intervened in these villages, removing several Catholic priests from their posts, and claiming that the Peace of Augsburg gave them the right to protect Protestants in this ecclesiastical territory.[19] In 1615, Palatine troops even occupied the Knightly Chapter villages for several weeks.[20] The Counter-Reformation was by any definition a failure here before the Thirty Years' War. Counter-Reformers faced similar limits on their efforts in many parts of Germany.

In the 1570s, Daniel Brendel von Homburg, the Archbishop-Elector of Mainz personally led an expedition to the Eichsfeld region of his principality, for the purpose of "recatholicizing" this district.[21] This was a major undertaking, as evidenced by the retinue of 2000 men who accompanied the Archbishop. As in Würzburg and elsewhere, Mainz officials began by reasserting and enforcing the Elector's secular authority in the Eichsfeld. Local officials were replaced, administrative procedures reformed, and new ordinances promulgated. The bishop then ordered all his subjects to return to the Catholic Church. However, "in doing so he avoided coercion or an overly forceful policy, in accord with the long-standing Mainz reform methods."[22] Von Homburg expressed confidence that visitations, schools, and especially the pastoral work of the Jesuits would persuade the Lutheran inhabitants of the Eichsfeld to convert to Catholicism. The results of this moderate policy were mixed. There was considerable resistance to attempts to enforce Catholic uniformity, but in the long run, inhabitants accommodated themselves to the demands of their prince, at least in public. It is sign of the superficiality of the Catholicism of the inhabitants of Duderstadt, for example, that the town became "once again a citadel of Lutheranism" during the Thirty Years' War.[23]

The difficulties faced by Mainz authorities in introducing Catholicism in Protestant villages and towns indicate that "recatholicization" is a misnomer for this effort. Many modern Church historians, like late-sixteenth-century Catholic leaders, assume that the restoration of Catholic practice was a relatively easy process of returning to a living tradition. Yet ending Lutheran religious services that had been in place for several generations was far from a simple matter, and in many places Catholic services were just a distant memory. Popular resistance, intervention by Protestant states, and a Catholic reluctance to use forceful methods meant that the conversion of Protestant populations to Catholicism was a long and difficult process. It proceeded only in fits and starts in most Catholic areas of Germany before the Thirty Years' War.

Moderate, even hesitant, Catholic princes and their officials could be found everywhere, even at the court of the Habsburgs, the preeminent Catholic family. As R. J. W. Evans has emphasized, the Emperors Ferdinand I and Maximilian II were, at most, lukewarm Catholics.[24] Between 1550 and 1600, a sophisticated humanism dominated the central European elite and Maximilian's court "represented the very image of educated moderation."[25] The emperors resisted papal interference in their territories and tolerated Protestant nobles in their service. There was certainly no centrally managed anti-Protestant policy.

The fragmentation of the Habsburg lands, even the German-speaking ones, meant, however, that local and regional leaders could pursue a Counter-Reformation program. In some regions, such as the Tyrol and Outer Austria (*Vorderösterreich*), the local elite remained loyal to the old Church, preventing the development of a strong Protestant movement.[26] In the Tyrol, Protestantism had two strands. The first was Anabaptism, which arose in the aftermath of the Peasant's War of 1525 and was savagely repressed by the authorities from the 1540s onward.[27] The second was a tendency for various groups, especially miners and townspeople, to support the "chalice movement" (*Kelchbewegung*), which advocated the distribution of communion in both kinds and was also strong in neighboring Bavaria (see Chapter 1). In the 1570s, Habsburg authorities, under the leadership of the Archduke Ferdinand, moved more forcefully against the latter groups, strengthened by the Council of Trent's firm position against communion in two kinds. The arrival of the Jesuits (1560), a new church ordinance (1566), the confiscation of Protestant books, and the removal of Protestant officials – all of this demonstrates the seriousness with which Austrian officials in this region moved against heresy.[28] In contrast to other Habsburg territories, neither the Estates, which were firmly Catholic in the Tyrol, nor episcopal authorities resisted this forceful use of state power.

The Counter-Reformation was well underway in the westernmost provinces of the Habsburg domains by the 1570s. It would have to wait until the 1590s in Inner Austria.[29] In 1598, the young Archduke Ferdinand (the future Emperor Ferdinand II) took power in Graz. The son of a Bavarian princess, educated by the Jesuits, and inspired by a recent visit to the Loreto shrine in Italy, where he had sworn an oath to root out heresy in his lands, the 19-year-old Archduke moved quickly and ruthlessly against Protestantism.[30] He immediately abrogated the "Pacification of Graz" signed by his predecessor in 1572, which allowed nobles to practice the religion of their choice. This was followed by the annulment of the privileges given in 1578 to the cities of Graz, Klagenfurt, Laibach, and Judenburg, in which the Habsburgs promised to leave Protestant preachers and schools undisturbed. The hallmark of the Inner Austrian Counter-Reformation was the "Religious Reform Commission" (*Religions-Reformationskommission*). These commissions were led by bishops and other churchmen and traveled through the countryside with a strong military force. The commissions' charge was to remove Protestant ministers and schoolteachers, install Catholic priests, destroy unapproved churches and cemeteries, and drive unrepentant Protestants into exile. Only nobles were left to practice Protestantism, although they were not allowed to hire or host preachers. In the space of a few years, Catholicism became the only public religion in Inner Austria and Protestantism had been driven underground or behind the gates of noble castles.

On the other hand, Lower and Upper Austria, the regions along the Danube from Vienna to the Bavarian border, experienced a long and complicated Counter-Reformation.[31] By the 1550s, Protestantism had a strong hold on the nobility and towns. Walter Ziegler calls the period from the 1540s to the 1580s the "the high point of evangelical religious life in Austria," pointing to the flourishing of educational institutions, the number and quality of noble and burgher libraries, and the production of written works as evidence of this thriving culture. He estimates that at this time about one-half of the parishes and about the same proportion of the population were Protestant.[32] Yet the Catholic Church never lost control of its religious institutions, including monasteries and bishoprics. Furthermore, strengthened by the Jesuit house founded in 1551, Vienna remained firmly Catholic throughout the period. Finally, the Habsburgs, whatever the religious views of individual rulers, maintained a commitment to a state church that was Catholic.

The support of the monarchy and the resources of the institutions of the Church provided a basis for a slow revival of Catholicism in Austria. In 1568, the monarchy created a *Klosterrat*, a Council on Religious Houses, aimed at reforming both the moral and the financial conditions of monasteries and convents.[33] Staffed by Viennese officials, the Council was certainly a tool of the state, and it moved to tax monastic resources for the Habsburgs. At the same time, the Council stabilized conditions within monasteries by restoring some discipline and, especially, gaining control over monastic finances. By 1610 or so, the monasteries of Upper and Lower Austria, with their vast estates, were well enough organized to serve as sources of Catholic patronage and as local focal points of the Counter-Reformation.

The Habsburg state was hampered in its support of Catholicism by the strength of Protestant nobles in the Austrian Estates, the regional parliamentary bodies. Much of the anti-Protestant effort fell, then, to a new generation of bishops and other Church officials. The leader of this group was Melchior Khlesl (1553–1631), son of a Viennese baker and a convert from Protestantism. Beginning in the 1580s, Khlesl accumulated a series of important ecclesiastical positions, including vicar-general of Passau, Bishop of Wiener Neustadt, Court Preacher in Vienna, and, eventually, Bishop of Vienna itself. Khlesl's anti-Protestant strategy was a mix of persuasion – he traveled from town to town preaching and encouraging the clergy and the Catholic elite to greater religious dedication – and an increasingly stringent use of punishments against Protestant preachers, especially in towns where they were not protected by powerful nobles. This program showed signs of strengthening Catholicism in Lower Austria by 1600.

Upper Austria, further from Vienna and more firmly controlled by the evangelical nobility, was little affected by Khlesl's efforts. The first real Counter-Reformation measures there occurred during the suppression of the 1594–1597 peasant rebellion, in which peasants had exhibited Protestant sympathies. Catholic authorities imposed an "imperial general Reformation," which officially limited Protestant preachers to noble castles. In general, however, anti-Protestant measures were muted in Upper Austria before the Thirty Years' War. The Catholic party did not really gain confidence before 1610.[34]

Beginning in the 1560s, the Wittelsbach Dukes of Bavaria and their officials moved much more consistently against Protestants than the Habsburgs did in Austria.[35] Although the Wittelsbach family never wavered in its support of the Catholic Church, Bavaria was not free of Lutheran influences. Small groups of Lutherans and Anabaptists could be found in Bavaria in the 1530s and 1540s, but the greatest threat to Catholicism developed between 1550 and 1565 and found most of its adherents among the nobility. This was the "chalice movement" (*Kelchbewegung*), which began with demands to allow the laity to take the chalice during the mass.[36] Duke Albrecht V was not opposed to this; he tolerated the practice of the lay chalice in the 1550s while also seeking concessions from the Pope to allow it to continue.

Lutheran-minded nobles soon pushed for greater religious freedoms, hoping to follow the Upper Austrian model and increase the power of the Estates at the expense of the Duke. The contest exploded at the Ingolstadt Diet of 1563, when the state moved quickly to suppress the so-called "noble conspiracy." Ducal officials asserted links between the heresy and treason and moved aggressively against anyone suspected of Protestant sympathies.

The years around 1570 constituted the turning point when the Bavarian state made a clear shift in policy from "cautious willingness to compromise to a decidedly confessional attitude."[37] From this time on, religious conformity was required of all subjects. In the 1570s, the Clerical Council (founded 1556), manned exclusively by secular officials, established wide authority over church affairs. A series of new ordinances from Munich flooded the duchy, including a Decree on Religion (*Religionsmandat*) requiring regular church attendance, a new school ordinance, and decrees establishing censorship. Clergymen, university professors, and state officials at all levels had to swear the new Tridentine "confession of faith" (an oath of religious loyalty), effectively making it impossible for Protestants, and even some humanist-minded Catholics, to take positions in state service. Regular visitations, mostly organized by secular authorities, served to implement these measures as well as supervise their effectiveness.

What is most striking about the Bavarian case is its precocity, not the fact that Bavaria became the leading Catholic state, or even the subordination of the Church to the state. Church reformers of various kinds had been active in Bavaria throughout the sixteenth century, the Duchy had a tradition of loyalty to the Catholic Church, and the dukes were especially concerned with the danger of rebellion fomented by Protestant-minded nobles. The early commitment of the Bavarians to a militant anti-Protestant policy and, in the long run, to a forceful Tridentine reform owed much to the leading role of the Society of Jesus.

The Jesuits

The first Jesuit College in Germany was founded in 1544 in Cologne. Over the next 75 years, the Society of Jesus became a major force in Catholic Germany. Partly through their work as preachers and pastors, but especially through their educational institutions, the Jesuits exerted enormous influence on the culture of the Catholic clergy and the Catholic elite.[38]

The Jesuits' "way of proceeding" contained within it many of the central strands of German Catholicism in the sixteenth century. The Society certainly sought to establish itself on the frontiers of Catholicism, challenging Protestants on their own ground, the cities, and with their own tools, sermons, the printed word, and individual devotion. In 1568, for example, the provincial of the Rhine Province expressed support for founding a new house in the predominantly Lutheran Speyer because the city was "surrounded by princes of the opposing religion."[39] Regular reports to Rome, the *Litterae Annuae*, always began with a list of conversions, usually accompanied by a description of one or more dramatic examples.[40] Even the persons of the Jesuits, black-robed, ostentatiously austere and celibate, highly educated and disciplined, were meant to be a provocation to the Protestants. In this the Jesuits succeeded!

Yet, as John O'Malley has reminded us, the Jesuits were more than just the "shock troops of the Counter-Reformation."[41] The Jesuit houses in Germany were founded by the Catholic elite, mostly bishops and princes, but sometimes cathedral canons and city councilors as well, for the purpose of reforming the Church. Indeed, by founding a Jesuit establishment, Catholic leaders specifically signaled their commitment to *Tridentine* measures rather than the more traditional humanist inspired reform. The earliest foundations, in Cologne (1544), Vienna (1551), Ingolstadt (1556), and Munich (1559) indicate the places where Tridentine reform gained its earliest supporters. Conversely, the later establishment of Jesuit houses in places such as Constance (1604) and Bamberg (1610) reflects skepticism among much of the Catholic elite about Tridentine reform, particularly in those parts of Germany.

The Jesuits were enormously influential in the late sixteenth century, especially with the clergy, in particular the episcopacy. The Jesuits ran the German College (*Collegium Germanicum*) in Rome, which opened in 1552 for the purpose of educating clergy to serve in Germany.[42] By the 1570s, the German College focused its efforts on educating noblemen destined to be cathedral canons and bishops. By the 1590s, a new generation of *Germaniker* had begun to assume important positions in the German Church. A number of the reforming bishops of this era and many of the suffragan bishops and vicars general who worked under them had studied at the German College.[43] By colonizing important positions in the German hierarchy, the *Germaniker* exerted an influence out of proportion to their actual numbers.[44]

Jesuit secondary schools and universities were also widely influential in Catholic Germany. Every Jesuit house, or college, came to manage a school, and every one of them claimed a rapid increase in numbers of students during the 1570s and 1580s. The Jesuit schools filled a need in many cities and developed a reputation, among Protestants as well as Catholics, as the most disciplined and rigorous schools for boys. The college at Trier claimed that the number of students there rose from about 200 in 1561, to 700 by 1570, to 1000 in 1577, and remained at that level for the next 50 years.[45] The number of students in Dillingen rose from 313 in 1563 to 760 in 1605.[46] Even assuming that the local Jesuits exaggerated the number of students in their care, it is clear that the Jesuit schools attracted students. The urban ruling class in cities such as Cologne and later in the Westphalian cities of Münster and Paderborn sent their sons to the Jesuit schools. In the biconfessional cities of Augsburg and Osnabrück, the Jesuit *Gymnasium* (secondary school) served the Catholic elite, while Protestant boys attended a Protestant school.[47] In some places, for example in the largely Lutheran city of Speyer, the Jesuits claimed that a large number of Protestants attended their schools and boasted that this gave them opportunities to convert impressible young people to Catholicism.[48] Finally, most Jesuit schools provided some financial support for poorer students in a conscious effort to attract the support of urban artisan classes.

The Jesuit schools trained future clergymen as well as the Catholic elite. The papacy created several pontifical seminaries in the German-speaking lands, at Vienna (1574), Graz (1578), Fulda (1584), and Dillingen (1585), affiliated with the Jesuits, and designed to train priests for the German dioceses.[49] These seminaries, together with the German College in Rome, came nowhere near training the numbers of priests needed for a reformed clergy. The Jesuits, therefore, consciously aimed their secondary schools at future priests as well, seeing it as their duty to develop their moral and religious characters while also immersing them in an intense world of Catholic practice and ritual.[50] By the years around 1600, a whole hierarchy of institutions were in place to train priests. Young men who had studied under the Jesuits were moving in steady numbers into the priesthood, initially in the towns, but gradually into the countryside as well.

The Jesuits also gained a place in German universities, which further expanded their influence. In 1549, the Duke of Bavaria asked Peter Canisius and two other Jesuits to teach in the theological faculty at the University of Ingolstadt. After a couple of years, Canisius, the so-called second apostle of Germany, was credited with revitalizing the moribund theological program. Furthermore, he set the stage for the Jesuit takeover of the Faculty of Arts, which was officially completed in 1585.[51]In

1563/1564, the Bishop of Augsburg gave the Jesuits control of the entire University of Dillingen. The kind of domination held by the Jesuits in Ingolstadt and Dillingen was exceptional. Although the Jesuit influence in the new university in Würzburg was extensive, Bishop Julius Echter von Mespelbrunn carefully maintained his authority and never allowed the Society to control all faculty positions.[52] The Jesuits taught in every Catholic university in Germany but, besides Dillingen, fully controlled only the newer universities at Molsheim in Alsace (founded 1618), Paderborn (1616), Osnabrück (1632), and Bamberg (1648).[53] Despite their undoubted influence, the Jesuits did not completely dominate Catholic education, and their influence declined after 1650.

The Jesuits provided vital support for Tridentine reform by educating the clergy; they also supported the work of papal nuncios and reform-minded bishops by serving as preachers, episcopal visitors, and reformers of monasteries. All these activities were in accord with the strongly pastoral emphasis of the early years of the order. German Jesuits found Loyola's *Spiritual Exercises* an especially valuable tool in reinvigorating religious life in monasteries. Abbots and monks in some of the most venerable and respected Benedictine and Cistercian houses, such as St Blasien, Weingarten, Ottobeuren, and Salem in the southwest, enthusiastically received Jesuit visitors and enacted important reforms of monastic life in response to the fathers' efforts.[54] By the 1580s, Weingarten, in particular, became a center of Jesuit-inspired monastic reform.

The Jesuits also developed the Marian Congregations as a method of remaking both the clergy and the Catholic elite.[55] The Jesuits promoted these brotherhoods for men across Europe, organizing them along professional and class lines. The congregations were found in towns and cities and spread rapidly in the 1580s and 1590s, often first appearing as sodalities for students at Jesuit schools. The first Marian Congregation in Bavaria was founded at the University of Dillingen in 1574. In Munich in 1584, 58% of members were students, 23% clergy, and 19% laymen.[56] Influential Catholic laymen, for example the Dukes of Bavaria, bishops, government officials, and mayors joined congregations in cities such as Cologne, Vienna, Augsburg, and Münster, and in Catholic territories such as Bavaria and the *Hochstift* Würzburg.

The Jesuit directors of the Marian Congregations consciously aimed to create a pious elite that would lead the rest of Catholic society. Members were encouraged to openly display their religious commitment through frequent communion, participation in public processions, recruitment of new members, and anti-Protestant activities. In Cologne, for example, members of the congregation were expected to spy on and report the activities of suspected Protestants.[57] In urban areas, the congregations spread down the social scale, and new congregations were founded with ties to artisan guilds. As Louis Châtellier has argued, the Jesuits ambitiously hoped the congregations would lead to " the conversion of the whole town by apostleship of like by like."[58]

The Marian Congregations greatly marked the religiosity and the sensibilities of the German clergy at all levels.[59] These brotherhoods complemented the work of the Jesuit schools and universities in training priests. Priests with ties to the congregations affected an ascetic personal style, displayed an activist commitment to Catholicism, demonstrated their piety openly and publicly, and understood themselves as an elite charged with converting others to greater religious devotion. By the first decade of the seventeenth century, priests of this kind could be found across Germany. The Jesuits also spread their message of religious renewal through their churches. Jesuit churches in Germany, as Jeffrey Chipps Smith has shown, were designed to demonstrate the central tenets of Catholic doctrine while also guiding and assisting the worshipper.[60] The Jesuit church in Munich was dedicated to the Archangel St Michael, a symbol of militancy that pleased the Jesuits' Wittelsbach patrons. It was "first and foremost a teaching church," favored by range of Munich's inhabitants, most of whom had some connections to the Jesuits, including students, clergy, courtiers, and members of Jesuit confraternities.[61] On the one hand, the church owed much to Ignatius Loyola's *Spiritual Exercises.* "Ignatius was first and foremost a sensualist " and he particularly wrote about the importance of seeing and sight and St Michael's was full of vibrant images that encouraged the visitor/worshipper to contemplate central moments in the life of Christ.[62] The church also "offered the individual a progress – a pilgrimage of discovery potentially leading to salvation, which gradually unfolded as worshippers moved through the church to the choir." The nave of the church was dedicated to the life of Christ, from his birth to the Passion "before culminating in the over-life-size statue of him as the judge of humanity at the apex of the high altar."[63] Finally, at the crossing and in the choir the church's iconography emphasizes the worshipper's "third and final stage of their spiritual evolution: union with God."[64]

Smith emphasizes that Jesuit churches were stylistically diverse, but that all aimed for a conceptual unity. In designing and building them, the Society sought to integrate itself into local communities by adopting local styles and hiring local builders and artist. But each church was obviously a

Jesuit church, with the omnipresence of the IHS monogram, and each was openly designed to teach Catholicism through an appeal to the senses.[65] The unity of the message of Jesuit churches also contrasted sharply with older Catholic churches, with their diverse decoration built in over centuries. The Jesuit architectural and artistic program highlights the strong pastoral component of the Society's project, while also reminding us of the Jesuits' sophistication and effectiveness.

Despite this effectiveness, before the Thirty Years' War, Jesuit influence in Germany was confined to urban areas, schools, and the courts of rulers. The Jesuits were almost unknown in the countryside, except where they served on the staff of an episcopal visitation. The growth of the order is, however, impressive. Between the 1550s and the 1650s, over 40 Jesuit colleges were founded in the German lands.[66] This growth is a sign of the commitment of important elements within the German episcopacy, and among Catholic princes and town councilors, to the reform measures enacted by the Council of Trent. The Jesuits were essential for the implementation of Tridentine reform.

Tridentine Reform, Catholic Reform

The Council of Trent

The reforming decrees of the Council of Trent provided the German Church with a blueprint for reform, and the policies of Carlo Borromeo, Archbishop of Milan, provided the model of an active Tridentine reform program. The Catholic leadership in Germany however had a skeptical view of Trent. In fact, although many bishops claimed they wanted to attend the Council, very few German churchmen of any rank had traveled to Trent. When the Council ended, most German bishops, abbots, and Catholic princes maintained a distance from its decrees, a reflection of traditional skepticism for Roman and papal policies.

Hansgeorg Molitor has argued that church reform in sixteenth-century Germany was essentially "untridentine."[67] He points out that the decrees of the Council were not widely published in Germany. Peter Canisius had little success in convincing bishops to do so, and a high-ranking papal delegation failed to persuade the Catholic estates or the Emperor Maximilian II at the Imperial Diet of 1566 to officially publish the reform decrees. The Duke of Bavaria told the papal legate that he supported the decrees on doctrine but that the reform decrees would be difficult to implement in Germany. Molitor further emphasizes that many German bishops failed to hold the provincial or diocesan synods prescribed by the Council for the publication of its decrees. In most cases, bishops were reluctant to hold such "dangerous" synods (as the Catholic estates at the Imperial Diet of 1566 called them). Synods implied that the assembled clergy, led by powerful cathedral chapters and monasteries, had the power to make and approve decrees. With this in mind, many bishops feared that such meetings would be an opportunity for the clergy to demand financial and jurisdictional concessions in exchange for publication of the decrees.[68]

Clearly Church reform in Germany was not in the narrow sense "Tridentine." Indeed, certain aspects of the Tridentine program were difficult to adapt to German conditions. Few German churchmen supported the expansion of papal authority promoted by the Council. Furthermore, cathedral chapters, exempt monasteries and chapters, and many princes and nobles strongly opposed the reforms that strengthened episcopal power. Even those bishops who saw the decrees as an opportunity to increase their powers and jurisdiction recognized that this effort posed considerable practical difficulties. German bishops themselves remained imbedded in the aristocratic Imperial Church, even when quite a number of them came to be educated in Jesuit schools, and rarely advocated extensive changes at the upper level of the Church. Successful reforms had to be adapted to local conditions and depended on "a high level of political pragmatism and a willingness to compromise."[69]

The rest of the Church hierarchy, especially the cathedral chapters and the monasteries, remained very traditional about reform.[70] For these men, the defense of privileges and exemptions often took precedence over the desire to reform the clergy. Cathedral chapters prevented reformist officials from disciplining the canons and often protected the lower cathedral clergy as well. Monasteries resisted efforts by episcopal officials to discipline priests working in parishes under monastic control and even more tenaciously fought attempts to investigate conditions within monasteries. All ecclesiastical institutions hesitated to provide financial support for seminaries, visitations, or new episcopal bodies, such as the clerical councils set up by some bishops.

Important Tridentine forces were nevertheless present in Germany. The Jesuits were of course the most prominent of these, but it should be remembered that the Society pursued its own goals. For example, the Jesuit aim of converting Protestants could conflict with the aims of reforming bishops who often hoped to avoid clashes with powerful Protestant neighbors.[71] At other times, the Jesuits' determination to educate a

Catholic elite could hinder their ability to train priests for service in country parishes. Even reform-minded bishops could complain vehemently about arrogance and independence of the Jesuits, as did Bishop Friedrich von Wirsperg of Würzburg in the 1560s and 1570s.[72]

The papacy itself pressed reform in Germany by appointing reformist canons to vacancies during "papal months" and by attempting to influence the election of bishops. Papal policies were, however, less than consistent, and the mutual suspicion between the German Church and the Curia always undermined Rome's influence.[73] As one historian explains, "if one spoke of reform in Germany, the answer [from German clerics] was always that one should start first of all in Rome."[74] The creation in 1572 of the *Congregatio Germanica* in Rome is another indication of the papacy's concern with affairs in Germany.[75] The cardinals in the Congregation sought to support Tridentine reform in Germany and operated primarily through the papal nuncios. Permanent nunciatures were established in Vienna (1560s), Graz (1580), and Cologne (1584), and the nuncios pressured the bishops to organize reforms. Felician Ninguarda, who served as a special "roving nuncio" in southern Germany from 1569 to 1583, was especially influential.[76] The nuncios, however, could not implement reforms themselves and often found themselves bogged down in political disputes, in attempts to influence episcopal elections, and in jurisdictional disputes within the Church. As outsiders (most of them were Italian), they represented the attempt to reform the German Church from the top down by creating a reform-minded episcopacy.

Reform of this kind, pushed by activist princes and supported by the Jesuits, sometimes dramatically disrupted traditional political and social arrangements.[77] In January 1570, Balthasar von Dernbach, just 22 years old, was elected abbot of the ancient monastery of Fulda. As abbot, Balthasar also became ruler of an important territory astride both vital trade routes and the confessional frontier between Catholicism and Lutheranism. Balthasar's colleagues, the noble canons of the monastery, elected him because he had distinguished himself as an efficient administrator during his short tenure as dean. To their surprise, Balthasar turned out to be an ardent Tridentine reformer and a committed supporter of the Jesuits.[78] Within a couple of years, the young abbot had turned political and religious life in his territory upside down.

Balthasar came to be deeply influenced by the Jesuits and acted on the belief that he was on a personal mission to restore Catholicism. The Jesuits mobilized a young, cosmopolitan, and activist group of supporters in

Fulda and worked with the abbot and his officials to remove priests' concubines, banish Lutheran pastors from country parishes, and enforce the abbot's authority in noble-dominated districts. This ambitious policy led to conflicts with the local noblemen, many of whom were Protestant. More than a confessional conflict, however, Balthasar's Tridentine reforms became a clash of political cultures and religious mentalities in Fulda. In 1576, a group of armed noblemen, Protestant and Catholic, supported by the Bishop of Würzburg, forced the abbot to resign. The parties in Fulda expressed different understandings of "religion." In the view of the abbot's opponents, Balthasar was guilty of giving too much "respect" to religion, of making it too central and important in his rule in Fulda. What he needed to do, in their view, was use more "discretion" in religious matters. These members of the Fulda elite wanted peace and order and, correctly, believed toleration was needed to achieve it. Balthasar, however, believed that his duty was to reform Catholicism along the lines of the Council of Trent. In doing so, as Gerritt Walther argues, he " not only gave Tridentine Catholicism an institutional basis – he made it social, politically, and intellectually attractive."[79] He was the ultimate victor. Restored to power by an imperial commission in 1590, he brought the Jesuits back to Fulda and returned, somewhat more carefully, to his policies of religious reform.

Balthasar's policies in Fulda were unusually extreme in the German context, and his successor followed a less aggressive program. In most places, the Tridentine phase of Church reform was really short lived, stretching from the 1570s up to the beginning of the Thirty Years' War. Even during this period, the reform program was usually limited, a kind of "transitional phase," characterized by a "coexistence of newer and older elements of Church reform," focusing on the reform of the clergy.[80] Tridentine reform did remain one aspect of German Catholicism into the eighteenth century, but it never defined how the Catholic leadership behaved. It is also too simplistic to describe German Catholicism as essentially Tridentine or to postulate that the clergy that came out of the reforms of decades around 1600 was truly "Tridentine," as the discussion of the reception of the reform program will show.

The reform of the clergy: Goals and methods

Although the German Church did not wholeheartedly embrace the reforming decrees of the Council of Trent, there was widespread support for a reform of the clergy. This reform, after a hesitant and doomed effort to improve the cathedral clergy, focused on the perceived moral and personal failings of parish priests, monks, and nuns. Echoing pre-Reformation humanist critiques rather more than those of the Council, reformers moved to eliminate sexual "crimes" (especially concubinage), drunkenness, absenteeism, and the general neglect of pastoral duties. These goals were in some sense "defensive," in that they aimed at correcting abuses, many of them long-standing and all of them targets of Protestant critics. Clergymen in Catholic Germany began to feel the impact of these reforms in the 1570s.

At the same time, most Church leaders recognized that a more ambitious effort to remake the clergy along the lines favored by the Jesuits would have to wait. It was certainly not possible to properly educate all priests, nor could the benefice system be reformed to pay parish priests properly. Under these conditions, it would be hard to create a real sense of professionalism. Most monastic establishments, the military orders, and the cathedral chapters would remain highly secular. Part of the problem was that it was difficult to institute the methods of reform mandated at Trent. Although bishops were willing to issue decrees demanding better behavior and performance from the clergy, they were reluctant to call synods, and few of them had the resources to organize a regular system of visitations. Funding for seminaries was hard to come by, and when staffing problems forced bishops to turn to the Jesuits to run them, cathedral chapters and monasteries often sabotaged their foundation. Of course, even the most reform-minded upper clergymen found reasons to avoid changing their own personal lifestyle. The widespread creation of an educated, professional clergy would have to wait until the late seventeenth century.

Clashes between Catholic princes and bishops also hindered the reform of the clergy. In the prince-bishoprics, Catholic secular and spiritual authority was combined in the bishop's hands. In some of them, as in Würzburg, and to a lesser extent Mainz, this concentration of authority allowed for a consistent reform of the clergy. Yet many bishops only governed small and fragmented territories, and reforms required the cooperation of secular authorities. Even in Bavaria, often considered the model of church/state cooperation, conflicts festered between the ducal regime and the Bishops of Salzburg, Chiemsee, Freising, Passau, and Regensburg. These difficulties were partially resolved with the signing of a concordat in 1583. This agreement was a compromise, but it did give secular authorities the right to supervise and tax the clergy. On the other hand, the Bavarian effort to create a new "Bavarian diocese" based in Munich failed, and the regime continued to have to coordinate religious policy with a variety of bishops.[81]

Provincial and diocesan synods increased the clergy's awareness of the decrees of the Council of Trent, and reports and publications from these meetings spread even to the many dioceses where no synods took place. Some synods, like the one convened in Dillingen in 1567 by the Cardinal Otto Truchsess von Waldburg, Bishop of Augsburg, have been called "exemplary for the implementation of the Council's decrees in the other German bishoprics as well."[82] Von Waldburg published the Tridentine decrees immediately before the synod so that the synod would be in a position to establish priorities adapted to the German context. The resulting decrees emphasized assuring the religious loyalty of the clergy, especially by ordering the swearing of the confession of faith. Beyond that, they reaffirmed the Catholic Church's commitment to the cult of the saints, the seven sacraments, and the authority of the hierarchy. Second priority was given to the reform of the clergy, with a focus on the goal of eliminating concubinage, absenteeism, and pluralism. Finally, the assembled clergy committed itself to founding a seminary, supporting Catholic universities, repairing churches, and reorganizing the episcopal bureaucracy. These decrees were typically German, in that they asserted the clergy's commitment to Trent, while really focusing on anti-Protestant measures and rather traditional admonitions to the clergy to improve its behavior.

Much of the clergy showed real enthusiasm for reform at the various synods held in the aftermath of Trent. The synod convened by the Bishop of Constance in 1567 was well attended and yielded an extensive set of statutes a year later.[83] Here too, the clergy supported anti-Protestant measures, accepted decrees aimed at eliminating concubinage and absenteeism, and discussed funding a seminary. The provincial synod in Salzburg in 1569 brought together clergy from the seven dioceses of the archbishopric, giving it considerable importance in south Germany.[84] The 1573 synod in Salzburg gave detailed instructions for the implementation of Tridentine decrees. Yet in all these cases, initial enthusiasm slackened as traditional problems and conflicts arose. The personal commitment to reform of many bishops was limited. The Bishop of Constance, for example, moved permanently to Rome after the 1567 synod, making it impossible for him to press for reforms, and there were few synods after the first post-Trent meetings. In Trier, there were no meetings after a synod in 1569, partly because of resistance from French officials, who did not want to concede authority to the bishops for those parts of the Trier Province that lay in France.[85]

Finally, as already discussed, synods were "dangerous events" for all parties. These gatherings gave the assembled clergy the power to assert itself in negotiations with the bishop. This was, of course, a threat to the bishops, who hoped that Trent would increase their power, not undermine it. Parish priests, who had little clout at the synods, correctly surmised that they would be the objects of many of the resulting decrees. Synods could also be dangerous for privileged institutions, such as the great monasteries of the southwest, which feared that an alliance of the lower clergy and the bishops might lead to a reduction of their privileges and to the taxation of their wealth. This threat was real enough in the discussions of how to fund the episcopal seminaries required by the Council of Trent.

In Cologne, papal nuncios struggled for 70 years to bring a seminary for the training of parish priests into existence.[86] As representatives of the popes, the nuncios faced resistance to their efforts from the Cologne clergy, which looked skeptically on initiatives ordered by Rome. The nuncios eventually secured the support of the Wittelsbach bishops of Cologne, Ernst von Bayern (ruled 1583–1612) and Ferdinand von Bayern (1612–1650), for this project, but the cathedral chapter led clerical opposition to a new seminary tax approved by the papacy. The seminary founded by the bishop in 1615 was small, trained only about three priests a year, and never received sufficient funding. It did not survive the Thirty Years' War.[87] Although the Cologne clergy did not support an episcopal seminary along Tridentine lines, the same men were not opposed to reforming the clergy. The cathedral chapter, monasteries, and other institutions funded and supported a range of schools designed to train better priests for service in the parishes, with some success by the 1620s.[88]

In the Bishopric of Speyer, plans for a diocesan seminary collapsed in the 1570s and 1580s amid conflicts between the bishops, the cathedral chapter, and the Jesuits.[89] In the 1570s, the cathedral chapter put pressure on the bishop to found a seminary. As early as 1561, the canons reorganized the cathedral school into a training school for parish priests, arguing that good priests needed a basic education in the humanities and the catechism in order to be successful pastors. The traditionalist Bishop Marquard von Hattstein did not support this school, preferring to provide stipends to attend universities to candidates for the priesthood. Yet in the 1580s, with the reform-minded Bishop Eberhard von Dienheim in power, the Speyer hierarchy could not find the resources to fund a full-fledged seminary. Part of the problem was the general poverty of this small diocese. A second issue was the canons' fear that a seminary would allow the Jesuits, who were the only possible teachers, to increase their influence in Speyer. As was the case elsewhere, the local clergy considered the Jesuits dangerously combative in the middle Rhine region where the powerful Calvinist Electoral Palatinate dominated.

Seminaries had come into being in some places in Catholic Germany by the Thirty Years' War. They indicate, above all, that the German Church was selective in its commitment to the decrees of the Council of Trent. On the one hand, most bishops and many cathedral chapters considered seminaries unproblematic; after all, they fit comfortably as part of a traditionalist, humanist-inspired reform of the parish clergy. On the other hand, the involvement of nuncios and the Jesuits made the seminaries a papal project and thus suspect. Finally, in many places, monasteries and chapters were not willing to make the financial sacrifice needed to found seminaries and bishops could not fund them alone. The seminaries were, as a result, slow in coming and too small to provide the large number of priests envisioned by the Tridentine decrees.

Visitations were the favored method of investigating conditions in the parishes and of reforming the clergy in Germany.[90] Episcopal officials, and on rare occasions bishops themselves, traveled through the countryside investigating the personal and professional behavior of the clergy, the physical condition of churches, cemeteries, and parsonages, and, less often, the religious and moral behavior of the population. These investigations led to the correction of some abuses on the spot as well as the formulation of a reform program after their completion. Visitations also involved the keeping of minutes and the writing of reports, which gave state and church a somewhat better grasp of religious conditions in the countryside. Most bishops, however, were unable to institute a regular system of visitations before the eighteenth century. As a result, the information they gathered was fragmentary and the reforms they instituted were usually inconsistent.

Visitations brought parish priests out of the isolation of their rural world and exposed their lives in new ways to the inspection of their superiors. Episcopal officials conducted 19 visitations in the rural chapter of Karlstadt in the Prince-Bishopric of Würzburg between 1596 and 1630. Furthermore, the dean of the chapter made further inspection tours between the episcopal visitations.[91] Here, as elsewhere, the initial visitations were extraordinary events. Between 1575 and 1580, officials from the Clerical Council in Würzburg attended meetings of the rural chapter, where priests gathered several times a year. At these meetings, priests were required to swear the *Professio catholicae fidei*, an oath of allegiance to the Catholic Church and answer questions about their lifestyle, mostly designed to uncover cases of concubinage. In the 1580s, the deans of the rural chapters visited individual parishes and questioned priests and parishioners. These inspections were apparently less than thorough, since episcopal officials conducted a more detailed visitation in 1593, the first complete trip through this district. On these visits, officials asked about the personal life of the priest, his performance of services and catechism lessons, the income of the parish and inspected the physical condition of the school and the church. These early visitations focused on concubinage, which was an obsession for Tridentine reformers in Germany. Concubinage was a matter of public knowledge and thus susceptible to correction from above. Once identified during a visitation, a priest guilty of concubinage could be warned, threatened, or removed. In the Karlstadt district, 26 of 29 priests had concubines in 1579; in 1600, there were few left and by 1620 open concubinage had been eliminated.[92]

After 1600, visitations in the rural chapter of Karlstadt became routine events. Between 1607 and 1624, for example, there were seven visitations, all conducted by the same visitor, following the same route, and generally asking the same set of questions.[93] In this period, the sense of crisis had faded, and the visitors were somewhat less concerned about the behavior of the clergy, although excessive drinking and inappropriate socializing remained a concern. The visitors put more effort into the mundane task of stabilizing the economic condition of parishes and improving pastors' incomes. Finally, in the decade before the Thirty Years' War, episcopal officials placed an emphasis on improving the quality of pastoral care. Priests now found themselves examined on the quantity and quality of catechism classes, sermons, and provision of the sacraments. In this district of the Hochstift Würzburg, we can clearly identify a shift from a "first phase" in the reform of the clergy that was aimed at correcting "abuses" to a second phase aimed at improving the quality of pastoral care.[94] This shift occurred in Würzburg, Bavaria, and perhaps on the middle Rhine (Mainz, Trier) around 1600; it would only occur after 1650 in the rest of Catholic Germany.

In the huge Bishopric of Constance, the visitations were much more chaotic and correspondingly had less influence on conditions in the parishes.[95] The bishops here conducted many visitations, but actually ruled only a small territory, so that they depended on the support, or at least toleration, of Catholic princes in order to conduct visitations. In some cases, as in the Austrian territories of Outer Austria (*Vorderösterreich*), secular officials not only supported visitations conducted by the bishops but also dominated them, sometimes at the expense of episcopal authority. In other places, for example in the parishes subject to the great monasteries and the military orders, visitors were sometimes refused admission to local parishes. According to Peter Thaddäus Lang, "the Constance visitors operated with considerably less discipline than their Würzburg colleagues, and the Swabian church overseers adhered much less [rigorously] to their list of questions."[96] The result was little unity in either the information gathered or in the reforms that resulted. In some places, the visitors apparently focused on the behavior of the priests, in others they investigated the conditions in the churches, while in yet others they attempted to arbitrate in legal and jurisdictional disputes.

If there was little system to the visitations in Constance, and thus little consistent Tridentine reform, in Speyer the visitation was a one-time event. In 1583–1584 Vicar General Beatus Moses led a visitation of almost all of the 30 parishes of the Prince-Bishopric.[97] This detailed and careful inspection produced several volumes of minutes. The vicar general followed up his investigation by moving aggressively against a number of priests he had found guilty of concubinage, gross neglect of duties, and absenteeism. Clearly inspired by Trent, as the cathedral chapter, the bishop, and the vicar general openly asserted, Moses' visitation jumpstarted a reform of the clergy. Yet there would be no other visitations until the 1680s! Unlike in Würzburg, but similar to what happened in much of Catholic Germany, visitations in the Bishopric of Speyer did not become a routine part of Church administration. Indeed, in most places, the bureaucratization of Tridentine Catholicism moved very slowly before the Thirty Years' War.

Church leaders of all confessions sought to create institutions that would enforce clerical discipline and religious norms. The Council of Trent clearly gave this duty to the bishops, and all bishops made some effort to revitalize the episcopal administration. After all, synods and visitations would have little impact if their decrees and reports were not enforced. Catholic leaders turned to the bureaucratic methods of their day, educated middle-class officials, councils, and ordinances.

Not surprisingly, Bavaria and Würzburg developed the most efficient ecclesiastical administrations. In both places, Church administration developed in tandem with, indeed as part of, state development. The key institution was the Clerical Council. We have seen how this institution took an important role in the suppression of Protestantism. These councils also helped enforce various episcopal decrees aimed at reforming the clergy. In Würzburg, these included new statutes for rural chapters in 1584 and a general church ordinance in 1589. The councils disciplined wayward priests, examined the qualifications of new clergymen, and adjudicated disputes among the clergy and between priests and their parishioners. Staffed primarily by middle-class men trained in canon law, in Würzburg, the councils worked closely with top officials of the episcopal administration, like the vicars general and the suffragan bishops and with state officials as well.[98] In Bavaria, the ties to the various episcopal administrations were more distant, but cordial and cooperative after the concordat of 1583.

Such an efficient administrative apparatus depended on the close cooperation of Church and state. In theory, all ecclesiastical princes were in a position to copy the Würzburg model, but in practice, they did not do so. In the western bishoprics, particularist forces led by the cathedral chapters made any extension of episcopal authority difficult, even if its purpose was church reform. In the Archbishopric of Trier, the cathedral chapter and several monasteries resisted efforts by the Archbishop/ Elector to raise new taxes, which were to be used not only for strengthening the episcopal administration but also for building fortifications and expanding the secular bureaucracy. The Archbishop's position as secular prince probably hurt his efforts to institutionalize Church reform. Ecclesiastical institutions resisted the development of a more efficient state, fearing a loss of their own autonomy as well as the rise in taxation that accompanied all state buildings.[99] The Archbishops of Trier pursued an energetic reform program without the benefit of an expanded administration and depended on the Jesuits to staff their visitations.[100]

In Cologne, new institutions only appeared in the episcopat of Ferdinand von Bayern (ruled 1612–1650).[101] Ferdinand expanded the role of the Church Council (*Kirchenrat*), giving it leadership in reforming the clergy. The episcopal administration also formed special reform commissions to travel to the countryside and institute reforms. In addition, Archbishop Ferdinand and the episcopal curia were intent on reducing the role of the archdeacons, who were dependent on the cathedral chapter and had traditionally supervised the rural clergy. The efforts at creating a more centralized episcopal administration were only partly successful. The Church Council was disbanded in 1616, with its duties left to the vicar general. The archdeacons, citing their traditional rights, remained influential into the eighteenth century. They retained, for example, the right of "approbation," that is the authority to turn over a pastoral position to a new priest.

In southwest Germany, the Bishop of Constance founded a new clerical council in 1594.[102] This council was clearly modeled on the Würzburg example, and its members, drawn from both the cathedral chapter and the episcopal administration, attempted to operate as the spiritual administration of the diocese. The Council was quite active in the 1590s, especially in the smaller Catholic territories around Constance. It investigated reports of concubinage and absenteeism and disciplined parish priests. The minutes of the Clerical Council show, however, that most of its time was taken up with jurisdictional disputes, such as conflicts between monasteries and the bishop over the right to collect certain fees, or disputes about priestly inheritances, and, of course, the endemic contention over the tithe. The situation was similar for the consistory of the Bishops of Passau, which was based in Vienna and functioned much like a clerical council. According to Rona Johnston, "the records of the Passau Consistory under Khlesl [the renowned Austrian church reformer Melchior Khlesl] are remarkable for the lack of evidence of a reforming spirit. They deal largely with cases of debt and disputed inheritance amongst the clergy   and there is no mention of the disciplining of unruly clergy   ."[103] Even when the institutions were in place, their ability to function over time as forces for the reform of the clergy was clearly limited.

In Catholic Switzerland, the papal nuncio Giovanni Francesco Bonomi promoted Tridentine reform at the expense of episcopal authority.[104] Bonomi, a disciple of Carlo Borromeo, the reforming Bishop of Milan, "undertook a rigorous course of visitations that sought to root out concubinage among the clergy, restore the recognition of ecclesiastical jurisdiction, reaffirm the enclosure of nuns, and regularize the bestowal of benefices."[105] The initial response of the clergy to Bonomi's efforts was negative, but the rulers of the Catholic cantons were more ambivalent. On the one hand, they resented his disregard for Swiss privileges, particularly local control of clerical appointments; on the other hand the cantons appreciated his willingness to criticize and bypass the ineffective Bishops of Constance.[106] In the long run, Bonomi's ongoing attack on the Swiss clergy in his reports to Rome reinforced Swiss efforts to establish their own ecclesiastical institutions, which included a permanent nunciature in Lucerne (1586) and an independent episcopal commissioner (1605). The result was not the strengthening of episcopal institutions and authority along the lines of the reforming decrees of Trent but a kind of devolution of that authority and its appropriation by the officials of the Catholic cities and cantons.

The reform of the clergy could only be fragmented and haphazard, given the varied and fragmented nature of Catholic institutions in Germany. To be sure, there were schools, seminaries, and universities, but not enough of them to remake the whole clergy. Most parishes were investigated at least once by episcopal visitations between 1565 and 1620, but visitations were not held regularly or consistently. Some bishops organized new institutions, like the clerical councils, to supervise and discipline the clergy, but these bodies were poorly financed and often possessed little real authority. The effectiveness of Tridentine reform, which focused on reform of the clergy, thus depended on the personal commitment of the bishops and their top advisors. Needless to say, the personal nature of reform further contributed to its inconsistency.

The reform of the clergy: Reception

Parish priests were the primary targets of discipline and reform. How did they respond to this effort? To what extent did they resist, accommodate, accept, or even internalize reform measures? Were priests more celibate, better educated, more attentive to their duties, and more loyal to the Catholic Church in 1620 than they had been in the middle of the sixteenth century? Since the reform program was itself inconsistent, the parish clergy's response was also varied. It is clear that the German clergy did not meet the high expectations of the most rigorous reformers. At the same time, the crisis situation of the pre-Trent period, which included widespread shortages of priests, absenteeism, and neglect of pastoral duties, had been at least partially overcome by the decade after 1600.

The reform of the clergy moved more slowly and more sporadically in Germany than it did in Italy and Spain. Nevertheless, priests everywhere had to respond to pressure in two main areas.[107] First, priests found their personal lifestyle under considerable scrutiny, with the initial focus on concubinage, followed by a concern for the nature of priests' social relations, their clothing, and their habits of drinking and eating. Finally, after about 1600, visitors wanted to know about the priests' personal piety, particularly about how often and to whom they confessed. Even in the most remote villages, parish priests were aware of these issues and were forced to respond in some way.[108]

The second focus of Tridentine reformers was on pastoral services. Reforming ordinances ordered priests to perform the sacraments as required by the Council, demanded that priests give sermons, and ordered them to teach catechism classes. Visitation questionnaires tended to focus in the early years (to 1600) on church services and the dispensation of the sacraments. The sacraments, in particular the Eucharist given in one kind, served to distinguish Catholic from Protestant services. In regions such as Westphalia, parts of Franconia, and Austria, the prohibition of communion in both kinds forced clergymen to make a confessional choice that they had often been able to avoid up to this point. Pressure on priests to improve sermons and introduce catechism classes came later, and reformers understood these as tools for deepening the religious knowledge and confessional commitment of the population.

Priests in some places resisted reform measures and a few even openly defended concubinage. In 1568, priests in the Breisgau region of Outer Austria claimed that they could not afford to pay housekeepers, making unpaid concubines necessary.[109] In Switzerland, concubinage was deeply entrenched and "a long-standing practice that defined the economy of many a parish priest attempting to live honorably with his domestic helper."[110] Such arguments were of little avail, for the clear prohibitions in the Tridentine decrees and in many synodal decrees and the long tradition of reformist attacks made it very difficult to defend publicly acknowledged concubinage. Furthermore, this practice could be reformed from above and episcopal officials could, and increasingly did, discipline concubinist priests.[111]

The clergy's response to Tridentine reform measures was conditioned by several factors. One issue was the extent to which each priest personally agreed with or supported the reforms. Jesuit-educated priests, for example, had usually internalized the values of the new celibate, educated, and confessionally committed clergy. The vast majority of the rural clergy, however, brought at most only a limited commitment to such values into the villages. These men considered the practical cost of disobeying orders coming from above, calculating, for example, the likelihood of being caught, the severity of possible punishments, and the like. Furthermore, priests had to consider the demands and concerns of their parishioners and neighbors. What were the costs within the village of enforcing new regulations or instituting new religious practices? Studies of conditions at the local level show that before the Thirty Years' War most priests remained firmly embedded in village culture, sharing the values of their neighbors rather than those of the urban clergy, the Jesuits, or reforming officials.[112]

The parish clergy of the western districts of the Archbishopric of Trier was very slow to adopt Tridentine models.[113] These priests remained peasant-priests into the late seventeenth century, sharing the day-to-day lifestyle of their neighbors. Their personal behavior was in some ways even less Tridentine. Concubinage, which had been almost universal in the 1570s, was never completely eliminated over the next century. Episcopal visitors regularly lamented excessive drinking by the parish clergy. Priests were also slow to fulfill their pastoral duties as understood by their superiors. They did provide sermons, something their parishioners wanted, and rarely taught catechism classes, which were in any case met with widespread popular indifference.

Parish priests responded to the reform of the clergy in much the same way throughout western Germany. Concubinage did not survive in Speyer and the Catholic southwest as long as it did in west Trier, perhaps because these regions were less isolated and secular authorities like the Habsburg government made a concerted effort to enforce celibacy.[114] Otherwise, priests did not and could not give up the lifestyle of the peasant-priest; indeed, Church officials with boring regularity lamented that rural priests drank, gambled, and socialized with other villagers.[115] Priests generally provided the pastoral services their parishioners desired, above all the mass with the elevation of the host, baptisms, annual confession and communion, processions, and celebration of feast days. Sermons were expected and provided but catechism classes were a failure, in Electoral Cologne as elsewhere in the west.[116]

In Würzburg and Bavaria, more efficient disciplinary structures forced priests to accommodate somewhat more quickly to reform measures.[117] In Würzburg, improvements in clerical incomes helped priests focus on their pastoral work rather than on farming activities. The fact that in 1619 a group of priests refused to socialize with a colleague who spent a lot of time in the inn is an indication that a distinct clerical culture was beginning to emerge.[118] In pastoral work, priests attempted to introduce the population to the practice of blessing the sick and to the sacrament of extreme unction, with little success before 1620.[119] Catechism lessons faced the same problems in Bavaria and Würzburg as they did in the west and priests often gave them up.

The reception of Tridentine reforms by the priests of Westphalia was slow and late. The intermingling of Protestant and Catholic practices, the influence of Protestant noblemen, and indecisive leadership from the bishops left the Catholic rural clergy with a lot of room to maneuver. This space made what one historian calls "a renewal of professional ethics" difficult and left rural parishes in the hands of men like the members of the priestly dynasty of the Deys, who served in a number of different parishes in the Bishopric of Paderborn across the whole sixteenth century.[120] Sons and nephews of priests used family connections to obtain the necessary education to become a priest, then succeeded to benefices held by family members. Many of the Deys were pluralists, holding several benefices at one time, and absenteeism was common among them. Imbedded in a network of friends, patrons, and clients, the Deys were old-style priests. In the late sixteenth century, their position became more tenuous, especially since individual members of the family maintained close ties with Lutheran neighbors. After 1600, Tridentine reform began to intrude on this world. "Out of necessity the Deys could pay lip service to upholding the minimum Tridentine standards, without however internalizing them."[121] They swore the Tridentine confession of faith and promised to serve their parishes diligently, yet still did not reside in their parishes. Only in 1613 was the last of the fourth generation of this dynasty removed from his position.

Clergymen in cities and towns responded more quickly and more positively to reform measures. Their response was, however, conditioned by local conditions. Beginning in the 1580s, the town council of the Catholic city of Überlingen on Lake Constance promoted the reform by reorganizing the clergy into a collegiate chapter (*Stift*) to enforce clerical discipline in the city.[122] The creation of a chapter, a traditional kind of corporate body, did not mesh well with the centralizing measures ordered at Trent, yet the city's priests supported these measures, in part because they improved the status and income of the Überlinger secular clergy. The bishop, however, was shut out of the process, making clerical reform in Überlingen essentially a local affair.

Developments in Cologne, the largest and most important Catholic city, were somewhat more complicated, but here too local needs and conditions modified the reception of Tridentine reform in significant ways.[123] By the 1580s, the Cologne clergy had a reputation among reformers for being free of "abuses" such as concubinage. Reformers, who included the papal nuncios based in Cologne, the Jesuits, some episcopal officials, and elements within the city council, then focused their efforts on improving the quality of pastoral services in the city. As in Überlingen, the city council in Cologne used its influence to improve the finances of the parishes. A 1580 papal bull assigned the incomes of 12 benefices in collegiate chapters to parish priests, requiring in turn that the priests be properly educated and reside in their parishes.[124] Although the chapters tenaciously fought this measure – one benefice did not go to a parish priest until 1699 – it demonstrated the city's commitment to pastoral work within the parish framework. Yet Cologne also remained a city of convents and monasteries, and many of them were active in pastoral work. As a result, after 1600 Catholicism in Cologne seemed to have two characteristics. One came close to the aims of the Tridentine decrees, since it included a revitalized religious life in the parish, exemplified by a greater respect for the secular clergy and a greater attention to parish conformity, with most people fulfilling their Easter obligation at the parish church. The second aspect was a wider, but rather diffuse religious revival, which marked the whole seventeenth century. This resurgence was often led by the orders, including the older mendicants as well as the Jesuits, who preached, organized processions, fostered the cult of the saints, and led new sodalities and confraternities. This aspect owed much to the city's traditional religiosity. As Franz Bosbach emphasizes,

> The renewal of the Cologne church into a pastoral and confessional church was – one can conclude – not a rebuilding on a strictly Tridentine basis, but rather a way of making use of a confessional reorientation toward all the conditions of being in the world, as they developed out of the specific urban traditions of Cologne.[125]

The initial response to the Council of Trent among the upper clergy of the Bishopric of Bamberg was negative. These men viewed the decrees as completely unrealistic and thus impossible to implement. The more intellectually inclined among them found that Tridentine measures did not accord well with their own irenical tendencies, while the practically minded feared that reforms would provoke hostile actions by their Protestant neighbors.[126] Similar reactions characterized the initial response to Trent across Germany. Yet in Bamberg and everywhere else in Catholic Germany, Trent gradually led to a revived Catholicism that came much closer to the Tridentine model of a pastoral church than had seemed possible in 1550.

Monastic reform

The reform of the clergy in Germany also included a broad effort to improve conditions in monasteries and convents. Urban monasteries and convents and abbeys in areas threatened by Protestantism were often critically short of monks and nuns by the mid-sixteenth century. The mendicant houses and convents in the city of Speyer, for example, were inhabited by only a handful of regulars in the 1580s.[127] Even when rural monasteries survived, they were often isolated when Protestant princes secularized neighboring houses. Complaints by church reformers about the moral and educational levels within monasteries were common, if at times exaggerated. Ultimately, Tridentine reform of monasteries aimed at two problems, a lack of respect for the monastic virtues of poverty, chastity, and obedience and an effort to enforce episcopal authority over monastic houses. In the last decades of the sixteenth century, abbots and abbesses, monks, and nuns responded positively to the first of these efforts and quite effectively resisted the second.

This ambiguity generally marked the monastic response to the Council of Trent. A call for renewal drew on vibrant observant and reformist traditions within almost every order. If many German monasteries were willing to undertake internal reforms, they wanted to do so on their own terms, while maintaining their traditions of independence from episcopal authority. This was particularly true in southwest Germany, where the old, like the Benedictines at Weingarten and St Blasien and the Cistericians at Salem, were wealthier and more powerful than the Bishops of Constance and never accepted the bishops' leadership in the region.[128] Furthermore, many monasteries and convents held incorporated parishes from which they gained considerable financial benefit. Not surprisingly, abbots' commitment to reform did not usually include a willingness to return resources to the parishes or pay parish priests better in order to improve the quality of pastoral care. Finally, the status, influence, and favor accorded the Jesuits by the Papacy, bishops, and Catholic princes gave the older orders a kind of inferiority complex about their place within a reordered Catholicism.[129]

The Papacy vigorously pursued monastic reform in the immediate aftermath of the Council of Trent. Nuncios were particularly active, visiting monasteries, and pressing abbots to reform their houses. In 1574, nuncio Felician Ninguarda visited the monasteries of Regensburg.[130] He went on to visit many houses in southern Germany in 1579, including the wealthy abbeys of Petershausen, Salem, Weingarten, Schussenried, Ochsenhausen, and Rot.[131] Ninguarda's efforts received some support within the monasteries, although changes came slowly. His efforts, for example, led to the reform of the female collegiate chapters of Niedermünster and Obermünster in Regensburg, but these houses did not produce reform statutes until 1608.[132] In other places, Ninguarda could effect little change. During his 1579 visit to Weingarten, the nuncio demanded that the abbot eliminate a range of abuses and enforce the vows of poverty, chastity, and obedience. Some reforms of the monastery's school were made. "Otherwise [writes the historian of Weingarten, Rudolf Reinhardt], everything remained as always: the abbot's economic management stayed the same, [and] the concubines remained in the abbey."[133] Nuncio Giovanni Francesco Bonomi's attempts to reform monastic houses in Catholic Switzerland met great resistance, although a less rigorous policy was better received in some southern German monastic houses.[134]

Some bishops attacked monastic problems in a high-handed manner. In Würzburg, von Mespelbrunn designated some monasteries as "unreformable," took over their property, and used it to support his university. In other cases, he interfered with elections of abbots, pressured monasteries to accept new statutes, and conducted unwanted visitations of abbeys.[135] As in other areas, von Mespelbrunn was unusually successful in exerting episcopal authority to reform monasteries. Most bishops found it very difficult, and often impossible, to overcome the privileges, financial resources, and political influence of monastic houses and impose new measures on them.[136]

Not surprisingly, reforms initiated from within monasteries were better received than pressure from the Papacy, nuncios, and bishops. We have seen how the Carthusian house in Cologne maintained its tradition of discipline and piety throughout the sixteenth century. In the 1560s and 1570s, under the leadership of an active abbot, the Benedictine house of St Emmeram in Regensburg began to attract a large number of new monks and became a center of anti-Protestant activity in the city.[137] In episcopal sees, such as Regensburg, Speyer, Cologne, and Mainz, cathedral chapters, by encouraging more festive services in the great cathedrals and more active pastoral work on the part of the chapter clergy, encouraged the revival of Catholic practice, despite their skepticism about Tridentine reforms.

The Benedictine abbey of Weingarten provides perhaps the most dramatic example of the interplay of the Tridentine impulse with more traditional forms of monastic renewal. Under Abbot Georg Wegelin (1586–1627), Weingarten experienced what Reinhardt has called "reform through Jesuit inspiration."[138] Wegelin studied with the Jesuits in Dillingen and maintained close ties with the fathers throughout his life. From this background, he brought a sense of Catholic consciousness, a strong anti-Protestantism, and a loyalty to the Roman Catholic Church to the abbey. The reception of these essentially Tridentine notions among the monks was, however, mediated by a revival of Benedictine self-confidence. Most obviously, Wegelin enforced with great rigor the traditional monastic vows, with regular reference to the history of the order. Furthermore, the monks developed, according to Reinhardt, a new identity as "religious," rather than as holders of benefices in a provisioning institution ("*Versorgungsanstalt*"). The Jesuits helped strengthen this new identity by leading the monks in Loyola's *Spiritual Exercises* and by teaching young monks in their schools and universities. A rigorous program of education and religious practice within the abbey further reinforced this identity, here again drawing as much on Benedictine tradition as on Jesuit models. Weingarten soon became an ideal for other abbeys in southern Germany, and its monks went to other houses to promote reforms. For all its influence, however, the Weingarten model of reform had its limits. Such a program depended to a great extent on the powerful personality and the political connections of Abbot Wegelin and it lost its vigor after his death. Furthermore, Wegelin clashed with the Catholic nobility of the region and with the institutions it dominated, such as the Order of Teutonic Knights and the female chapters. Here again, we see the limits of Tridentine-inspired reforms.

In the late sixteenth century, monasteries and convents, like the parish clergy, recovered from the crisis that had reduced their numbers, discipline, and reputation in the wake of the Reformation. This revival was the result of the cautious acceptance of some of the reform measures of the Council of Trent and the revival in some places of older monastic models of religious life. Abbots and monks, abbesses and nuns also made a hard-headed analysis of the threats posed by Protestantism, reform-minded bishops, secularizing Catholic lords, and ambitious Jesuits, and decided to strengthen discipline within their houses, reorganize their finances, and pay more attention to relations with subjects and parishioners. If some monastic houses, for example the commandaries of the military orders, remained inattentive to new trends within Catholicism, a general monastic revival was well under way by 1620.

Despite its obvious importance, the Council of Trent did not, as the German Church historian Hubert Jedin thought, produce an almost miraculous revival of Catholicism.[139] In many places, the Council initiated a process of reform; in other places it reinvigorated existed reform tendencies. In all cases, the impact of Tridentine reform was conditioned by German realities, realities that included of course the existence of Protestantism, but also the secular role of the ecclesiastical institutions, and the fragmentation of political and ecclesiastical authority. Ultimately, the reception of Tridentine reform was determined by its encounter with everyday life in the village, town, monastery, and parsonage.

The Reform of Popular Religion, Confessionalization, and the Creation of Catholic Identity

Tridentine reformers, like Protestant leaders, always considered the reform of the clergy as the first step in a more general reform of society. A reformed clergy was expected to guide the laity to a better understanding of what it meant to be a good Christian. Sermons and catechism lessons, together with stronger disciplinary measures, would lead to the moral and the religious improvement of the population as a whole. Moral reform brought new regulations that would lead peasants and townspeople to internalize the values and virtues propagated by the Church. This effort focused on eliminating sexual sins (adultery, premarital sex), drunkenness, gambling, and other "irresponsible and licentious behavior" (*Leichtfertigkeiten*). Religious reform meant above all encouraging churchliness, that is the willingness and ultimately desire of people to practice their religion within the framework of the institutional church. The key to this effort was encouraging and requiring certain practices, especially the sacraments, while also suppressing unofficial and "superstitious" practices.[140]

This reform of lay and popular religion was linked to "confessionalization," which is a term coined by modern historians to describe the cooperation between church and state officials in enforcing religious unity and promoting the development of confessional identity.[141] "Confessionalizers" shared many of the aims of the Tridentine reformers, but they were more directly engaged with changing the lifestyle of the wider population. Although these men were often honestly concerned with the religious salvation of those they considered under their care, princes and their officials also considered religion a very effective tool for creating more orderly, disciplined, and obedient subjects. At its most basic level, confessionalization led to the enforcement of confessional unity. We have seen how effective this could be in some places, such as Bavaria and the Prince-Bishopric of Würzburg. As Catholic confessionalization progressed, especially in Bavaria and some of the Habsburg lands, state and Church officials enacted ordinances requiring attendance at church services and demanded that priests maintain parish registers, at least partly in order to keep track of nonconformists. They also enacted new regulations concerning marriage, sexual activity, gambling, drinking, and other "immoral" behavior and made an effort to enforce them. Here we see a concern for social discipline, perhaps not as strong as in Lutheran areas and not on the scale found, for example, in Calvin's Geneva, but nonetheless real and with sometimes traumatic effects for peasants and townspeople.

These two programs, the reform of lay religion and confessionalization, were often supported by the same people. Particularly in the period 1570–1620, they also appeared to be two aspects of the elite project to impose its moral values and religious practices on the wider population.

There were, however, inherent fissures in this alliance, beginning with the different priorities of the Catholic Church and the Catholic states. Furthermore, the clergy, especially priests at the local level, found that ordinances and disciplinary measures often had a harmful effect on popular loyalty to Catholicism. Some clergymen realized that churchliness and Catholic identity could best develop if they encouraged traditional practices, such as pilgrimages, the cult of the saints, processions, and Eucharistic piety. Tridentine-minded Catholic leaders and confessionalizers in state bureaucracies viewed many of these practices quite skeptically. Processions, for example, tended to be organized by laypeople in guilds, by confraternities, or by village communities, and they could often be disorderly and difficult to control. This skepticism about popular religion reinforced the elite inclination to press forward with a reform/ confessionalization program organized in a hierarchical fashion, at least through the middle of the seventeenth century.

Tridentine reform of lay religion, the reform of popular religion

The program to reform popular Catholicism in the late sixteenth century was very ambitious; of course it failed to realize most of its goals. This obvious point makes an analysis of the "success and failure" of reform fairly uninteresting. For this reason, the emphasis here will be on the reception of these reforms, for only those policies that received the support of influential or broad groups of people – parish priests, town and village leaders, men and women parishioners – became part of everyday religion at the local level.

Was this reform intended to change the way people practiced Catholicism, or was its goal to cement popular loyalty to Catholicism? In Germany, in the presence of a real Protestant threat, the latter goal tended to take priority. Of course, many proponents of reform did not think that the two aims were in any way incompatible, yet at the local level it became apparent that there was considerable tension between aggressive efforts to change popular practice and the development of churchliness. Indeed, disciplinary measures could easily antagonize people and drive them away from attendance at services. This dynamic led German Catholic leaders to be relatively tolerant of popular practice. As a result, laypeople had a greater ability to resist changes they found unacceptable or even just unattractive and to encourage those practices they liked.

Some Catholic leaders quickly grasped the usefulness of catechisms for the religious education of the wider population. Drawing on the late medieval tradition of catechetical instruction, Catholics responded to

Protestant polemics as early as the 1540s with new catechisms. These works reflected the moderation of Catholic policy by becoming "far more subdued [than before the Reformation] in defining the duties lay people owed to their clerics."[142] It was the Jesuit Peter Canisius who most clearly understood the effectiveness of Protestant catechisms, particularly those of Luther himself, and responded by publishing his own catechism.[143] Very well received from the first, with over 200 editions published between 1556 and Canisius' death in 1597, Canisius' catechism was widely used across Catholic Germany into the nineteenth century.[144] The simple question and answer format, partially copied directly from Luther's catechisms, was primarily used in classes for children. Taught everywhere the Jesuits went in Germany, and then later by the parish priests trained by the Jesuits, Canisius' catechism came to strongly mark Catholic culture.[145] Yet, like all attempts to reform popular religion, popular reception was mixed.

Visitation records give some sense of both the priorities of Church reformers and the ways in which their program was received.[146] Most sixteenth-century visitors were primarily concerned with the clergy. When they did turn their attention to the religious life of laypeople, they focused their questions on the presence of Protestants. A reform of lay religion only really began when visitors and ecclesiastical officials investigated popular participation in the sacraments and in catechism classes. Visitations indicate that people sent their children only sporadically to catechism classes before the mid-seventeenth century and adults never attended the lessons, despite efforts to get them to do so. Church leaders found it somewhat easier to encourage laypeople to partake of all the appropriate sacraments, but because the mass and transubstantiation were potent markers of a Catholic service, they placed particular emphasis on the Eucharist.

The basic requirement was that all adults confess and take communion once a year, at Easter time. In the 1580s and 1590s, visitors questioned priests about those who failed to fulfill the Easter obligation, assuming, at least in mixed confessional regions, that those who did not take Easter communion were Protestants.[147] Reformers were further distressed with the general casualness – they called it disorder – during church services, especially in country parishes. In the villages around Cologne, there were two problems during services: "in the first place, unreliability and a lack of punctuality at the beginning and end of the mass, and, secondly, a lack of attentiveness in between."[148] In the village of Otterstadt, in the Rhine valley outside Speyer, a priest complained that "when he is just reading the mass, before the sermon, they [the villagers] do not come in for the mass, instead they stand outside in front of the church and peer inside like dogs [peering] into the kitchen."[149] The parishioners in Otterstadt did not want to miss the elevation of the host and waited until the last moment to rush into the church to witness this key moment. This practice was common, and reformers saw its elimination as a marker of more orderly services. In this they would be disappointed, at least in the countryside, where even in the early eighteenth century there was a lack of solemnity and punctuality during Sunday services.[150]

Reformers also wanted to encourage more respect for the Eucharist. Visitors regularly inspected the condition of the perpetual light, which was supposed to burn continuously next to the monstrance that held the consecrated host.[151] The failure to keep this light burning indicated a lack of respect for the Eucharist and a general neglect of the upkeep of the church. Conversely, the proper maintenance of the light was a sign of good parish organization, proper financial management (since the oil for the light was expensive), as well as a proper reverence for the Eucharist. Visitors went on to inspect the inside of churches with great interest. Their concerns were several. Churches and chapels in disrepair made services difficult, and the Tridentine focus on pastoral care made reformers sensitive to the ways in which parish resources were used or misused. Visitors, ecclesiastical officials, and, increasingly, parish priests also sought to separate the sacred and the profane more clearly. This goal could be most easily realized in and around the church itself.[152] Thus, churches were cleaned and decorations repaired and replaced. Altars were consecrated, chalices and other *paramenta* put in order, and nonreligious activities banned from the church and, if possible, the churchyard. It was more difficult to "sacralize" cemeteries, but reformers ordered walls built around graveyards and sought to ban the grazing of livestock there.

More ambitious Tridentine reformers, such as the Jesuits, hoped to encourage a more intensive lay participation in the sacraments, particularly the Eucharist. In urban areas they claimed considerable success. The number of communicants in the Jesuit chapel in Cologne rose from 15,000 in 1576 to 45,000 in 1581 and to over 100,000 in 1635.[153] The growing number of communicants surely indicates that the Jesuit effort to encourage more frequent communion had some success among city dwellers. The ruling class of the small Catholic cities of the southwest, such as Rottweil and Überlingen, embraced this program as well, while also taking full control of the local church.[154] In the countryside, by contrast, there was no shift toward more frequent communion before the late seventeenth century. A similar trend can be found with respect to the other sacraments. Baptism, which had been considered indispensable by the laity long before the sixteenth century, remained a vital part of popular religion, even as church reformers moved, with some success, to "cleanse" it of unofficial practices, such as the multiplication of god-parents. Extreme unction, by contrast, was unknown in many parts of Germany, considered very dangerous for sick people, and rarely prac-ticed.[155] New ordinances failed to force people to accept this sacrament. Confirmation appears to have a more confusing history. Unknown in some places, it gradually gained acceptance in others.[156]

The effort to reform lay religion also aimed at controlling or even eliminating popular accretions to official practice. Franz Bosbach argues that reforms of this kind in Cologne – he points to decrees forbidding passion plays and efforts to regulate processions and other celebrations of feast days – led to a more controlled religious life in the city. These "reforms" conflicted with other aspects of Catholic revival, in particular the clerical encouragement of a more active and elaborate religious life.[157] As mendicants encouraged processions, Jesuits organized religious plays, and laypeople embraced a revived cult of the saints, others – episcopal officials, city councilors, and still other Jesuits – advocated disciplining religious practice. This tension in Catholic reform, present throughout Europe, was particularly pronounced in Germany where the Catholic Church faced the Protestant challenge on a daily basis.

The city fathers of Cologne were faced with an exuberant religious life so that perhaps an effort to control some aspects of popular practice seemed necessary to them. In the later sixteenth century, parish priests and even the reform-minded episcopal officials in the German country-side were rarely worried about a surfeit of devotion. In some parts of Germany, the Church promoted pilgrimages with little hesitation, seeing them as a way of creating and strengthening churchliness. In the centrally governed principalities of Bavaria and Würzburg, authorities actively promoted new shrines and worked to revive old ones. Publicists working for the Dukes of Bavaria were especially active promoting pilgrimage shrines as they developed a wider notion of *Bavaria Sancta*, the special status of the Duchy in the history of Christianity.[158] Martin Eisengrein's *Our Lady at Altötting*, the most famous book by the Bavarian propagandists, was a work of confessional polemic defending the reality of miracles against the Protestants, while aggressively promoting Altötting as the "national shrine" of Bavaria. These efforts contributed to a revival of pilgrimage piety in Bavaria after about 1570.

The attitude of reformist clergymen toward pilgrimage piety is clearly demonstrated in the case of Dettelbach, a Marian shrine in Franconia.[159] In some ways, Dettelbach perfectly fulfilled the aim of encouraging more active devotion while controlling popular excesses. Although the shrine had its origins in a 1504 miracle and had popular roots, it had never experienced a period of rapid and uncontrolled growth as did many other late medieval shrines. Bishop von Mespelbrunn of Würzburg was pleased that Dettelbach had always been well controlled by the clergy and that it was located near Protestant areas so as to attract pilgrims from non-Catholic territories. The bishop also wanted to encourage a Marian shrine, to complement the nearby Eucharistic shrine at Walldürn, which was under the jurisdiction of the Archbishop of Mainz. Despite episcopal support, which included funds to build a new church in 1610, people only came to Dettelbach in modest numbers before the Thirty Years' War.[160] This would change after 1650, when all shrines, including Dettelbach, experienced an explosion of popularity.

Shrines were a concern to Church officials because they could undermine parochial conformity, one of the centerpieces of the reform decrees of the Council of Trent.[161] The decrees were explicit and open in their motives.

> The holy council commands the bishops that, for the greater security of the salvation of the souls committed to them, they divide the people into definite and distinct parishes and assign to each its own and permanent parish priest, who can know his people and from whom alone they may licitly receive the sacraments.[162]

For city dwellers, parochial conformity meant marrying, baptizing their children, and confessing and taking communion at the parish church, rather than at a mendicant church or from a priest affiliated with a confraternity. Villagers generally had little choice but to take the sacraments from their parish priest, but some did confess at shrines or to neighboring parish priests.

Parish conformity was difficult to enforce in Germany. Part of the problem was the weakening of ecclesiastical organization in the wake of the Reformation, which left some parishes vacant and reduced the incomes of others. Privileged monasteries and other institutions resisted giving up the incomes and influence that came with hearing confessions and could rightly argue that they filled a necessary role assisting overworked parish priests, especially during the Easter rush. Many late-sixteenth-century parish priests were themselves reluctant or unable to handle the keeping of parish registers and other tasks that came with true parish conformity. In places such as Cologne, which experienced a revival of Catholic religious life after 1570, the very success of reform made parish conformity difficult. Gérald Chaix emphasizes that the "spiritual and social variety which in the case of Cologne characterized Catholicism on its way toward renewal."[163] This variety could lead believers away from the parish, as they participated in pilgrimages, processions, confraternities, and sodalities, much of which was promoted by the Jesuits and others. Parochial conformity was, then, an ideal rather than a reality, and part of the problematic relationship between the enforcement of clerical control and the promotion of a more expansive religious practice.

Confessionalization, social discipline, and the reform of popular religion

The Tridentine decree on parish conformity quoted above, with its admonition that bishops install in each parish a "parish priest, who can know his people and from whom alone they may licitly receive the sacraments" demonstrates another tension within Catholicism. Was the parish priest a pastor, the good shepherd of his flock, or was he an agent of a (distant) church and state who should discipline and rule his people? There is no question that elements within the Catholic Church shared the view of much of the European elite that the population needed to be better disciplined. Whether we call these efforts "social disciplining" (Gerhard Oestreich, Michel Foucault), "acculturation" (Jean Delumeau), "civilizing" (Norbert Elias), or the "reform of popular culture" (Peter Burke), its proponents favored expanding the role of religion into areas previously beyond its reach.[164] The effort to "christianize" sexuality, for example, was not new, but the very real attempt to enforce the marriage decrees of the Council of Trent was an innovation. Catholic authorities were less strict than their Protestant contemporaries in many other areas, such as the suppression of Carnival, Sunday dancing and drinking, and other forms of popular sociability, but they too wanted to hem in popular "excesses."

The Catholic reform of marriage, based on the *Tametsi* decree of the Council of Trent, was quite conservative. The Tridentine reassertion of clerical celibacy and the council's vigorous affirmation of the religious value of celibacy and virginity were firm rejections of Luther's praise of marriage. *Tametsi*, like Protestant marriage ordinances, did seek to prevent "clandestine marriages," that is marriages promised and consummated without parental approval, while also enforcing the Church's monopoly of the regulation of marriage.[165] The decree stated that couples were to declare their intent to marry openly, in public, and in the presence of their parish priest. They were to publish banns and to marry in their parish church. Priests were ordered to keep marriage registers and compare them with baptismal registers in order to identify children born too soon after weddings. As in Protestant areas, parents often supported the regulations aimed at preventing clandestine marriages. On the other hand, a second goal of preventing sexual relations before marriage often clashed with popular marriage customs, such as allowing engaged couples to sleep together, as a test of sexual compatibility and fertility. Rules limiting the number of godparents to one of each gender also radically changed the common practice of having many godparents.[166] Moreover, the reassertion and enforcement of marriage as an unbreakable sacrament could, and did, clash with popular practice, which often tolerated remarriage in the case of abuse or abandonment.

Tridentine marriage reform was potentially a very effective tool for social discipline. However, the effort to publish and enforce the *Tametsi* decree exposed the essentially conservative nature of the Catholic Church, the general inefficiency of many Catholic territories, and the unwillingness of priests and officials to challenge entrenched social practices. In Electoral Mainz, couples were expected to pass a marriage exam, a test of religious knowledge, before the wedding, but those who failed the exam were reexamined and allowed to marry anyway.[167] Evidence from Electoral Cologne shows that the marriage decree was published only after considerable delay in 1627, that priests and the laity resisted its implementation, and that the archdeacons who ran the local ecclesiastical courts refused even in the eighteenth century to enforce it. If a parish priest refused to marry a couple, citing, for example, improper publication of the banns, the archdeacons would allow a different priest to conduct the marriage.[168] Tridentine marriage reform was also received skeptically in regions where young couples traditionally slept together before the wedding. Elimination of this practice would have required a concerted and efficient alliance of priests, local officials, courts, state bureaucrats, and parents. Such an alliance was impossible in ecclesiastical territories before the Thirty Years' War and rarely found even after 1650.

An effort was made to regulate and discipline popular behavior in other areas as well. Gérald Chaix identifies a strong "criminalization of society" in the city of Cologne, beginning in the middle of the sixteenth century.[169] The city council led this effort, and studies of court cases indicate a focus on suppressing violence, protecting property, disciplining sexual behavior, and enforcing religious conformity. Some of this "brutal repression" coincided directly with the goals of reformist church leaders in Cologne, like the Jesuits and the nuncios. These groups supported such social disciplining by emphasizing the sinfulness of sexual crimes, excessive drinking, violence, and gambling from the pulpit, in confraternity regulations, and during confession.

In Cologne, then, secular and religious authorities worked, apparently hand in glove, to create a disciplined, confessionalized, Catholic society. Chaix, however, points to a number of factors that took almost all the teeth out of this program. First, the "apparatus of repression" was far too weak to effectively discipline such a large city and the police force in Cologne was very small compared to those of Florence and Bordeaux.[170] Effective social discipline therefore required the active participation of the wider population, as informers and even enforcers of the new regulations. The size and diversity of the city and the ability of the artisan class to mobilize politically through its guilds made such participation sporadic. For the same reason, the city council was reluctant to push such measures too hard.

Secondly, despite its façade of Catholic uniformity, Cologne was a religiously diverse city. Not only did several Protestant communities survive official repression, but Catholicism in the city was remarkably pluralistic. The mendicant orders, for example, gained influence by promoting many traditional practices at the same time as the Jesuits were forming new Marian sodalities and advocating a new, austere, and individualized piety. Chaix also emphasizes that the survival of traditional clerical structures – he points to collegiate chapters, monasteries, and benefice priests – prevented the creation of a professionalized secular clergy that might have been inclined to serve on the front lines of a disciplining process.

The impact of disciplinary measures was therefore limited. Decrees aimed at taming Cologne's famous Carnival were not enacted until 1617 and 1644. The city's official and regulated bordellos were closed only in 1591, when the City Council responded to a public protest by the Cathedral clergy; but then the Council did little to eliminate unofficial prostitution. Such citywide measures were also slow in coming, Chaix argues, because the diversity of the city made it hard for secular and religious reformers to create effective methods of imposing discipline. In everyday life, individuals and groups of neighbors developed a great variety of strategies of resisting, accepting, and molding disciplinary measures that greatly complicated the whole process of "social disciplining."

The reform of popular culture was even more difficult in the country-side than in a city like Cologne. The rulers of the Electorate of Mainz believed that rural people engaged regularly in "dancing and other frivolous behavior," and that *Spinnstuben* ("spinning rooms," evening meetings of young people) were dangerous and sexually charged gatherings.[171] *Leichtfertigkeit*, which can be translated as frivolousness, casualness, or carelessness, became a favorite word in the ordinances and decrees of this period. The term carried the implication of both licentiousness and economic irresponsibility. *Leichtfertige* people would have unwanted children, never find good jobs, and end up as beggars in need of public support.[172] In response to this concern, decrees outlawed dancing on Sundays, during church holidays, and during all of Lent. Carnival, in the view of the authors of the 1615 Mainz Police Ordinance, was a particularly good opportunity for licentiousness and a general lack of discipline. Other situations, for example the celebrations of baptisms and weddings, could easily lurch out of control.[173] "The reform of popular culture," as presented by Peter Burke, was under way.[174] Historians of Mainz (and other regions), however, present no evidence that rural populations changed their behavior along the lines demanded in the decrees. Instead, they emphasize a revival of Catholic religiosity led by the Jesuits and the Capuchins and focused around confraternities and pilgrimages, especially the revival of the shrine of the Holy Blood at Walldürn.[175]

During the decades leading up to the Thirty Years' War, Catholic princes, bishops, and town councils across Germany promulgated "reform" decrees like the one in Mainz. That 1615 ordinance carried the typically ponderous, but revealing title of "Renewed and further explained Reformation and Ordinance/ In his Electoral Grace's *Erzstift*, in cities and in the countryside/ how sacred church services should be held/ how the most blessed Sacrament should [be received and honored]/ and how other religious practices and prohibitions should [be handled] by ecclesiastics and laypeople."[176] The ambitions of the program were considerable, and its supporters believed that there was a seamless connection that ran from religious devotion and orthodoxy to social discipline and order, to economic well-being and prosperity, and finally to political obedience and unity. Reformers were of course disappointed that peasants and townspeople accepted new rules and restrictions on their daily lives less than enthusiastically. In fact, it is fairly clear that "moral reform" could not succeed if imposed from above and that an overly energetic policy of reform could in turn hurt religious reform, for religious change depended to a great extent on the ability of clergymen in the parishes to adapt reforms to local conditions. The slow pace of the reform of the clergy in much of Germany meant that this process was just beginning when the Thirty Years' War struck the Catholic heartlands of Germany, Bavaria, the southwest, and the Rhine valley in the 1630s.

Did Catholic Germany experience confessionalization in the period 1570–1620? Certainly, there was a concerted effort of Church and state authorities to create and enforce religious unity in Catholic territories. At this level, confessionalization had some success, more so in the more tightly governed territories (Bavaria, Würzburg, Tyrol), much less so in Westphalia and Austria. The second level of confessionalization was the attempt to create celibate, educated, and ultimately professionalized clergymen who could operate as agents of Church and state. This goal was overly ambitious and very elusive, and the realities of everyday life and the structures of ecclesiastical life in Germany, especially the benefice system, made it impossible to realize. Still, the reception of reform by the clergy was mixed and important changes did result. The virtual elimination of public concubinage, the rising educational standards of most priests, and the increasing emphasis on pastoral work created a new dynamic in the parishes, which would create a new kind of clericalism and churchliness after 1650.[177]

For many historians of Germany, confessionalization is closely linked to social disciplining. The Catholic Church had a more tolerant view of much of popular religion than Protestantism and consciously sought out the high ground of tradition in its conflict with the other confessions. The reaffirmation of good works, transubstantiation, the cult of the saints, pilgrimage piety, prayers for the dead, and other popular religious practices proved effective tools for creating Catholic identity and churchliness. Many churchmen recognized that disciplinary measures – outlawing dancing, celebrations after weddings and baptisms, ending Carnival – could be counterproductive. As H.R. Schmidt points out, "Counter-Reformation and popular piety moved closer together, in complete contrast to Protestantism, where the disciplining effects of the church and its distance from popular culture were emphasized."[178] Germany was not fertile ground for an austere, Borromean style Tridentine reform, as the Jesuits seemed to realize as they plunged, for example, into the religiously pluralistic world of Catholic Cologne. The weakness of the reform of popular culture in Catholic Germany became one of the strengths of post-1650 Baroque Catholicism, when many popular elements in Catholicism were embraced, promoted, and deployed in order to create a deeper popular loyalty to Catholicism.

Chapter 3: The Thirty Years' War

The victories of Catholic armies in the early years of the Thirty Years' War provided Catholic authorities with the opportunity to restore Catholicism in a number of Protestant regions. The Emperor's Edict of Restitution of 1629 further ordered the reestablishment of many monasteries and convents that had been taken over by Protestant states in the late sixteenth century. These years of Catholic triumph were short lived, and in the 1630s, Protestant armies under Swedish leadership restored the military balance in Germany. Even after France joined the anti-Habsburg alliance, neither side was able to achieve a decisive military victory. Meanwhile, marauding armies destroyed much of Germany. By the 1640s, the population had declined by about one-third and by as much as 50% in some regions. Many basic social institutions, including the Catholic Church, were badly disrupted and the damage was psychological as well as physical. Across Germany, the confidence of the Catholic elite – even in regions not directly touched by the war – was badly shaken by what many came to see as the destructive consequences of confessional militancy.

By the 1630s, it was clear that the reform of the clergy that had begun in the 1570s and 1580s had lost momentum. In places such as Bamberg or Westphalia, where reform had gotten underway after 1600, the war ended reform soon after it began. Disciplinary measures aimed at the laity also lost much of their vigor. Enormous tax burdens, wartime destruction, and general insecurity led to the collapse of seminaries, universities, and schools, the end of episcopal visitations, and the breakdown of ecclesiastical administration. Perhaps, most importantly, a massive shortage of priests developed. Priests were attacked by raiding Protestant soldiers, and armies on all sides frequently plundered and destroyed churches, parsonages, monasteries, and convents. Catholic leaders in regions not directly affected by the war (like the Tyrol, Catholic Switzerland, and parts of the Northwest) could attempt to continue reforms, but they found that the war had weakened many vital sources of support. The Papacy and the nuncios were fully occupied with the conduct of the war and had no resources for local matters. The Jesuits had to flee Protestant armies and abandoned many of their colleges. The network of Catholic educational institutions that had been built up in the decades before the war fell apart, contributing to a decline in the numbers and educational level of the clergy.

A growing cultural and psychological crisis exacerbated these practical difficulties. The conquest and forced conversion of Bohemia, the Catholicization of the Upper Palatinate, and the attempted conversion of the Rhine Palatinate in the 1620s, capped off by the Edict of Restitution, had briefly created considerable confidence in Catholic Germany. In the 1630s, Catholic defeats caused the rapid collapse of this confidence and tended to reinforce conservative tendencies in the German Church. Leading churchmen sometimes accused the Papacy and the Jesuits of pursuing overly ambitious anti-Protestant policies, and conservative clerics frequently withdrew into the traditional policies of maintaining the privileges of the Imperial Church. When the war ended, the German episcopacy and the cathedral chapters were pleased that the Peace of Westphalia in 1648 stabilized the Empire and secured the existence of the ecclesiastical states. Militancy had been discredited, and while confessional identities remained strong, the Catholic elite no longer favored confessionalized politics at the imperial or even the regional level.

Although the Thirty Years' War ended the "Age of Confessionalism" for the German elite, it was an important stage in the spread of Catholic identity to the wider population. The wartime experience may have caused a greater personal commitment to religion; it certainly led to a burst of pilgrimage and processional piety as communities sought divine protection. Because of the shortage of priests, much of popular religious life took place with limited clerical participation, a situation that reinforced existing tendencies toward communally organized religious practice. At the end of the war, communities in the more devastated regions turned to Catholicism to help integrate the immigrants who moved from less devastated places in pursuit of peacetime prosperity.

A new religious synthesis, Baroque Catholicism, thus began to develop during the Thirty Years' War, and it reinforced the rise of popular confessional identity in Catholic Germany. Certain key characteristics of Baroque Catholicism – a tendency toward elaboration and expansion of the liturgy, the central role of pilgrimage, processions, and the cult of the saints, and an active, participatory role for the laity – were of course not new. Yet during the war, the Catholic elite seems to have backed away from the austere piety of Tridentine Catholicism, making space for the more flamboyant aspects of popular religion. The reduced role of the Jesuits and the expansion of the Capuchins, known for their pastoral work and popular preaching, began during the war and symbolized a new focus within Catholicism. The trend toward Baroque religiosity that began in the 1630s and 1640s would come to dominate Catholicism in the second half of the seventeenth century.

The Edict of Restitution, 1629

The Edict of Restitution represents the high water mark of Catholic restoration during the Thirty Years' War. As Robert Bireley has demonstrated, this decree was the work of Catholic militants, led in Munich by Archduke Maximilian's Jesuit confessor, Adam Contzen.

> For them the war was a holy as well as religious one; that is, it was fought not only to advance religious interests but at the behest of God and with the promise of his assistance. They discerned in the Catholic triumphs the call of God's Providence, and his promise of aid to reclaim the ecclesiastical lands seized by the Protestants since 1555 in alleged violation of the Peace of Augsburg.[1]

The Edict attempted to enforce a strict Catholic interpretation of the ecclesiastical reservation: all church property taken by Protestants since 1552 and all Catholic territories secularized by Protestants since 1555 would be returned to the Catholic Church.[2] In theory, the Edict returned 2 archbishoprics, 12 bishoprics, and 50 major monastic houses to the Catholics. Members of the Wittelsbach and Habsburg families were quickly appointed to seven of the bishoprics, and the monastic orders moved monks into quite a number of monasteries, especially in the conquered Protestant territories in southern Germany, like the Rhine Palatinate and Württemberg.

The restoration of monasteries brought into relief conflicts within the Catholic Church itself. The old orders – especially the Benedictines and Cistercians – demanded the restoration of their houses, seeking, in effect, a return to conditions as they had been before Martin Luther.[3] The orders immediately clashed with the Jesuits and their supporters in Rome, in the episcopacy, and among secular rulers. The Jesuits and many bishops hoped to employ the resources of the monasteries to support more Jesuit houses, episcopal seminaries, and a variety of other projects. To be sure, at one level this was a conflict over the spoils of victory. At another level, however, it was a conflict between competing visions of German Catholicism. The Jesuits and their supporters saw the gains of the war as a catalyst for creating a reformed and militant Church with a strong pastoral focus *and* a commitment to converting Protestant populations to Catholicism. Many in the older orders, however, imagined (in the words of Wolfgang Seibrich) "a (total) restoration of the Imperial Church, a re-creation of the ecclesiastical and ecclesio-political conditions of the High Middle Ages, as they imagined them to have been, more from wishful thinking than from historical knowledge."[4] Seibrich further argues that the "restorative" program of older orders, by promoting tradition and the diverse heritage of the Middle Ages, provided a partial counter-balance to the increasingly bureaucratized and centralized confessional Church.

Seibrich probably overestimates the differences between the older orders and the reformers. After all, by the 1620s, the Jesuits had trained many of the abbots of the large south German abbeys. The important reform movement that radiated out from the Benedictine house of Weingarten between the 1570s and the war was openly Jesuit-inspired.[5] Furthermore, many monasteries were deeply involved in pastoral work and in some cases clearly adopted Tridentine values in dealing with their parishioners and subjects.[6] What is certain is that the restoration of monasteries did not lead to a revival of traditional monasticism and did little to change the confessional landscape in Germany.

The effort to restore the many monasteries in the Duchy of Württemberg indicates the difficulties, and the possibilities, set in motion by the Edict of Restitution.[7] Since the Reformation, the secularized monasteries had become an important element in the political and social landscape of the Lutheran Duchy, especially as schools, orphanages, hospitals, and other institutions, and their return to the Catholic orders threatened to disrupt the development of the Württemberg state. At the very least, the prelates would gain representation within the estates, but they also hoped to gain extensive political and financial immunities for the abbeys. The "maximalist position" taken by some orders envisioned that the Catholic orders would take full possession of all the monasteries and their incomes. This would take away extensive resources from the Lutheran ministers, many of whom were at least partially supported from monastic sources.

Not surprisingly, Württemberg officials struggled to prevent such a program from becoming reality. In 1629, they were often successful, out-maneuvering the imperial commission charged with enforcing the Edict. The Württembergers employed a variety of delaying tactics, such as filing a series of legal actions in Vienna. Divisions within the Catholic camp slowed restitution as well, as several bishops and the Jesuits all sought to obtain the income of at least some of the monasteries. In the summer of 1630, however, the Emperor insisted on restitution and troops were ordered to help install the monks. At Maulbronn in September 1630, for example, an imperial commission accompanied by a contingent of soldiers enforced the turnover of the Cistercian monastery to the Catholics. Masses were held in the church and local officials were informed that the monks planned to install priests in the surrounding villages and convert the population to Catholicism. When Swedish armies abruptly ended this experiment in 1631, this effort was in full swing. Although there were no more than four or five monks in Maulbronn, too few to restore the full panoply of monastic life, there were ten Catholic priests at work in the countryside around the abbey.

Conflicts over the Edict of Restitution were fought out at the local and regional levels. In 1630, the Bishop of Speyer proposed, without success, that most of the revenues from the restored monasteries be used to fund an episcopal seminary and to support other pastoral activities.[8] The Jesuits occupied the former Cistercian convent of Heilsbruck in the Palatinate between 1623 and 1646, using it as a missionary outpost for the conversion of the surrounding Protestant population. Meanwhile, the Benedictines, Cistercians, and Augustinians occupied a number of mon-asteries, although in all cases they could only send a couple of monks to each house. Finally, the Catholic occupying powers in the Electoral Palatinate around Speyer, the Spanish, Bavarians, Austrians, and French appropriated monastic resources for the upkeep of their armies. Catholic authorities clearly worked at cross-purposes, making any real "restora-tion" impossible.

The situation in Württemberg and Speyer was repeated across Germany, especially in the south. The old orders were overwhelmed by the project of restoring so many monasteries, having neither the personnel nor the financial resources to maintain the restored, but often isolated, houses.[9] At the same time, pamphlet wars raged, pitting Catholic against Catholic.[10] Bishops criticized the "idleness" of the Benedictines and other orders, and the orders responded that episcopal efforts to take monastic incomes ignored the wishes of the donors and thus violated imperial and divine law. The Jesuits, often with support from princes, claimed that they were the only organization that could really undertake the long and difficult job of restoring Catholic unity in Germany. The Edict of Restitution caused many problems and, in the end, effected little change.

The Conversion of Protestant Populations

Especially in the 1620s, the war provided Catholic authorities with control over considerable Protestant populations. Bavarians, Austrians, and various prince-bishops used this opportunity to attempt to convert these people to Catholicism, a process historians often called "recatholicization," but which in fact usually meant a complete change of religious practice for people who had no memory of Catholicism. The success of "Catholicization" (as I shall call it) generally depended on the ability of the Catholic Church and Catholic secular officials to deploy military force to remove Protestant ministers and force the initial "official" conversion of the population. The permanent conversion of the population, however, could only occur if Catholic priests were installed and maintained over a long period of time. During the Thirty Years' War, such conditions only applied in a few places.

Probably the most effective Catholic effort to convert Protestants occurred in the Upper Palatinate (*Oberpfalz*). This territory was occupied by Bavarian troops early in the war, and the Emperor granted it to Maximilian of Bavaria as a reward for his leadership in defeating Elector Frederick of the Palatinate. Residents of the Upper Palatinate had experienced a confused confessional history long before the Bavarians began a concerted program of converting them to Catholicism.[11] A strong evangelical movement had gained many adherents in the region by the 1540s and the territorial elite supported the official adoption of Lutheranism in the 1550s. By the 1590s, Lutheranism was firmly established and strongly defended by territorial estates when Palatine officials based in Heidelberg attempted to impose Calvinism. During their initial occupation of the territory after 1623, Bavarian officials exploited the resentments of the Lutheran residents against the Calvinist officials and ministers. In the long run, the Bavarians pursued a careful but determined policy of Catholicization. Protestant ministers and teachers were removed, priests were installed in the parishes, and Jesuit and Capuchin preachers and missionaries traveled the countryside. The conservative Lutheranism of the majority of the population and a widespread hostility to Calvinism may have created a popular mentality more conducive to Catholicism; Bavarian soldiers certainly made any open resistance futile.[12] The depth of Catholicization in the Upper Palatinate by the 1650s, however, cannot be doubted and was the result of what Walter Ziegler calls "the slow, careful, and strongly religious oriented introduction of the Catholic confession in territories that became Bavarian."[13]

Ziegler contrasts the Bavarian conversion of the Upper Palatinate with the "often formal and more superficial, also of course sometimes violently imposed confessional changes in Austria after 1618."[14] The victory of the Catholic army at the Battle of White Mountain in December 1620 allowed the Habsburgs to embrace a vigorous anti-Protestant policy.[15] The rebellion of the Bohemian estates, the election of the Calvinist Palatine elector Frederick as King, and the support given to the Bohemian rebels by the Protestant estates of Upper Austria confirmed the new Emperor Ferdinand II's belief that "Protestantism equals disloyalty." Already known for his ruthless anti-Protestant policies as Archduke in Inner Austria, after White Mountain Ferdinand decided, as R. J. W. Evans emphasizes, to eliminate all forms of Protestantism from his territories, including the moderate pro-Habsburg Protestantism found in many places.[16] This program was most brutal in Bohemia, where it began in June 1621 with the execution of 27 leaders of the rebellion and the confiscation of the property of all rebels. According to Evans, the Counter-Reformation in Bohemia was "by the standards of the time thorough and certainly tough."[17]

Bavarian troops occupied Upper Austria in the 1620s and enforced Ferdinand's edicts aimed at the full suppression of Protestantism. In 1624 Protestant pastors were evicted, in 1625 a general confession of faith was required of all officials, and in 1627 nobles were given a choice of conversion or immigration.[18] In 1626 an extensive peasant rebellion erupted in Upper Austria. The *Gravamina* (or complaints) of the peasant rebels focused on the "Reformation Decree" of that year. This decree ordered the removal of any remaining Protestant pastors, transferred control of church endowments and treasuries from town councils and rural communes to Austrian officials, ordered guilds to participate in Corpus Christi processions, and demanded that all subjects convert or emigrate.[19] The root causes of this rebellion and later ones in the 1630s were economic as well as religious and social, but the protests attest to the extent to which the conversion of the population disrupted society at all levels.

The conversion of Protestants in Vienna and Lower Austria proceeded in a less draconian fashion than in Bohemia and Upper Austria. Here the tradition of reformed Catholicism was stronger, Protestantism was weaker, and many nobles had remained loyal to the monarchy in the crisis of 1618–1620. Capuchin and Jesuit missionaries were active, but ultimately here too Ferdinand abrogated the rights of Protestant nobles to maintain ministers and hold services in their homes and pressured them to convert to Catholicism. Non-noble subjects, whether townspeople or peasants, had no option but to conform.[20] The Counter-Reformation as an anti-Protestant movement in the Habsburg lands came late and fairly suddenly; as a result it led to an extensive wave of emigration, especially from the region of Upper Austria ob der Enns, estimated to have involved as many as 100,000 people.[21] Catholicism would only gain the allegiance of the entire population of Austria in the years after 1650, with the fuller development of monarchical Baroque Catholicism.

Catholic armies occupied the Electoral Palatinate for much of the war, opening this Calvinist territory on the middle Rhine to efforts to convert the population to Catholicism. Unlike in Bavaria or in Austria, there was no territorial church in this region. Instead, bishops, the Jesuits, and the occupying powers, Spain, Austria, Bavaria, and France, each followed their own policies.[22] The first stage of Catholicization generally involved establishing legal and ecclesiastical authority in formerly Protestant areas. As we have seen in the case of the restoration of the monasteries, this process could be fraught with conflicts, especially between bishops and secular rulers. In the Rhine Palatinate, the questionable legal position of the Bavarian regime in the 1620s, the Swedish invasion of the 1630s, and the collapse of state authority under wartime conditions after 1635 exacerbated these conflicts. Nevertheless, in many places, Catholic rulers, supported by military forces, had sufficient authority to proceed to the second stage of conversion, which involved removing Calvinist ministers and installing Catholic priests.

The success of Catholicization in the Upper Palatinate, Austria, and Bohemia depended on the use of state authority, punitive ordinances, especially those requiring conversion or exile, and sometimes extensive use of military force. This element was mostly missing in the Rhine Palatinate. Somewhat ironically, given their reputation for confessional militancy, the Spanish occupiers of the left (or western) bank of the Rhine made no effort to force the population to accept Catholicism.[23] The Spanish considered their occupation a matter of military expediency, had no long-term interest in ruling this region, and did all they could to avoid conflicts with the population. The French and the Bavarians were somewhat more active, supporting several small Jesuit establishments in the towns of Neustadt, Bretten, and Germersheim. The Jesuits were especially active in the 1620s and claimed some success in convincing country people to come to Catholic services and even take Catholic communion.[24] These successes were cut short by the Swedish military occupation in the early 1630s and, especially in the 1640s, by financial problems, war-weariness, depopulation, and a shortage of priests. Wartime Catholicization did create a Catholic minority in the Protestant Palatinate; it did not, however, change the confessional geography of the region in a significant way.

The conversion of Protestant townspeople and villagers to Catholicism could have some permanency if Catholic authorities proceeded carefully and consistently. Thus, from 1623 on, officials of the Archbishop of Mainz moved to convert the Calvinist population of a number of districts on the Bergstrasse, in southern Hessia, which had previously been governed by the Electoral Palatinate.[25] As elsewhere, Calvinist ministers were removed and Catholic priests installed. Here Capuchin friars rather than the Jesuits supported the work of the priests, a sign of things to come, as the Capuchins eventually supplanted the Jesuits in many places in Catholic Germany. Still, the ultimate conversion of the Bergstrasse was only assured when negotiations at the Peace of Westphalia in 1648 left the region under the rule of Mainz. Over a period of decades, the Bergstrasse became predominately Catholic.

Catholicism gained ground in the border regions of the Franconian bishoprics of Bamberg and Würzburg during the Thirty Years' War as well. In villages governed by Imperial Knights, Catholic military and political dominance in the 1620s allowed bishops to enforce their rights of patronage and to appoint Catholic priests in parishes with majority Lutheran populations. As elsewhere, it was difficult for these priests to change the religious practice and beliefs of the population. A shortage of priests meant that the newly Catholicized parishes were generally served by a priest from a neighboring parish, hardly a situation conducive to conversion.[26] Here too, the changing fortunes of war prevented a consistent policy, and the shortage of priests became especially acute in the 1640s. The strong traditions of communal resistance to "counter-reformation" measures also continued in this area, hindering Catholic policy.[27] The ultimate success and failure of Catholicization depended on the negotiations at the Peace of Westphalia, and Catholicism gained a hold only in those villages where Catholic priests remained in place after 1648.

The War, Tridentine Reform, and the Rise of Baroque Catholicism

Despite the difficulty of Catholicization in many places, we should not be too quick to discount conversion. After all, the war permanently changed the confessional makeup of the Habsburg lands, turning them into the Catholic strongholds they would remain into modern times. The war did not, however, end the religious division of Germany; indeed the Peace of Westphalia strengthened and expanded the constitutional status of the confessions.

The war also changed Catholicism internally. Perhaps, most dramatically, the crisis of the war led to a crisis of Tridentine Catholicism. A key aspect of the Tridentine program in Germany was the effort to convert Protestants. Associated with the Jesuits, this program was militant and provocative in confessionally divided cities as well as in rural regions. Many Germans, Protestant and Catholic, blamed such religious militancy for the excesses of the war. By the 1640s, few members of the Catholic hierarchy supported new attempts to convert Protestants, and after the war such efforts were rarely part of the official Church program. The generation of bishops who came to power during and shortly after the war was best represented by Johann Philipp von Schönborn, bishop of Mainz, and Würzburg, known for his cosmopolitanism, religious moderation, and his willingness to compromise with Protestants.[28]

This decline in militancy occurred at the local level as well. Confessionally charged polemics were common in the confessionally mixed city of Hildesheim, and the region around it, in the decades before the war.[29] These confessional conflicts meant that both Catholics and Lutherans experienced the early years of the war, until the mid-1630s or so, as a *Konfessionskrieg*, or religious war. By the 1640s, however, survival strategies dominated everyone's day-to-day life and Catholics of all social classes abandoned religious militancy. Indeed, active cooperation between Catholics and Protestants (and between soldiers and civilians) was not unusual and increased as the war dragged on.

The pastoral focus of Tridentine reform was not abandoned during the war, but almost everywhere it became impossible to carry out. For two decades at least, from the Swedish invasion of 1631 until the early 1650s, the Church suffered from an acute shortage of priests and other clerics. In the Bishopric of Bamberg, to cite one example, 40% of the parishes were without priests in 1642.[30] Those priests who remained in their posts struggled to provide basic pastoral services, often a difficult task when they had two or more parishes to serve. Disciplinary and educational structures ceased to function, leaving priests isolated and subject to a variety of pressures. There is some evidence that the incidence of concubinage increased in the latter stages of the war, and it is clear that Church officials did not look too closely at the educational qualifications of candidates for vacant positions. Most seminaries ceased to function and the pool of priests committed to the full pastoral program of Trent shrank.

The long and devastating war led to a shortage of clergymen, a weakening of Church institutions, and a decline in elite militancy; it also caused a widespread social collapse and a strong sense of spiritual crisis at all levels of society. The wave of witch hunts, which peaked in Catholic Germany in the 1620s, was one manifestation of this crisis, as was the burst of popular pilgrimage piety during the war.

Witch hunts

Studies of the witch hunts in Germany indicate that religious conflict was only rarely directly responsible for outbreaks of witch-hunting.[31] An exception may have occurred in 1616–1617, when the Bishop of Würzburg, Julius von Mespelbrunn, moved to convert the town of Freudenberg to Catholicism. During this heavy-handed Catholicization – a typical instance of von Mespelbrunn's procedures – more than 50 "witches" were executed, suggesting that witch trials may have been used to eliminate recalcitrant Protestants.[32] In general, however, the victims of witch hunts in Catholic territories were Catholics, not Protestants.

Religious tensions were high in Germany from the 1580s on, and this charged atmosphere contributed to the outbreak of large-scale witchcraft trials. Within Catholic Germany, the growing political and constitutional conflicts with Protestants, conflicts that would lead to the outbreak of the Thirty Years' War, were only part of the heightened sense of religious crisis. We have seen how Tridentine reform, often led by the Jesuits, caused conflicts among Catholics and in the long run undermined moderate, humanistic forces within the hierarchy. Tridentine reformers, whether active in Church or state, privileged militancy in all spheres; such people were often as gravely concerned about the danger posed by the devil as they were about the threats of the heretics.[33] As Lyndal Roper points out, "part of the vigour of these men's attacks came from their sense of belonging to a beleaguered minority who understood the peril their society faced better than the common herd."[34]

Although all confessions persecuted witches, after about 1590, Catholics became more active witch-hunters than Protestants. During most of the sixteenth century, says Erik Midelfort, "all three major confessional groups were split between a strongly providential point of view (the *Episcopi* tradition) and a strongly fearful point of view (the *Malleus* tradition)."[35] This tension meant that "moderates" in the *Episcopi* tradition, who viewed most natural disasters (plagues, harvest failures, and the like) as divine tests or punishments, were initially able to prevent major witch hunts. After 1590, however, the *Malleus* tradition, which gave the devil great and growing power in the world, came to dominate in Catholic regions, partly because the moderate position was generally associated with the works of Johann Weyer and Johannes Brenz, both Protestants. According to Wolfgang Behringer, jurists and theologians "brought up in the spirit of the Counter-Reformation" pressed for more prosecutions, and Catholic universities such as Dillingen and Freiburg turned the old *Malleus* tradition into a "de facto dogma."[36]

Catholic and Protestant demonologists generally agreed on the threat of witches and witchcraft, which came to be understood as "particularly pure" transgressions against the First Commandment.[37] Catholic intellectuals, however, had "   doctrinal commitments that, like the belief in purgatory and the invocation of saints, gave ancillary encouragement to spirit activity" and required that they make careful distinctions between proper and improper rituals.[38] This difficult intellectual position contributed to the intensity and chaotic nature of witch-hunting in Catholic Germany, particularly in the prince-bishoprics, where thousands of "witches" were executed.[39] The link between militant Catholicism and witch-hunting is, however, more of a tendency than a consistent connection. For example, although most Jesuits supported witchcraft prosecutions, sometimes very actively, there were also influential opponents of witch-hunting within the Society of Jesus.

One of the most dramatic and saddest examples of a large witch craze occurred on the eve of the Thirty Years' War in Ellwangen, a small Catholic ecclesiastical territory in Swabia.[40] Although they were influenced by witch trials in neighboring territories, authorities in Ellwangen jealously defended their own legal and political independence. Thus, after the trials started, there was no higher legal or political authority to restrain, or possibly end, the craze once it got out of hand. The Ellwangen trials did quickly lurch out of control in 1611 in a classic fashion. Local people accused a 70-year-old woman of using witchcraft to kill cattle, whereupon she was arrested and eventually tortured. This began a cycle of torture, denunciations, further arrests, confessions, and more torture.

It has been estimated that between 300 and 400 persons were executed in Ellwangen between 1611 and 1618.[41]

Many studies of witch hunts in the early modern period have outlined the complex interplay of popular and elite beliefs, economic and social crisis, as well as the judicial methods, especially the use of torture, that underpinned hunts such as the one in Ellwangen. Heightened religious feeling was certainly part of the context in which the Ellwangen panic developed. The Jesuits arrived in Ellwangen in 1611, just before the craze began, and they no doubt increased the confessional awareness in this city with close Protestant neighbors. As the trials progressed, investigators developed questionnaires that asked the accused to "say the Lord's Prayer, the Ave Maria, the Creed, and the Ten Commandments, but then moved on directly to the question of who seduced her into witchcraft."[42] The assumption was that weakness in one's knowledge of the faith might make one vulnerable to the seductions of the devil. On one occasion the Jesuits used "exorcism, holy oil, and other Catholic ceremonies" to try to cure a 7-year-old girl who claimed to be participating in witch's sabbaths. Those who ran the trials clearly considered witchcraft a consequence of poor levels of confessional commitment in Ellwangen and therefore turned to the Jesuits to help solve the problem. At the same time, they countered the immediate threat with a "ferocious witch hunt."[43]

The Catholic Prince-Bishoprics of Würzburg and Bamberg experienced extensive witch panics during the Thirty Years' War, particularly between 1626 and 1630. Here, argues one historian of the region, "the intensification of the witch hunts was closely linked to the severity of confessional conflict."[44] As we have seen, the militant bishop of Würzburg, Julius von Mespelbrunn, personally promoted witch prosecutions in some areas. Witch-hunting in Franconia peaked, however, during the Thirty Years' War, in a deadly combination of confessional fervor and bureaucratic efficiency.[45] The prince-bishops cooperated in the prosecutions and their officials developed new methods of hunting witches. "Malifice Commissions," commissions staffed mostly by jurists, which traveled from town to town organizing investigations and trials, were especially effective. In the three Bishoprics of Bamberg, Würzburg, and Eichstätt, an "absolute peak of prosecutions in South Germany" was reached in the 1620s, with about 3000 people of all social classes as victims. The executions only came to an end following the intervention of the Emperor and the Imperial Chamber Court.[46]

The Suffragan Bishop of Bamberg, Friedrich Förner, personified the link between forceful Catholic confessionalization and witch-hunting. Förner initially made a name for himself as cathedral preacher in Bamberg and as a fierce opponent of Prince-Bishop Johann Philipp von Gebsattel (ruled 1598–1609), a moderate, old-school bishop who was accused of having Protestant tendencies. Förner maintained close ties with von Mespelbrunn, with the rector of the *Collegium Germanicum* in Rome, and with Duke Maximilian of Bavaria: in short, he was a member of the new generation of Catholic leaders who, deeply influenced by the Jesuits and Tridentine reform, favored forceful anti-Protestant policies.[47] In the 1620s, Förner led policies aimed at converting formerly Protestant districts to Catholicism, including the quartering of troops in recalcitrant villages. He also helped organize an "intensification and deepening of churchliness and piety" in Catholic areas, which the Jesuits, in particular, considered essential. At the same time, Förner was the "evil genius of [witch] prosecution," who organized witch-hunting commissions and pressed local officials to move aggressively against witches. He was perhaps best known for delivering sermons that whipped up fear of the power of Satan and encouraged denunciations.[48] Catholic militancy, the crisis of the Thirty Years' War, and the witch craze were closely linked in Franconia.

The example of Bavaria demonstrates that forceful Catholic politics did not necessarily lead to large-scale witch hunts. Wolfgang Behringer has shown that there were two parties at the court of Duke Maximilian in Munich, which he labels the "moderates" and the "persecutors."[49] Maximilian himself vacillated on the issue of witch prosecutions through-out his long reign (1598–1651) and neither party dominated Bavarian policy. The moderates were for the most part patricians and nobles who dominated local government, although some were found at the highest level of government. Although they never denied that witches existed, the moderates pointed to abuses of process in witch trials, especially the prosecution's overdependence on denunciations and torture. Behringer argues further that the persecution party overlapped with "the intransi-gent Jesuit party," led by Adam Contzen, the powerful Jesuit confessor of the Duke. This group favored "religious extremism" in foreign policy, and "rigorous social discipline and persecution" in domestic policy. "Religiously motivated confrontational politicians," they also tended to be more often of middle-class origin than the moderates.[50]

Each witchcraft case that came to the attention of officials in Munich led to a clash between the two parties, usually followed by consultations with universities in Italy and in other parts of Germany. There could be a range of outcomes. In the period 1601–1604, for example, the moderates were in a strong position and were able to quash several trials. The work of Adam Tanner S.J., whose anti-persecution position came to dominate the theological faculty at the University of Ingolstadt, was important for the success of the moderates in this period. Tanner's writing also founded a whole school of moderate Jesuit scholars, which culminated in the work of the most influential Catholic opponent of the witch hunts, Friederich von Spee. At other times, however, the prosecutors gained the upper hand, as when they succeeded in publishing the *Mandate against Witchcraft and Superstition* in 1612. This mandate combined an intense fear of witchcraft (in "baroquely violent language" according to Behringer) with an attack on various kinds of popular magic and superstition.[51] Yet the *Mandate* did not lead to a witch panic in Bavaria, because many government officials neglected to publicize it, bishops opposed it, and many priests refused to read it from the pulpit when ordered to do so. The closest Bavaria came to widespread witch-hunting was during the late 1620s, the most tense period of the war, when 39 people were executed in the region around Wemding. Ultimately, the very strength of the Bavarian state prevented extensive hunts. Officials generally moved carefully and slowly, which prevented the kind of local panic that was so dangerous in Ellwangen. As good bureaucrats, they were concerned with proper legal process, consulted their superiors at all times, and found witch trials disagreeable and very time-consuming. The result was that there was little chance for ad hoc processes and procedures to develop, especially the liberal use of torture. It was this sort of administrative looseness that made the trials in Franconia so destructive. The Bavarian state followed an activist policy of Tridentine reform and Catholic confessionalization, but it did not hunt witches very enthusiastically.

The worst outbreaks of witch-hunting occurred during the Thirty Years' War, but the prosecutions did not disappear completely until the middle of the eighteenth century. The tiny Upper Swabian territory governed by the Premonstratensian Abbey of Marchtal experienced periodic witch hunts throughout the early modern period. In the 1580s and 1590s, 46 witches lost their lives, in a territory with a population of about 700. "At least" five more people were executed in the 1620s, and then several more in the 1740s.[52] The persistence of witch-hunting in smaller Catholic territories reflects the looseness of governance structure and the close proximity of those structures to the local people, who always made the first complaints against witches. The intensity of local religious life and the belief in the constant activity of the supernatural forces in everyday life – whether they were witches and demons, or God, Mary, and the saints – certainly contributed to the willingness of both villagers and government officials to execute people, mostly older women, as witches.

Pilgrimages and processions

Another important and widespread religious response to the war was the expansion of pilgrimage piety. Pilgrimages and processions to shrines in an effort to seek divine protection and intercession were, of course, a tradition in times of crisis, and the Thirty Years' War was no exception. As we have seen, however, pilgrimages and processions could be more than traditional. In the context of confessional conflict, they were overtly Catholic, and in a confessionally mixed city or region they could be militantly aggressive. Finally, these practices were popular in the sense that most pilgrims were peasants, yet the Catholic elite, clerical and lay, often supported and promoted new shrines and processions.

Elite promotion can be seen most dramatically in the rise of the cult of Loreto. The Jesuits promoted this cult with great enthusiasm after the Society took over care of the shrine in northern Italy.[53] Both Maximilian of Bavaria and the future Emperor Ferdinand II visited Loreto in the 1590s and developed special ties to the shrine. The Jesuits and these princes supported the building of Loreto chapels during and after the Thirty Years' War.[54] During the Protestant siege of Constance in 1633, the population put the city under Mary's protection and vowed to build a Loreto chapel, which was completed a number of years later under Jesuit sponsorship.[55] The cult of Loreto was, it seems, a south German phenomenon, and it reinforced ties with Italy and Rome, since many Catholic leaders stopped in Loreto during trips to the Vatican.

The shrine of the Holy Blood at Walldürn, in Franconia, experienced a typical history during the Thirty Years' War.[56] The shrine experienced a high point in popularity during the 1620s, the result of a long campaign of clerical promotion supported by the activities of the Capuchins, who opened a house in Walldürn in 1628. In the 1630s and 1640s, the ravages of war dramatically reduced the number of pilgrims. The money in the endowment fund of the shrine, which reflects levels of donations by pilgrims, reached 2500fl. in 1630, only to fall to 800fl. by 1650.[57] Walldürn continued to attract pilgrims in the worst years of the war, but not at the levels of the 1620s, the years of Catholic victories.

During the crisis of the 1640s, the population's "expectation of miracles" increased dramatically in Westphalia. Werner Freitag has shown how the number of miracles reported at the Marian shrine of Vinnenberg rose steadily between 1641 and 1649. As a result, pilgrims began to come to the shrine from further and further away. Vinnenberg gained its reputation in the 1640s, but its real period of popularity was in the half century after 1650.[58] The pattern was similar in southwest Germany, where a number of shrines were founded during the war, went into decline in the 1630s and 1640s, only to be revived in the later seventeenth century.[59]

A widespread outburst of pilgrimage piety would have to wait for the period after 1650. Popular enthusiasm for new shrines was sporadic and usually local during the Thirty Years' War. Furthermore, the disruptions of war hindered clerical efforts to build up or support shrines. Nevertheless, we can see in pilgrimage piety important aspects of a developing Baroque religiosity. Communal pilgrimage processions, a hallmark of German Baroque piety, apparently first developed in the region around Walldürn in the 1620s.[60] In the late 1630s, the Franciscan administrators of the Franconian shrine of Dettelbach encouraged a shift away from the earlier Counter-Reformation emphasis on confessional conflict. Their program, found in pamphlets and other writing, increasingly emphasized the "strengthening of one's own belief and the cultivation of popular piety."[61] At Dettelbach, the Franciscans also promoted the cults of a number of Franciscan saints at the shrine; this effort is part of the tendency to continuously elaborate religious practices in Baroque Catholicism.

Perhaps the most significant consequence of the war was a decline in religious militancy among the German elite. This trend is well known in the older scholarship on the Thirty Years' War period. Theodore Rabb points to the declining importance of religion in international affairs during the war itself and argues that "after the 1660s, killing in the name of faith was virtually unknown."[62] The effect of the war was probably more profound in Germany than elsewhere in Europe. Hajo Holborn puts it bluntly: "In the highest classes of society a great deal of skepticism about the truth of traditional religion had crept in as a result of the war which led to a secular opportunism in thought and action."[63] With Catholic Germany, the elite, especially the upper clergy, turned away from anti-Protestant polemic and began to view policies aimed at converting non-Catholics with skepticism. According to Ernst Walter Zeeden,

[confesssionalism] now became a constant, which one counted on; but it was a constant that was not a defining force as it once had been. From the middle of the seventeenth century until its end, the confessional moment faded more and more away. In the eighteenth century, it [confessionalism] only played a subordinate role and was the object of widespread criticism.[64]

By the 1640s, Catholic leaders were much more willing to compromise on religious issues than they had been early the war. Johann Philipp von Schönborn, Prince-Bishop of Würzburg (from 1642) and Worms (from 1663) and Elector-Archbishop of Mainz (1647–1673), was the dominant figure in the Imperial Church from the 1640s on and an example of this element among the upper clergy.[65] Schönborn was a key figure in the peace negotiations that ended the war, during which he gained the enmity of papal representatives for his willingness to compromise on religious issues. In particular, Schönborn proved willing to solve religious issues at Westphalia, rather than at a later date, even if this situation gave the Protestants some advantages. After the war, he followed a policy of balancing French and Austrian interests, often forming alliances with other smaller German principalities in order to exert some influence. Schönborn's policies aimed at gaining and maintaining peace in the Empire.

Schönborn no doubt desired peace for its own sake; he also understood that war threatened to destroy the Empire and with it the Imperial Church. In fact, the German Church gained great security and stability from the Peace of Westphalia. Like the Peace of Augsburg, it left the institutions of the Imperial Church – the prince-bishoprics, cathedral chapters, imperial abbeys, and military orders – intact. Furthermore, after 1648, the right of princes to determine the religion of their subjects was further circumscribed by the setting of 1624 as the "normal year." This rule meant that in the future, subjects would be allowed to practice their religion as they had in 1624. In part, this rule meant that princes could no longer force their subjects to change their religion.[66] Furthermore, the Peace led to a stabilization of confessional frontiers and a lowering of religious tensions. The confessional map of Germany was fixed in 1648 and would remain largely unchanged until the aftermath of World War II.

The Peace of Westphalia also defused the religious situation in Germany by "legalizing" it. The Imperial Diet could no longer rule on religious matters by majority vote, but instead divided into confessional groups (the *corpus Evangelicorum* and the *corpus Catholicorum*) for separate deliberations, with all differences resolved by negotiation. This formal, legal, and constitutional structure coincided with the elite desire to reduce religious tensions. In a sense, what had once been issues that led to heated debates about Christian freedom and spiritual truth were now handled in a very practical way. This solution succeeded in diffusing confessional conflict for most of the period after 1648.[67]

The Catholic party, especially the leaders of the Imperial Church outside of Bavaria and Austria, considered the treaty a victory. Of course it was a compromise and the Catholics could no longer hope to reconquer or convert large Protestant populations. On the other hand, "the peace ended forever the latent threat, under which the prince-bishoprics had stood since the Reformation, as well as the very real threat that peaked in 1632–34 [when the Swedes conquered many Catholic territories]."[68] The security provided by the treaty allowed particularist tendencies within the German Church to grow stronger in the period after 1648. Furthermore, cathedral chapters no longer believed that it was necessary to elect Wittelsbach or Habsburg bishops, thus loosening the links between the great Catholic dynasties and the Imperial Church. Finally, because both the Papacy and the Society of Jesus rejected the religious compromises of the Treaty, they lost considerable influence among the Catholic elite.

The declining role of the Jesuits and the Papacy led to more particularism, a further decentralization, and a wider variety of political policies and religious practices within Catholic Germany. This new cultural context can be understood as "self-containment" or (perhaps less positively) as a "turning inward."[69] Certainly, the localism and particularism had always been a characteristic of much of Catholic Germany. After 1648, however, German Catholics, especially outside a few cities such as Munich, Vienna, and Cologne, were more isolated from developments elsewhere in the Catholic Europe, especially compared to the period around 1600.

The Thirty Years' War set the context for the full flowering of Baroque Catholicism. The diffusing of confessional conflict that came with the end of the war allowed the Catholic elite to back away from disciplining the population, freeing up reserves of popular piety. Popular Catholicism, especially in the countryside, had developed a new affinity for the miraculous in the crucible of war, which was given free rein after the war. Furthermore, the shortage of parish priests from the 1630s to the 1660s and beyond left many communities to develop and elaborate their religious life with relatively little clerical interference. The strong presence of the supernatural and the miraculous in pilgrimage piety, the importance of popular initiative, and the extensive elaboration of religious practices would be the essential characteristics of Baroque Catholicism in Germany.

Chapter 4: The German Church after 1650

German Catholicism developed in two main directions after the Thirty Years' War. On the one hand, the basic institutional structures of the Imperial Church and the confessional state remained very stable for at least the century after 1650. At the same time, both church and state moved away from militant confessional politics and activist intervention in local religion. The confessional state, even in its most developed forms in Austria and Bavaria, became more bureaucratic in practice, while turning more and more to propaganda and education in its efforts to "improve" the religious life of the people.

The second trend in German Catholicism was the development of a vibrant religious practice and a baroque culture that transcended social and regional differences. Catholics across Germany embraced pilgrimages, confraternities, the cult of the Virgin Mary, and an increasingly elaborate liturgy, most of it practiced within the framework of the approved Church practices. Meanwhile, the development of devotional literature, church music, schools, and the building of churches and monasteries spread baroque culture to all levels of society. Catholic culture developed its own characteristic forms, often in contrast to Protestantism, but its most important structures after 1650 were its dynamism, its continued regional diversity, and its churchliness, that is the predominantly church-centered nature of popular practice. Because of the dynamism of Baroque Catholicism, the close church–state ties that characterized the "confessional state" and the stability of Church institutions did not lead to a rigid orthodoxy.

This chapter will examine developments within church and state institutions, emphasizing the stability and increasingly bureaucratic nature of these institutions. There were also some important developments in the character of the clergy. As a consequence of new educational institutions, more stable career paths, and better financial conditions, the professional performance and social status of parish priests improved markedly. The role of the religious orders within German Catholicism also evolved. On the one hand, the older orders such as the Benedictines claimed a place as vital elements in rural religion, especially in southern Germany. On the other hand, the Jesuits declined in importance in many places, often losing influence to the Capuchins, who especially benefited from the explosion of pilgrimage piety.

Chapter 5 examines the structures of Baroque Catholicism, with an emphasis on the religious practices of the population as a whole and the vitality of Catholicism at the local level.

The Reichskirche

The Peace of Westphalia stabilized the constitutional structure of the Holy Roman Empire and secured, for the next century at least, the continued existence of the institutions of the Imperial Church. Stability and security, together with the decline of religious conflict with Protestantism, led in turn to a sense of confidence and even self-satisfaction at the higher levels of the Church in Germany. The sense of crisis and the fear of further Protestant gains that energized Catholic leaders in the decades around 1600 faded after 1650. Furthermore, the fear of secularization by the large secular states declined, at least until the middle of the eighteenth century.

The constitutional and institutional stability of the Empire was especially important for the ecclesiastical states. These states were not inconsequential. In the early eighteenth century, 65 ecclesiastical princes governed 3.0–3.5 million subjects (about 12% of the population of the Empire), and about 14% of the land.[1] Some of these states were important middle-sized territories, like the Archbishop-Electorate of Mainz, which had 300,000 inhabitants. Other ecclesiastical principalities were tiny, like the many monasteries of the southwest whose territories were really clusters of villages with a few hundred to a few thousand inhabitants. Stability and complacency led to two somewhat contradictory developments in religious affairs in these states. On the one hand, ecclesiastical rulers saw less need to impose the kind of disciplinary measures designed to "clean up" local religious practices. On the other hand, these states, following the lead of the secular states, worked to build more active and efficient secular administrations.

The "incubator" of the Old Reich allowed particularism to dominate the Imperial Church, thereby enhancing the local character of German Catholicism.[2] Tridentine reformers, especially the papal nuncios and the Jesuits, had tried to counter this tendency by pushing the German Church to adopt the Tridentine model. If this effort had some success before the Thirty Years' War, after 1650 few German bishops modeled themselves after Carlo Borromeo, and cathedral canons, abbots and abbesses, monks and nuns were much less inclined to accept the need for far-reaching church reforms. The secular clergy, both among the non-noble officials in episcopal and state service and among the parish priests, was the one group that continued to look to the Council of Trent as a guide for their personal and professional lives.

German prince-bishops did not completely abandon the ideal of the pastoral bishop, but most found the role of secular ruler more to their liking. Some became quite active in imperial politics after 1650. This trend began during the Thirty Years' War, when in 1632 the Archbishop-Elector of Trier, Philipp Christoph von Sötern, abandoned the Catholic-Imperial coalition to form an alliance with the King of France.[3] Von Sötern feared the expansion of Habsburg power and believed the French would be a useful counter-force in the Empire. He should perhaps not be overly criticized for underestimating the long-term French threat; furthermore, in 1635 the archbishop was captured by imperial forces and spent 12 years in prison!

Von Sötern's foray into European and Imperial politics was taken up (with more success) after 1650 by Johann Philipp von Schönborn, the Archbishop-Elector of Mainz. Called by his admirers the "German Solomon" for his successes in the negotiations that produced the Peace of Westphalia, von Schönborn was the founder of an ecclesiastical dynasty that would give its name to the whole period.[4] After 1648, he worked to organize the smaller and middling states of the empire into a "Third Germany" that could serve as a political balance between France and Austria.[5] Von Schönborn initially feared Habsburg power and organized a "Rhine Union" in 1658 that included France, but after 1661 he reversed course, supporting the Habsburgs against the ever more threatening Louis XIV.

Johann Philipp's nephew, Lothar Franz von Schönborn, was also active in Imperial politics. As Prince-Bishop of Bamberg and Mainz from the 1690s until his death in 1729, von Schönborn kept a number of clear goals in mind.[6] A primary concern was to maintain the Empire in its current configuration, as a federal union of independent territories. The prince-bishop was also convinced that warfare was the greatest danger to the smaller states of the Empire. By the 1690s, of course, France was the greatest military threat, although von Schönborn continued to fear the Protestant powers as well. Like his uncle, Lothar Franz believed that associations of smaller states were needed to prevent the destruction of the Empire and, furthermore, that the ecclesiastical principalities should take the lead in such groupings. His success in organizing these associations contributed to the revival of various regional imperial institutions such as the Imperial circles (*Kreise*) that were so important to the survival of the Empire through the eighteenth century.[7]

Of course the Schönborns had a familial interest in the survival of the Empire and the Imperial Church. Indeed, the von Schönborn family is one of the great success stories of the German Church.[8] This Franconian noble family exploited its connections with the Church to expand its wealth and landholdings until it was one of the richest noble families in Germany. Along the way, the von Schönborns achieved first free imperial status and then were made counts in 1701. Members of the family held 33 positions in various cathedral chapters: 12 of these men became bishops, and one, Damian Hugo, was made cardinal. Alfred Schröcker has shown how the von Schönborn bishops used their patronage – control of appointments to administrative positions in the *Hochstifte*, influence in the elections of bishops and even emperors – to secure property and wealth for the family and positions in the church for nephews. In particular, the von Schönborns cultivated ties with other noble families that were active in the Imperial Church in order to divide the spoils and secure control over the key Episcopal sees.

Developments in the cathedral chapters also reflect the security and even complacency of the Imperial Church.[9] The *Domkapitel* had always been predominantly aristocratic – the cathedral prebends in Cologne and Strasbourg were reserved for counts, those along the Rhine and Main for free imperial knights – but over the course of the seventeenth and eighteenth centuries, the chapters systematically excluded non-noble canons.[10] Furthermore, the chapters became more reluctant after 1650 to admit members of princely families such as the Habsburgs and Wittelsbachs. The canons no longer felt the need for princely protection, as they had in the period 1580–1620, when a number of princes were elected bishops. Noble canons also entered the chapters at a younger and younger age (13–14 years old in the "knightly chapters" in the west, 22–24 years in the other "noble chapters"), and they increasingly held benefices in two or more chapters. Few canons performed the ecclesiastical or liturgical functions associated with their positions, leaving those duties to middle-class officials. These trends are all signs that there was little concern with Tridentine decrees about age or clerical qualifications for canons.

As they had for centuries, cathedral chapters continued to fill two roles. They were *Versorgungsstätten des Adels*, that is, institutions that provided well-endowed benefices for sons of noble families and allowed them to live a lifestyle appropriate to their rank. It was even possible, with good planning, the application of patronage, and a little luck, to be elected bishop and thereby achieve princely status. Cathedral chapters also had a political function in the ecclesiastical states, where they functioned as a kind of representative body, with the duty to help the bishop govern the territory, while also restraining his power. Both these functions gained in importance after 1650, for several reasons.[11] The competition for positions in the chapters intensified as some noble families converted to Catholicism, while others had larger families, which meant more young men competed for a fixed number of positions. At the same time, stability in the Empire meant a declining interest in Church reform and reduced the canons' (already limited) interest in spiritual matters. The chapters' social and political functions, together with a growing tendency to recruit canons from the regional aristocracy, also meant that the cathedral chapters contributed forcefully to the particularism of the German Church.

The heavy engagement of prince-bishops in Imperial politics and in the administration of their states was mirrored at the regional level by the smaller ecclesiastical princes. The great abbeys, commandaries of the Teutonic Knights, and the collegiate chapters were increasingly well organized in defending their "liberties." In Swabia, for example, the abbots of the richest abbeys were active in the affairs of the Swabian Circle, which helped them work with the neighboring secular lords to protect their independence.[12] Leaders of the Imperial Church of the seventeenth and eighteenth centuries generally withdrew from engagement with wider notions of reform within the Catholic Church and instead immersed themselves in German and regional politics. This focus led them to develop the administration of their own principalities and brought them into more conflict with the increasingly organized secular states.

Confessionalization after 1650

Catholics living in the larger states, secular and ecclesiastical, had to deal with increasingly efficient and well-organized states. As before the Thirty Years' War, princes and their officials embraced "confessionalization," policies aimed at creating religious unity, a disciplined clergy, a financially solvent church, and a pious and obedient population. The difference between the policies of Catholic leaders of the later seventeenth century and those of the princes in the decades around 1600, like Julius Echter von Mespelbrunn the (in)famous Bishop of Würzburg, was first of all one of tone. The urgency that marked the "Counter-Reformation era" was gone, replaced by a sense of security and a bureaucratization of the confessional state.[13] Furthermore, after 1650, this new atmosphere led Catholic leaders to turn away from policies oriented toward social discipline and to give priority to methods of persuasion, propaganda, and representation.

The Catholic Church, because of its status as an international organization, could never be fully incorporated into the state, as was the case in Protestant principalities. However, in the ecclesiastical territories, especially the larger *Hochstifte*, prince-bishops held both secular and ecclesiastical authority. In these territories, there could be a real unity of purpose between church and state. Some prince-bishops attempted to take advantage of this congruence of power and authority.

Münster

Christoph Bernhard von Galen, the Prince-Bishop of Münster from 1650 to 1678, followed policies designed to create a model confessional state.[14] Von Galen was an energetic and ambitious ruler who embraced both state-building and Church reform. Because Münster had not experienced much reform before the war and because of the destruction of the 1630s and 1640s, the bishop had to start from the beginning. He began by working to remove occupying Protestant troops from the towns of the *Hochstift* followed by a concerted effort to root out Protestant inhabitants, especially in the city of Münster, where he ordered Protestants to be excluded from public office.

Von Galen considered himself a Tridentine bishop, on the model of Carlo Borromeo, and began his episcopate by publishing the decrees of the Council. In classic fashion, he followed the publication of the decrees with a series of "reform synods" where the bishop often personally admonished the clergy to obey Trent.[15] As Manfred Becker-Huberti points out, reform synods were quite unusual in the late seventeenth century, but von Galen held them twice a year for 28 years! The synods were followed up by episcopal visitations. Between 1654 and 1656, the bishop personally visited 54 of the larger parishes in his diocese (about one-third of the parishes visited), while his officials visited all the rest of the diocese.[16] This was one of the few times a German bishop personally conducted visitations and it apparently had considerable impact on local people.[17]

Von Galen also attempted to put institutions in place that would ensure the continuity of reform. Here he was less successful because he faced considerable opposition from the cathedral chapter and from the arch-deacons. The latter had traditionally exercised ecclesiastical jurisdiction at the local level, for example investing new priests and adjudicating marriage cases. As required by Trent, von Galen attempted to take these powers away from the archdeacons. In this he failed, as the archdeacons had the support of the cathedral chapter; instead he tried, with a bit more success, to subordinate the archdeacons to the bishop.[18] Furthermore, in an attempt to bypass the archdeacons, von Galen revived a moribund clerical council (*geistliche Rat*), but it never gained any real authority.[19] Von Galen also failed, despite a variety of plans, to find the financial resources to open a seminary.

The example of Münster shows that in many ways little had changed since before the Thirty Years' War. The impact of Tridentine reform depended on the person of the bishop. An activist like von Galen might have a considerable impact on the lives of the clergy, and perhaps even the population as a whole. On the other hand, even the combination of secular and episcopal power in the hands of a prince-bishop could not overcome the power of cathedral chapters and great monasteries and many essential Tridentine institutions could not be created. The structure of the Imperial Church continued to limit the development of the ideal confessional state. In most of Catholic Germany, there was little of the kind of reform pushed by Bishop von Galen.

Cologne

Although they were all members of the Bavarian Wittelsbach family, the archbishop-electors of Cologne did not create a well-developed confessional state in their territory. It is telling, for example, that the decrees of the Council of Trent were only incorporated into diocesan law in 1662 and that an episcopal seminary was not created until the eighteenth century.[20] Nevertheless, an effort to restart Tridentine reform occurred in Cologne and, as in many German dioceses, a 1662 diocesan synod attempted to inspire a new reform impulse.

Church authorities used regular visitations as their primary method of controlling and reforming local Catholicism. Over the course of the seventeenth century, however, the visitations became increasingly structured, routine, and bureaucratic. Around 1700, for example, diocesan officials developed a printed list of questions, allowing the visitor to fill in the results of his investigation. Furthermore, the forms were often sent to parish priests in advance so they could fill them out before episcopal officials came to visit. As Thomas Paul Becker points out, episcopal archivists loved the printed forms and carefully saved them: "To be sure, this improved archiving is a sign of the tendency to change the visitation from a ceremonial act to a bureaucratic act."[21]

Secular authorities in Cologne did little to help visitors. Any absolutist tendencies on the part of the archbishop-electors were undermined by the powerful cathedral chapter, and this limited state-building in Cologne. Officials ignored recommendations and decrees inspired by visitations and the punishments imposed were often minimal. If there was little confessionalization here, at least relations between episcopal visitors and those they investigated (parish priests and the local population) were cordial and relaxed. Again, as Becker puts it, "   in a small state with weak central authority, neither the behavior of the population nor the pressure from the authorities was of the kind to give rise to strong emotions [about religious practice]."[22]

Visitations in Cologne, and elsewhere, increasingly focused on the material and financial condition of parishes, a further indication of the bureaucratization of the confessional state.[23] This new focus came at the expense of concern about heretics and meant fewer questions about the quality and work of the clergy as well. In a sense, as many scholars argue, the interest in buildings, decoration of churches, and finances is a sign that the confessionalization process had (logically) reached an "advanced stage." In the 1650s, to be sure, a concern with material conditions was necessary in the wake of the Thirty Years' War.

Würzburg

Developments in the Franconian bishopric of Würzburg followed a similar pattern. Here again, bishops attempting to strengthen the ecclesiastical state faced entrenched resistance from the cathedral chapter. The canons played a role in the appointment of many important state officials, approved new taxes, and governed the *Hochstift* in the absence of the bishop. In this context, the power of the bishop depended on "the personality, the desire for power, and the tactical ability of each individual bishop."[24] Some administrative rationalization took place in Würzburg in the late seventeenth century, particularly in the financial bureaucracy. Overall, however, the *Hochstift* was relatively decentralized and under-administered, having, for example, no intermediate officials between the central government and local officials.[25]

Under these conditions, Church reformers could not expect the consistent and effective support of secular officials. In any case, Bishop Johann Philipp von Schönborn (ruled Würzburg 1642–1673) was not inclined to reinstitute the aggressive anti-Protestant policies of the pre-war period. Von Schönborn, known for his willingness to compromise with the Protestants, even devised plans for the reunification of the confessions.[26] Within the dioceses he governed (Mainz and Worms, as well as Würzburg), von Schönborn clearly preferred persuasion to force. He did produce a new church ordinance for Würzburg in 1668, based on the 1584 rural statutes of the Counter-Reformation bishop Julius Echter von Mespelbrunn, but most of von Schönborn's policies emphasized revitalizing the liturgy. The bishop wrote and published new hymns and advocated a preaching style based on scripture. Like many bishops of this era he also ordered the publication of new liturgical books. After 1650, the *Hochstift* Würzburg was certainly a confessional state in a formal sense, which meant that Protestant inhabitants were not tolerated and church attendance was mandatory, but neither the church nor the state showed much interest in extensively regulating (or disciplining) local religion.

Similar developments took place in the smaller ecclesiastical territories in western and southwestern Germany. The bishops of Augsburg, for example, demonstrated little interest in church reform, and the small *Hochstift* they governed was lightly administered and dominated by a powerful cathedral chapter.[27] Several mid-eighteenth-century episcopal decrees demonstrate the focus of church policy. The bureaucratic impulse is reflected in a 1749 decree ordering parish priests to submit statistics about the number of confessions heard and the number of masses said. In 1764 priests were admonished to preach each Sunday and holiday, hold catechism lessons, and keep proper parish registers.[28]

In southwest Germany, the Bishops of Constance continued to send episcopal visitations into the countryside. This regular activity is a sign that the Tridentine impulse remained important in Catholic Germany. As in Münster, Church officials, especially in the clerical council in Constance, continued to invoke the decrees of the Council and lament the ways in which the local church did not measure up to Tridentine models.[29] The reports produced by the visitors, however, were usually remarkably terse lists of benefices, priests, confraternities, and financial resources. Here too, there was a tendency to make the work of church administration bureaucratic and routine.

Bavaria

Even the largest Catholic secular states, Bavaria and Austria, moved away from religiously oriented politics. Bavaria remained a deeply Catholic confessional state, but as Alois Schmid puts it, "in the period of court and enlightenment absolutism the religious basis of politics was no longer as dominant as it had been in the early period of confessional absolutism, when the Church gave goals and direction to the state."[30] Indeed, princes and officials in Bavaria now saw Catholicism almost exclusively as a tool for strengthening loyalty to the state. This shift was most obvious in foreign policy, where the Bavarian electors found themselves caught between France and Austria. In the 1740s, Elector Max III Joseph even abandoned the traditional French alliance to fight with the Protestant powers, England and Holland![31]

Ecclesiastical structures in Bavaria were further stabilized in the century after 1650. The clerical council, which had exerted considerable influence over policies before the Thirty Years' War, developed an increasingly bureaucratic character. The membership of the council was stabilized at seven ecclesiastical and three secular members. In the early eighteenth century, subcommittees were created, with a panel for converts, a deputation for administering the "Turkish taxes," and a censorship committee. Soon thereafter, the Council organized its own chancellery and archives. Founded to promote and manage church reform, the clerical council had become a normal, indeed unremarkable, part of the central administration in Munich.[32]

Although the Bavarian state continued to seek the creation of an exclusively Bavarian diocese, it also strengthened its position vis-à-vis the eight bishops who exerted ecclesiastical authority in Bavaria. A series of agreements, called *Rezesse*, were negotiated regulating the Concordat of 1583; in most cases, these agreements strengthened the hand of state officials and limited church privileges.[33] Conflicts between church and state were never of course put to rest, but there was a certain ritualistic character to the disputes over taxes and jurisdiction.

As the Bavarian state became more bureaucratic – and correspondingly less active and interventionist – the court and the ruling Wittelsbach family continued to develop and promote a particular Bavarian religious style.[34] The *Pietas Bavarica* owes much to Archduke Maximilian I (ruled 1598–1651), whose personal piety became legendary after his death.

Maximilian and his successors promoted Marian devotions of all kinds, symbolized by the *Mariensäule* (Marian pillar) on the Marienplatz in Munich, which was copied in other Bavarian cities and towns. Pilgrimage shrines, especially the Bavarian "national" shrine at Altötting, were another central feature of the *Pietas Bavarica*. The Wittelsbach promotion of these practices was personal: the princes and their families went on pilgrimage, participated in processions and public church services, joined confraternities, and named their daughters – and sons – Maria. They also gave financial and political support to particular practices, funding, for example, the importation of relics from Italy and the construction of new monasteries at pilgrimage shrines. Most visibly, the Bavarian state supported the construction of churches and monasteries, above all in Munich, but also in the countryside. In the long run, the promoters of the *Pietas Bavarica* aspired to move beyond the court and the city of Munich and hoped to influence the Bavarian population as a whole.

> The decisive impulse came from the princely court, which was inspired by the conviction that religion is not at all a personal or private affair of princes, but rather that it had a political and statist dimension. For this reason, the court consciously took its religiosity into the public space, in order to encourage similar behavior among the subjects.[35]

Here again, we see late-seventeenth-century princes and state officials showing a preference for persuasion and propaganda, rather than disciplinary measures in religious matters. Along the same lines, the Bavarian state supported the extensive Jesuit missions to the countryside in the first half of the eighteenth century. These missions were oriented around preaching, confession and communion, and incorporated dramatic theatrical displays.[36] The confessional state did not relinquish its dominance over religious matters in the century after 1650, but it turned to new, less rigorous methods of promoting Catholicism.

Austria

In the Habsburg lands, state officials continued to be very active in religious affairs, at least in the first decades after the Thirty Years' War. Habsburg officials in Silesia, where there was a large Lutheran population, continued to resort to the traditional "Counter-Reformation" methods that they had perfected in Bohemia during the war. "Reformation commissions" were sent into the region where they ordered the expulsion of Lutheran ministers, forced the appointment of Catholic priests, closed

Protestant churches, and even ordered the quartering of soldiers to pressure the population into abandoning Lutheranism.[37] The Habsburgs, like most other rulers in this period, continued to consider religious uniformity an important characteristic of a strong state.

Despite the persistence of a militant tendency, Catholic authorities in Austria also turned increasingly to persuasion and propaganda. The activities of the Jesuits illustrate this trend well.[38] Although they participated in the Reformation commissions and served as missionaries to Protestant regions, the Society focused its efforts on the urban population and the nobility. Jesuit schools and universities dominated Catholic education in the Habsburg lands, and generations of urban patricians as well as the aristocracy of this multinational empire experienced this practical yet deeply Catholic education. Robert Bireley points out that Catholic political theorists reinforced this trend by arguing for

> patience in the process of winning over people and underlined the positive measure to be employed: clergy of high moral quality, effective preachers, genuine care for and adaptation to the people, and education.[39]

Furthermore, as in Bavaria, the Austrian state was increasingly characterized by the commitment of the ruling family to particular forms of religious practice rather than the use of repression against dissenters. The *Pietas Austriaca* of the Habsburgs was, in fact, a close cousin to the piety of the Wittelsbachs; it was also an integral part of Baroque Catholicism in Austria.[40] When the leading Jesuit playwright Nicolaus Avancini produced a play in Vienna in 1659 called *Pietas victrix sive Flavius Constantinus Magnus de Maxentio Tyranno Victor* ("The victorious piety of Flavius Constantine the Great the victor over the tyrant Maxentius"), he was of course equating the Habsburgs with the great Christian Emperor of the fourth century.[41] At one level, the message of the play was simple: the piety of the Habsburgs was the virtue that brought them victory! Somewhat more profoundly, the *Pietas Austriaca* also reflected the political theory of the time, especially that of Justus Lipsius (1547–1606), who argued that an absolute monarch would only succeed if he maintained popular support, or reputation, which owed much to the personal piety of the ruler.[42] The Habsburgs were presented as models of the pious princes who had earned the loyalty of their subjects through their religious virtue.

The *Pietas Austriaca* may have functioned to justify the power of monarchy and the imperial family, but it was also a concrete ensemble of religious practices.[43] As in Munich, the Viennese court practiced an ostentatious piety oriented around the cults of the Eucharist and the Virgin. The Corpus Christi processions in Vienna became major displays of court ritual in the seventeenth century. Marian devotions owed much to the Bavarian example. The Austrians, for example, copied the Marian pillars that were so popular in Bavaria. Emperor Leopold was particularly known for his devotion to the Immaculate Conception, and several generations of Habsburgs supported and developed the national shrine at Maria Zell. As Wolfgang Zimmermann points out,

> The idea that the rule of the Habsburg family was a result of its piety, of the *pietas Austriaca*, and thus grounded in God's grace, did not remain limited to a matter of theoretical reflection in court circles. Instead, it became a form of dynastic propaganda, praise for the Emperor directly appointed by God, which was passed on and thus popularized.[44]

The piety of the imperial family served as a model for all of Austria, spreading from the court to ever widening parts of the population. The *Pietas Austriaca* was not, however, static. Jean-Marie Valentin, in his study of Jesuit theater, identifies a major transition in the *Pietas Austriaca* in the decades after 1650, as reflected in the plays presented in Austria, especially in Vienna.[45] The Jesuits were certainly mainstays of the *Pietas Austriaca*, supporting and developing the notion of the special religious and imperial mission of the Habsburgs. Avancini and his colleagues wrote and produced a series of plays known as the *Ludi Caesarei* ("Plays of the Emperors"). The prince of these plays is "a soldier of God who refuses to compromise with the adversaries of Christ, and who wants nothing but the happiness of his subjects." In the conflict between good and evil, the good prince is conscious of his choices and his ability to sin, yet he fights (and usually wins) the good fight. The *pietas* of the good princes (always equated with the Habsburgs) wins out over the *impietas* of the tyrants, increasingly linked to the Turks.[46] If some of this myth dated back to the sixteenth century, Valentin sees the "*pietas austriaca* of the reign of Leopold and the *Austria gloriosa* of the baroque" as something new in the late seventeenth century. No longer focused on Germany and the Protestant threat, Austria was turning east in preparation for defeat of the Turks and the conquest of the Danubian basin.[47]

The transition from a policy of confessionalization characterized by the use of disciplinary measures to a milder form of state-sponsored religious persuasion was never complete. Both aspects of confessionalization remained important in Catholic Germany well into the eighteenth century. The well-known expulsion of the Protestant farmers of the alpine valleys above Salzburg in 1732 by the Catholic archbishop-prince shows that princes could still resort to force.[48] Nevertheless, the tendency to employ the tools of persuasion and propaganda, combined with increased bureaucratization, reduced the forcefulness of confessionalization, especially as experienced at the local level.

The Parish Clergy

The reform of the parish clergy that began in the late sixteenth century continued and accelerated after 1650. Furthermore, it can even be said that parish priests experienced and supported the beginnings of a "professionalization" of their work unlike anything their predecessors had experienced. These priests, through their sermons and teaching of the catechism, their administration of the sacraments, their leadership of the parish, and their personal example, exerted wide influence over the development of Catholic life at the local level. Yet the creation of this new parish clergy, the most dramatic development within the German Church in the early modern period, continued to be constrained by the experience of everyday life in villages and towns. In particular, priests' standards of living and social status – even their influence over parish affairs – remained tied to the dynamics of an essentially unchanged benefice system.

The character of the Catholic clergy in the period after 1650 was deeply influenced by the Tridentine decrees. The enforcement of celibacy and parish residency, the elimination of pluralism, improving educational levels, and the internalization of the model of the "good shepherd" (*pastor bonus*) characterized parish priests in most of Germany.[49] As we have seen, reform had begun before the Thirty Years' War, especially in cities and towns, but the war had badly disrupted reform, especially by causing a great shortage of priests and making it necessary for priests in many places to serve several parishes at a time.

Professionalization was related to the process of Tridentine reform. It designates the development of standardized educational qualifications for clerical positions, an internal hierarchy within the profession, clearly understood career paths, strong professional discipline, and a sense of corporate loyalty. The Catholic secular clergy moved in this direction more slowly than the Lutheran pastors, but elements of professional structures *and* attitudes developed after 1650, even if they were not firmly in place until the later eighteenth century.[50] As a modern sociological term, professionalization may seem misleading, but it usefully highlights important aspects of the development of the parish clergy.

Reform and professionalization have to be understood in the context of the priest's life in the parish. Some aspects of the lives of parish priests changed little between 1500 and 1800. Almost all priests lived off the income of a benefice and in most country parishes this income was paid in kind. As had been the case for centuries, many priests had to manage their benefices, collect tithes, and sometimes even farm the parish property. Conflicts over the tithe were particularly endemic. This system engaged priests continuously with their peasant neighbors and made it difficult for priests to stay out of local conflicts. Other aspects of daily life, including personal interactions, the hiring of servants, local political disputes, and conflicts over the organization of religious life, shaped how a priest fulfilled his pastoral duties. Most Catholic priests came from urban and small town backgrounds, which may have helped them stay out of local conflicts in the countryside, but everyday life still weighed heavily on them.[51]

Tridentine reform of the clergy

By 1700, parish priests in Germany had met the basic demands of the reform decrees of the Council of Trent: they were celibate, reasonably well educated, lived in their parishes, and were generally attentive to their pastoral duties. The period after 1650 was vital for this development, which can be credited to the bishops and, especially, the Jesuits, who were so influential in Catholic education in this period. The elimination of concubinage, as we have seen, was almost complete before 1620. There may have been some revival of this practice during the war – about 25% of priests in one district near Cologne lived with women in the 1620s and 1630s – but episcopal authorities could and did punish priests who kept concubines.[52] Very few priests were punished for concubinage after 1650, and this reflects a real decline in sexual misconduct. As Werner Freitag points out, "hidden numbers (of concubines) can be ruled out, for in this area the supervision by superiors and the community was very careful."[53]

The enforcement of clerical celibacy was of course only part of a larger effort to reform the lifestyle of parish priests. In the decades around 1600, some priests adopted the clothing and daily habits promoted by Tridentine reforms, but most parish priests remained essentially pea-sant-priests. After 1650, however, the project of "civilizing the clergy" gained momentum. Priests wore the cassock and behaved in a dignified manner in daily life. They avoided inns and taverns, the company of women, and local conflicts. Episcopal ordinances even forbade priests from wearing wigs or powdered hair during services.[54] Few priests con-tinued to farm the parish fields themselves, a key step in setting the clergy apart from the rest of rural society.[55] Of course some priests failed to meet the requirements of this model of behavior. It was often the parishioners who reported their pastors' failings to higher authorities, as when in 1667 the villagers of Schönau asked for the removal of their priest, a violent man who was raising dogs and a young wolf in the parsonage of this Black Forest parish.[56]

Parish priests received a better education after 1650 than in the prewar period. This process had also begun before the Thirty Years' War and advanced slowly but steadily in the later seventeenth century. The Tridentine goal of training priests in episcopal seminaries was never completely realized, but many dioceses finally founded seminaries in the eighteenth century, for example in the dioceses of Cologne, Trier, Paderborn, Augsburg, and Constance.[57] Other dioceses, such as Münster and Würzburg, had organized episcopal seminaries in the late sixteenth century, but these barely survived the Thirty Years' War.[58] The growing number of seminaries was one way in which more priests were educated to be Tridentine priests.

Developments in Würzburg after 1650 show how complicated seminary politics could be in German dioceses. In 1654, Bishop Johann Philipp von Schönborn turned over the leadership of the seminary to the "Bartholomites." This group had been organized in the 1630s by Bartholomäus Holzhauser (1613–1658), a parish priest who had served in parishes near Salzburg, in the Tyrol, and at Bingen on the Rhine near Mainz.[59] Holzhauser's *Institutum clericorum sæcularium in communi viven-tium*, also known as the "communists," was a congregation of secular priests who vowed to live communally in groups of two or three in the parishes, without private property, and without any female servants. Holzhauser was especially interested in having the best members of his congregations take over management of seminaries, where they would educate a new generation of priests on the model of the Institute.

Although Holzhauser was much admired by many in the German Church, including members of the von Schönborn family, in 1679 the new Bishop of Würzburg, Peter Philipp von Dernbach, took control of the diocesan seminary away from the Barthololomites.[60] Apparently the bishop considered the Institute a threat to his authority and resented the Bartholomites' close ties to both the cathedral chapter and Bavaria. After von Dernbach's death, the Bartholomites once again took over management of the seminary in Würzburg, but they only stayed until 1693, when the bishop once again took control. In 1703, the episcopal seminary in Würzburg was subsumed under the University. The tangled history of the Würzburg seminary highlights the ongoing difficulties that plagued these institutions, particularly the conflicts between cathedral chapters and bishops that prevented the founding of many seminaries. At the same time, the rise of the Bartholomites indicates that by the late seventeenth century some parish priests were willing to organize clerical education themselves. A new clerical culture was forming, and it was not just imposed by reform-minded bishops but was also the consequence of several generations of Jesuit-inspired clerical education.

Seminaries did not, however, train the majority of Catholic priests. Most priests were educated in Jesuit secondary schools and at the (mostly) Jesuit-dominated universities.[61] Almost all priests who served in the Vechta district of the Bishopric of Münster (studied by Werner Freitag) attended the Jesuit *Gymnasium* in the city of Münster.[62] By the eighteenth century, the majority of parish priests had also completed a 4-year university course in theology. Freitag argues that priests "went through a unified, specialized professional training which was much more extensive than that of their predecessors."[63]

In Trier, the system of educating priests was especially fragmented.[64] The Jesuits ran a small seminary in Trier, the *Lambertinum*, which was endowed in 1673, but it only had space for 24 students. In 1723, another seminary for 12 students was founded in Koblenz. Other young men who wanted to be priests sought support from a variety of endowments in Trier while they pursued their theological studies at the university. Most must have studied in Jesuit secondary schools. Only in 1773, after the dissolution of the Society of Jesus, did the bishop find it necessary to fund a full-blown seminary, with places for over 70 students.

Priests in the countryside around Cologne were also primarily graduates of a Jesuit *Gymnasium*, supplemented by several years of university study.[65] The level of education also rose there in the later seventeenth century. In 1663, 22% of priests had not attended university, but by 1684 all parish priests in this region had several years of university education behind them, and 17% had advanced theology degrees. In Thomas Paul

Becker's words, "the tools of a priest educated in this fashion can be more or less equated with the level of education of a graduate of a humanistic secondary school of our times."

The Jesuits also formed the Tridentine clergy through the Marian sodalities they organized in most Catholic German cities. Best known were the congregations of students, whose members were often future priests. Some Marian Congregations, like the "Major" in Munich, came to be dominated by clergymen by the eighteenth century. The Munich Major had clerical members from its founding in 1584 (23%), but by 1673, 30% were priests, rising to 54% in 1727.[66] The Jesuit directors of the congregations aimed at creating a Catholic elite, through aesthetic devotional practices, frequent communion, and religious reading and discussion.

Louis Châtellier's research on the Jesuit sodalities shows that the Jesuits promoted two models of congregations across Europe. Small, purely clerical, and often secret congregations – the "small coterie" – were more common in France. In Germany, the Jesuits focused on organizing larger congregations – the "big battalions" – where priests mingled with pious laymen and students.

> The desire to isolate the young cleric from the world, as a prelude to the isolation of the curé in the village, was a factor operative in this French example, which was much less influential in Germany and the Rhineland. The analysis can be taken further, and we may wonder whether these two models of associations do not in fact reveal two forms of Tridentine Catholicism.[67]

Although greatly influenced by the Jesuits as well, the culture of the German parish clergy was less elitist, milder in demeanor, and more tolerant of popular culture than that of the more austere French priests.

In the century after 1650, parish priests embraced the model of the good shepherd, the *pastor bonus*. In sermons, especially those given on the second Sunday after Easter based on John 10–11 (*"Ego sum pastor bonus"*), preachers emphasized moderation, simplicity, and concern for the needs of parishioners.[68] Holzhauser taught priests the following list of virtues:

> 1. Christian gentleness in word, deed, and gesture; 2. humility combined with respectability of dress, the power of the word, grace of appearance, and spiritual dignity; 3. affability; 4. demureness, the

imperative companion of affability: 5. humor; 6. kindness that lets others go first, shows much obligation, and keep peace with everyone.[69]

The image of the good shepherd could be found in the pious literature of the period and also became an important iconographic motif in Baroque art. As Wolfgang Zimmermann reminds us, the good shepherd was often contrasted with the bad shepherd, frequently called in German the "bad hireling or bad mercenary."[70]

The promotion of this model, and its general acceptance by the parish clergy, coincided with long-standing lay demands for active, resident priests who dependably fulfilled their pastoral duties. Such demands had been a central part of the drive for a communal church in the pre-Reformation era.[71] In particular, as Peter Blickle has emphasized, rural communes and town councils wanted resident priests, they demanded that the tithe go to the priest who was providing pastoral services, and they advocated an "equitable (or low-cost) church (*wohlfeile Kirche*)," where priests could not charge fees for pastoral services.[72] This movement had its greatest impact, and left its deepest roots, in southern Germany and Switzerland. Indeed, Blickle has argued that the triumph of a communal Catholic Church in the Forest Cantons of Switzerland in the fifteenth century explains the limited appeal of the Protestant Reformation there in the sixteenth century.[73]

This communalist tradition remained important in southwest Germany too in the seventeenth and eighteenth centuries.[74] Peasant communes protested when priests failed to fulfill their pastoral duties. They demanded that priests be available at all times for baptisms and deathbed confessions, that they provide frequent masses and sermons, and that they participate in processions and communal pilgrimages. In the eighteenth century especially, villagers pressured higher authorities to establish more parishes in order to improve the quality of pastoral services. Communalism was thus combined with a kind of clericalism, characterized by a general respect for the person of the priest and an acceptance of his indispensability for most Catholic practices.

There were, of course, conflicts between priests and parishioners, and the episcopal archives contain many petitions demanding that priests be removed, usually accompanied by letters from priests defending their work, words, and behavior.[75] Nevertheless, the consensus between priests and people over the centrality of pastoral work did much to prevent widespread anticlerical outbursts. Conflicts were unlikely if priests even attempted to conform to the sentiments expressed by the Capuchin

Prokop von Templin as he took over a new parish in the 1660s: "it is most of all important that we – that is me and my dear congregation – explain to each other how we would like to organize the situation so that everything will be in order and go well."[76]

Professionalization?

Reform of the clergy could shade into a process of professionalization. Werner Freitag has presented this thesis most cogently. While not denying the charismatic character of the Catholic clergy, Freitag, following Max Weber, argues that the parish clergy increasingly displayed the character-istics of a rationally organized professional bureaucratic class.[77] These characteristics include rational rules for appointment to a position (com-petitive exams), clear hierarchies and career paths, a professional ethos, remuneration by fixed cash salaries, and enforcement of professional discipline. Aspects of professionalization can be easily identified. After 1650, for example, admission to the priesthood required (*de facto* if not always legally) at least some university education. Many bishops also instituted competitive exams for priests seeking pastoral positions. By the eighteenth century, career paths had also become clearer, with priests being promoted from poorer to wealthier parishes.[78]

German bishops had some success strengthening episcopal authority after 1650. Even in the large and decentralized Bishopric of Constance, the clerical council and vicar general were quite active. The minutes of the clerical council in the early eighteenth century show the bishop's officials disciplining individual priests, organizing commissions to inves-tigate conflicts in the parishes, and discussing how to deal with the grow-ing number of hermits in the diocese.[79] Certainly officials in Constance faced opposition to episcopal centralization from both state officials and the monasteries, but the church hierarchy was functioning more ration-ally and actively than ever before.[80]

As we have already seen, the creation of a professional ethos, or, put differently, the development of a clerical culture, was primarily the achievement of the priests themselves. The development of more regular educational patterns created a common experience for young priests. Clerical culture was then reinforced and maintained by clerical confra-ternities and meetings of rural chapters, which were increasingly common and regular after 1650. Priests also built up personal ties by confessing their sins to each other on a regular basis. Furthermore, in many regions, priests went to a local Jesuit or the Capuchin house for confession and to attend spiritual retreats.[81] These monastic houses thus became local centers of clerical culture, while giving clerical culture in the surrounding area a Jesuit or Capuchin flavor.

While it is true that the parish clergy began to look and behave more like a professional class, especially in the eighteenth century, this new ethos could never completely capture the Catholic clergy. Obviously, the Catholic priest kept his charismatic sacral character, marked above all by his celibacy. Priests also maintained an all-important monopoly on the distribution of the sacraments. The population seems to have generally accepted the idea that the priest was indispensable for proper functioning of local religious life. Furthermore, while the Protestant clergy internalized the role of teacher and popular educator in this period, Catholic priests (as Andreas Holzem emphasizes) considered themselves primarily servants of the cult (*Kultdiener*) and liturgical specialists (*Liturge*), as well as representatives of the Catholic Church in general.[82] We should not, therefore, embrace too enthusiastically the notion of the professionalization of the parish clergy. The limits of this model are even more apparent if we look at the everyday experience of priest.

The power of everyday life in the parish

This vision of a "professional" priest, doing his best to meet the demands of the *pastor bonus* model, while living in reasonable harmony with his parishioners is, of course, overly romantic. The everyday experience of the priest in the parish did much to undermine, or at least alter, this happy vision. Most significantly, the benefice system required priests to manage property, obey noble and monastic patrons, and hire subordinates to perform pastoral services when the parish was too large. The everyday world in which most parish priests worked was rural, often isolated, and deeply traditional. As we consider the priest in his parish, we also need to be cognizant of the wide range of contexts in which pastors worked. The priest working in the Catholic metropolis of Cologne had very little in common with the impoverished parish priest in a mountain hamlet in the Black Forest.

Ulrich Pfister posits that the clergy of the confessionally mixed Graubünden (Grisons) region of Switzerland experienced only a partial transition to a professional priesthood.[83] Priests found that they could not easily hold themselves aloof from peasant society – they could not be the "socially dead persons" envisaged by the Council of Trent – for a variety of reasons. Even in the eighteenth century, some priests considered their pastoral duties a "side activity" as they were forced to support themselves by farming. Those priests who were able to live off the income of their benefices still had to manage their property, collecting rents and tithes from their neighbors. Furthermore, most priests in Graubünden were local men, often from elite families, and their family ties often implicated them in local political conflicts, as did the necessity of gaining communal support in order to be appointed to a parish in the first place.

Graubünden was on the extreme edge of the German-speaking world, and most German priests lived in less isolated and decentralized regions. Nevertheless, across Germany, they confronted aspects of the challenges their colleagues faced in the Swiss mountains. The close economic inter-dependence of priest and parishioners is the most obvious. Almost every country priest, and many urban ones as well, received their upkeep from a variety of sources (tithes, rents, fees for services), many of them paid in kind. Incomes certainly rose in the seventeenth and eighteenth centuries as economic conditions improved generally, but they also varied widely from parish to parish and over time. Priests benefited from good harvests and suffered during poor ones.[84] Parsonages were also important sites of consumption, especially in times of economic growth, as priests and parish patrons repaired buildings, purchased furniture and decorations, and laid in food and drink.[85] In the first half of the eighteenth century, a large-scale building boom supported many artisans, especially in the regions of south Germany where wealthy abbeys built new churches, parsonages, and extensive baroque monastic complexes.

Tithes were always a source of conflict between priests and parishioners, especially where priests had to go into the fields and supervise the collec-tion. Methods of collecting tithes varied widely. In some places, state officials collected the tithe and then redistributed it to priests. In regions such as the southwest and the Rhineland, where many parishes were incorporated into monasteries, collegiate chapters, and military orders, those institutions collected the tithe. This aspect of the benefice system often infuriated parishioners, because these (often distant) ecclesiastical institutions took a portion of the tithe, lowering the income of the parish priest.[86] Priests living in incorporated parishes were however insulated from conflicts over the tithe; in some places priests worked together with their parishioners in an effort to increase the share of the tithe that was sent back to the parish.

The benefice system remained the most traditional aspect of German Catholicism and it undermined almost every aspect of the reform of the clergy and its (tentative) professionalization.[87] By giving a variety of parish patrons a major role in the appointment of parish priests, the benefice system limited the ability of bishops to control access to the priesthood.

Patrons often included powerful nobles, for example in Westphalia, cathedral chapters, and monasteries, especially in the south. Ecclesiastical institutions that controlled many parishes could become mini-bishoprics. The abbots of Salem, a powerful and wealthy Cistercian abbey near Lake Constance, had its own system of education and promotion for priests in its patronage parishes. Priests in that region could ignore the bishop while pursuing a career within Salem territory.[88]

Monasteries could also undermine the quality of pastoral care provided in the parishes they controlled. Many monasteries, especially it seems the Benedictine houses, found it expedient and inexpensive to appoint monks as parish priests. Monks had always served as parish priests, but many monasteries increasingly resorted to this practice during the Thirty Years' War when there was a severe shortage of secular priests, and they continued it after the war. The most serious problem with this practice was that monks often did not reside in the parishes they served. The Benedictine Abbey of St Blasien, in the southern Black Forest, appointed many monks as pastors in the seventeenth and eighteenth centuries. When these monks/priests did not reside in their parishes, their parishioners protested vigorously and they often received the support of episcopal and Austrian authorities against the monastery.[89] Until the late eighteenth century, however, St Blasien continued to send monks out from the monastery on Sundays and feast days to say mass and hear confessions.

The benefice system was also very rigid and could not be easily adapted to a growing population or new economic realities. As the population rose, especially after 1700, there was an increasing need for more parishes and more priests. It was not easy to create new parishes in the context of the benefice system. One problem was that a variety of authorities often had financial interests in a parish. When the villagers of Seebronn, an Austrian village in southwest Germany, petitioned their overlords and the bishop in the 1770s for a resident priest, they ran into the opposition of the largest tithe-holder in the village, the University of Freiburg.[90] The University had no interest in turning over a portion of the tithe for the support of a resident priest in Seebronn. The project was further complicated by the fact that five other individuals and institutions also held portions of the tithe. This sort of situation was common throughout western and southern Germany, where centuries of development had created a dense and complex benefice system.

One solution to the rigidity of the benefice system was to create alternative ways of providing services.[91] Many villages built filial churches and chapels in order to have services in the village. Some filial churches came to be served by resident priests; in other cases parish priests had to travel from one church to the next for services. In mountainous regions, priests sometimes alternated services, holding mass in one church one week and in a different church the following week. Bad weather, illness or physical infirmity, or plain laziness could wreak havoc with this sort of schedule. Alternately, priests could hire assistants or vicars to serve filial churches and chapels. Not only did this solution create (more) hierarchy within the clergy, but many assistants were poorly trained and tended to move to other positions as soon as possible. Taken together, this context made it hard for priests to perform their duties with the diligence demanded by the Council of Trent.

Ultimately, it is apparent that the daily lives of priests hindered, undermined, or even prevented the adoption of a Tridentine model of a parish priest. Furthermore, the benefice system, which was intimately tied to the structures of the Imperial Church, was particularly ill suited for adaptation to a notion of the clergy as a profession. The necessities of everyday life in the parish and the institutional structures of German Catholicism, not the personal failings of clergymen, limited the "modernization" of the parish priests.

Despite these qualifications, Wolfgang Brückner, the preeminent religious folklorist in Germany has argued that between 1570 and 1770 a new kind of priest was in place in the parishes, especially in southern and western Germany.

> This [development] was about a change in conditions from late medieval pastoral practice in the countryside, about the disciplining of the parish clergy through a seminary education, through the requirement of residence, and through the general enforcement of celibacy, as well as the positive value placed on these [characteristics] by the society.[92]

Furthermore, by the seventeenth century, there was a surplus of well-educated priests available for the parishes, supplemented by the revived religious orders and the new orders, especially the Jesuits and Capuchins. The result, according to Brückner, was that "the possibility for a continuous catechizing of the Catholic population of all classes and estates was now in place."[93]

We should also remember that parish priests had many duties beyond teaching and catechizing. The "good shepherd" was supposed to serve as well as guide his flock and he had to compromise with the demands of his parishioners. As we will see, the focus of Baroque piety in Germany was on public and dramatic practices – the mass, pilgrimages, processions – which meant that the priest's primary role was that of indispensable server of the sacraments and performer of the liturgy. At the same time, the sacrament of confession, that powerful tool of priestly control over the laity, appears to have been less central in Germany than in France in the same period.[94] Catholicism was in the process of becoming more of a "priest's church," but the parish priest's power and influence were limited by the kind of religion practiced by the bulk of the population.

It is an oversimplification to characterize the history of the Catholic clergy in the early modern period as primarily the transition from a traditional to a Tridentine clergy. Nor did the parish clergy experience a straightforward development from a premodern (even "feudal") estate to a modern professional class. Elements of both trends were present, especially after 1650, but the experience of most priests lay somewhere on the continuum between traditional and Tridentine and between estate and class.

The Monasteries and the Orders

Although the number of monks and nuns in Catholic Germany was small compared to Italy and Spain, members of religious orders personified Catholicism for Protestants and for enlightened thinkers in the eighteenth century. Monasteries and orders did, in fact, play an important role in Catholic regions, a role enhanced by the structure of the Holy Roman Empire and the particularism of German Catholicism. In the era of Baroque Catholicism, the great monasteries of the "old orders" became religious centers, enhancing the sacral landscape by building new churches and convents, and promoting many of the characteristic aspects of Catholic religiosity, including pilgrimages, confraternities, and the cult of the saints. Friars and, especially, nuns did much the same in cities and small towns, providing a place for men and women of modest background who wanted to live an active religious life. Meanwhile, the Capuchins, practitioners of an active and popular pastoral mission, supplanted the Jesuits as the leading reforming order in this period, an indication of the distance most German Catholics took from the austere personal religion favored by the Society of Jesus.

The old orders

After 1650, German monasteries of the contemplative orders came to symbolize the triumphant Catholicism of the Baroque. The Benedictine, Cistercian, Augustinian, and Premonstratensian abbeys of southwest

Germany, Bavaria, Austria, and Franconia, all built new complexes of residences, administrative buildings, warehouses, wine cellars, and churches. These building projects employed thousands of workers and many of the leading artists, architects, builders, and decorators of the age. Most of the greatest artistic achievements of the German Baroque, such as the Wieskirche in Upper Bavaria or the pilgrimage church of Steinhausen in Upper Swabia, both designed and decorated by the Zimmermann brothers, were paid for by the monasteries.[95]

The artistic achievements of the old orders reflected the confidence of the Catholic elite after 1650. This was also a period of revival of discipline and a liveliness of spiritual life in many monasteries, which continued well into the eighteenth century. Male and female houses had no difficulties recruiting new monks and nuns. Twelve monks lived in Schussenried in 1650, 22 in 1683, 29 in 1710, and 30 in 1802. There were 25 nuns and 11 lay sisters in Heggbach in 1720 and in 1780 28 nuns and 10 lay sisters.[96]

Monks and nuns often lived comfortably, even luxuriously, especially in the eighteenth century. It is true that most abbots and abbesses enforced the basic rules of their orders; at the same time, monastic life became increasingly comfortable, especially in the wealthier houses.[97] Abbots built up full-blown courts, with all the necessary officials and courtiers. The abbots of Salem were famous for the quality and quantity of the carriages and horses they maintained. Ordinary monks and nuns lived better too, and the cells in the newly built abbeys were well appointed, roomy, and heated. Food and drink, and the traditions of hospitality, were especially cultivated, at least according to one of those ubiquitous English traveler, who, during a trip through Upper Swabia, wrote of the monks at Weingarten: "Eating and drinking is the main activity of these men   ."[98]

The flowering of the monasteries depended on great wealth, but also owed much to the particularist and fragmented nature of the Old *Reich*. Extensive building projects were often part of the ongoing competition between monasteries, or between monasteries and bishops, as well as efforts to demonstrate the power and wealth of the abbey to its subjects and clients. Most monasteries also built ostentatious *Kaisersäle* (Emperor's halls) to demonstrate their loyalty to the Habsburgs and the Empire.[99] Such worldly concerns cannot easily be distinguished from the desire to honor God with beautiful buildings and churches. The confidence, even the presumption, of the abbeys is perhaps best exemplified by the statement over the entrance to the monastery of Ottobeuren in Upper Swabia: "*Haus Gottes und Pforte des Himmels* (God's House and the Gate to Heaven)."[100]

Yet it is also fair to say that the abbots and abbesses understood their building projects as primarily "houses of God," not lordly residences.[101] They built new parishes churches in the villages around the monastery and each abbey supported at least one important pilgrimage shrine. For example, through the 1730s and 1740s, the abbot and monks of Salem, the Cistercian abbey on Lake Constance, fought a long jurisdictional battle with the city of Überlingen in order to move the important Marian shrine of Birnau to monastic territory. With Überlingen defeated, Salem spent huge sums of money to build a new chapel overlooking the Bodensee, a gem of Roccoco architecture and decoration.[102]

Despite the wealth of many of these monasteries, which was enhanced by increasingly efficient methods of estate management, such projects put a severe strain on the finances of some houses. In 1733, Didacus Ströbele, the abbot of Schussenried in Upper Swabia, was forced to resign his position because of the debts incurred in the building of the pilgrimage church of Steinhausen. Other monasteries were often forced to move slowly on major building projects. The Benedictine abbey of Zwiefalten, for example, began to make plans for a new church and abbey in the 1690s, but the new church was not consecrated until 1765.[103]

The monasteries, once criticized by Tridentine reformers as backward, developed into centers of learning that challenged the Jesuit domination of Catholic education. The Benedictine houses took the lead in this area, coming together in 1623 to create a Benedictine university in Salzburg.[104] The university gained in influence after the Thirty Years' War and south German abbots sent young monks to be educated in Salzburg rather than at the Jesuit universities at Ingolstadt and Dillingen. According to R.J.W. Evans, the university also " proved increasingly attractive to clerics and nobles who sought a freer syllabus and an alternative set of authorities."[105]

The monks trained in Salzburg returned to their monasteries and led an ongoing intellectual revival. Swabian, Bavarian, and Austrian monasteries built up large libraries in the eighteenth century. The Bavarian monastery of Polling, for example, had a library of 80,000 books, and each of the Swabian monasteries had collections of 15,000–50,000 volumes, libraries that compared favorably to the largest library in the German-speaking world, the Court Library in Vienna with 170,000 volumes.[106] The libraries supported a range of intellectual activities, focusing of course on theology and philosophy, but including studies in history, languages (with a special focus on "oriental languages"), and a range of natural sciences. Indeed, despite their rural and often isolated locations, the monasteries participated in all the intellectual movements of their day. Friedrich Nicolai, one of the leading lights of the Berlin Enlightenment, wrote about Martin Gerbert, the Abbot of St Blasien, after a visit to the Black Forest abbey in 1781.

> Where can monasticism be seen in a better light than there [at St. Blasien]? An abbot, who is very learned, a true friend of mankind and an agreeable socializer, learned monks, a beautiful library, a splendid building without pomp, full of comfortable apartments, polite and cordial interactions, romantic surroundings, peace and leisure; it appears that everything has come together there that a learned man could ever ask for.[107]

The monasteries, especially in southern Germany, were centers of elite Catholic culture. At the same time, monasteries and convents remained embedded in local religious, social, and economic life. As such, monastic houses functioned as important intermediaries in Baroque Catholicism: "close to the people, of course, but also distance." Benno Hubensteiner's somewhat romanticized vision of the place of monastic houses in Baroque Bavaria makes several important points.[108] The monks from the old orders lived out their lives in their monastery, perhaps leaving to study, but living for long years in one place. They developed links with the local population, sometimes as pastors in country parishes and frequently as promoters and participants in local pilgrimage cults. Benedictine monks, for example, often served as pastors during the Thirty Years' War, and then stayed on after the wartime emergency was over, partly because this practice saved the abbey's money and partly because of the enhanced importance of pastoral work in the post-Tridentine Church. By the early eighteenth century, more than one-third of the monks at the great Austrian abbey of Melk were doing pastoral work outside the monastery.[109] Premonstratensian and Augustinian monks had always been active in pastoral work and continued to be in this era.

These "popular" aspects of monastic life contrasted with the luxurious lifestyle in the convents and with the attention to learning that characterized monastic life. The great abbeys with their theaters and libraries, *Kaisersäle* and reception rooms, consciously displayed their wealth and power and acted as lords and rulers. The eighteenth-century building projects certainly provided employment to many artisans, but since they were funded out of taxes and fees and often led to an increase in *Fronarbeit* (forced labor), they also led to peasant rebellions.[110]

In religious style and practice as well, monasteries were intermediaries between the Church and the population. The interplay of monastic promotion and popular devotion at pilgrimage sites provides the most obvious example of this process. In Westphalia, the Benedictine nuns at Vinnenberg promoted the Marian cult that centered around a miraculous picture in their church to the nearby population, but the cult was important for the identity and collective life of the convent as well. Villagers came in procession to the shrine, but the nuns also took the picture in procession around the convent asking for divine protection.[111] More modestly, the Franciscans in Ehingen on the Danube served pilgrims coming to worship a particle of the True Cross held in their church.[112] In 1718, when the Premonstratensians at Schussenried decided to acquire a "catacomb saint" from Rome, they turned to several artisans from the Allgäu region resident in Rome for assistance in finding an appropriate body. Once the body of St Valentine was brought to the abbey in Upper Swabia, the abbey sought indulgences in order to bring people to their church to revere the relics.[113]

The social composition of the monasteries contributed further to their role as intermediaries. It should not be forgotten that even the wealthiest Benedictine houses were not aristocratic. In Bavaria, monks were mostly sons of well-off artisans and merchants, only occasionally the sons of wealthier peasants, and never from noble families.[114] In Upper Swabia, aristocratic monks could be found in the Princely Chapter of Kempten, but in most houses the monks' fathers were artisans and officials from the many small towns of the region.[115] Furthermore, by admitting sons of landed peasants and poorer artisans, "monasteries were an important instrument of upward social mobility."[116] Ultimately, the election of abbots meant that the sons of modest families could rise to the rank of Prince of the Empire. Some, like Anselm II Schwab, abbot of the Cistercian abbey of Salem from 1746 to 1778, embraced their status with enthusiasm. Anselm sought and acquired the title of Privy Councilor to the Emperor, had himself addressed as "*Excellentissimus,*" a title normally reserved for princes, and, from the quality of his carriages to the food at his table, lived in a courtly style comparable to that of other German princes.[117]

Female monasticism

Female monasticism fulfilled a similar role within Baroque Catholicism to male monasticism. However, the experience of nuns in the period after the Thirty Years' War was considerably different from that of their male counterparts. Church authorities began already in the last decades of the sixteenth century to implement the decrees of the Council of Trent putting all convents under the control of male clerics and requiring the strict enclosure of all female religious, that is the confinement of nuns within the walls of the convent. Although these measures were never fully implemented, they still meant a major transformation of the lives of most nuns.

There was considerable tension between this move to control the persons of nuns, as well as their property, and the desire of the nuns themselves, (supported by some Catholic leaders) to practice an active religious life. Nuns participated in the dynamism of Baroque Catholicism, taking part in religious services, caring for the poor and sick, and serving as teachers, all activities not easily compatible with enclosure. This tension, between the passive role accorded female religious and the active nature of Catholic religious life more generally, became even more acute in the eighteenth century as Catholicism experienced a gradual feminization that included a growth in the numbers of nuns.

Like the monasteries, some of the older houses, particularly among the Benedictines and Cistercians, were very wealthy, ruled monastic territories, and possessed wide-ranging privileges and exemptions from episcopal authority. Some aristocratic abbesses claimed princely titles and personally managed their abbeys with great engagement. These structural factors meant that female monasticism in Germany never fully reflected the aims of Tridentine inspired reform. The Cistercian houses in southwest Germany, for example, strongly resisted the full implementation of enclosure in the late sixteenth century. The nuns appealed, with considerable success, to family members among the nobility for support against the monastery of Salem, which, as the "paternal house," was leading reform efforts. In the seventeenth century, the Abbey of Wald required each nun to bring a considerable sum of money into the convent, which allowed for a comfortable lifestyle for all the nuns.[118]

As Anja Ostrowitzki has pointed out, "one can hardly speak of the restoration of enclosure. Rather, the new arrangements consisted of the complete shutting off of many convents for the first time, and in much sharper form."[119] Resistance to enclosure continued in some houses for decades and was not everywhere enforced even at the end of the seventeenth century. Abbesses and other convent officials left the houses to supervise their property or to participate in representative bodies, as did the abbesses of Frauenchiemsee, Geisenfeld, and Kühbach in Bavaria.[120] Traditions of hospitality, especially toward family members, could not easily be changed, especially among nuns of noble and burgher background, who hosted visiting members of their family in the convents.

The nuns in two Franciscan tertiary houses in Munich, the Ridler and Pütrich convents, were forced into a strictly enclosed lifestyle in the decades after 1600.[121] These nuns had appeared frequently on Munich's public streets, especially as participants in funeral processions. It took decades for authorities to enforce enclosure on these nuns, who had family connections at court and among Munich's ruling class. By the 1620s, however, the convents were fully enclosed, which forced the nuns to adopt new values and lifestyles. Some nuns internalized the new values and the convents deployed the importance of virginity favored by the Tridentine Church to improve their status. Now protected by enclosure, the nuns' virginity could not be doubted, which in turn enhanced the value of the prayers the sisters offered for the salvation of family members and benefactors, including the Wittelsbach princes. At the same time, many nuns resisted enclosure, for example by refusing to participate in the new Latin liturgy or by adapting extreme forms of meditation copied from Theresa of Avila and the Carmelites.

While some nuns contested enclosure, other female religious embraced an active lifestyle. In the same period as the enclosure of the Franciscan tertiaries in Munich, the "Institute of English Ladies" founded and led by Mary Ward, the English nun and follower of the Jesuits, opened a school for girls in the Bavarian capital.[122] Supported by the Bavarian state, the school continued to function after the abolition of the Institute by the Pope in 1631. Patronized by Munich's elite, the English Ladies eventually opened houses and schools in Augsburg (1662), Burghausen (1683), and five other locations in the eighteenth century. As Ulrike Strasser argues, the English Ladies supported the gender policies of the Tridentine Church, teaching "normative femininity" and (passive) female piety. Yet at the same time, the Ladies rejected enclosure, "living as religious women in the world and engaged in self-development and the development of other women through education ."[123]

The English Ladies were often called "Jesuitesses," which was both an attack on their "presumption" and a reflection of the influence the Society had on them. The Ursuline nuns in Cologne also responded to the Jesuit call for an active religious life in the world and rejected enclosure for religious women.[124] These women taught catechism classes in schools, lived in their own communities, and took vows of celibacy. The Ursulines even engaged in liturgical practices, without the participation of male clerics, for example going in procession to church on St Ursula day, where they then gathered in the choir and lit candles at the high altar. During Lent, the Ursulines engaged in a "spiritual meal" that included biblical readings and eating of blessed almond cake.[125] Despite their clear violations of ecclesiastical regulations and their rejection of enclosure, the Cologne Ursulines carved out a space for religiously active women that presaged the activities of nuns in modern Catholicism.

The diversity of female monasticism is apparent when one compares the lives of the women in the rich rural abbeys of south Germany with the Cologne Ursulines teaching catechism and primary school classes, or with the nuns in the Franciscan or Dominican tertiary houses. The abbess of the St Fridolin abbey in the south German town of Säckingen held a princely title, was the lord of villages, the manager of large estates, and the final judge of her own court. In the minutes of the Abbey's chapter meetings, the choir nuns discussed the appointment of priests to the convent's incorporated chapters, the building of churches and parsonages, the management of land holdings, and the regulation of life in the convent.[126] The women's collegiate chapter at Buchau was even more aristocratic. The abbess and 12 canonesses there were from the highest level of the nobility, mostly imperial countesses. In the fifteenth century, the chapter acquired independent status and was represented at the Imperial Diet. The chapter ruled a number of villages in small territory around the abbey. Although they fulfilled their basic liturgical duties, the canonesses lived comfortably in a very secular style. As a modern historian states, "the religious importance of Buchau should considered limited." Despite extensive property holdings and a large income, the chapter built up huge debts in the eighteenth century, the result of a massive building program in the post-Thirty Years' War period.[127]

The Franciscan and Dominican tertiary houses found in every small town in southwest Germany are evidence of a different aspect of the female monasticism. Most of these convents developed out of the Beguine tradition, which was strong in the lands along the Rhine in the fifteenth century. Many of these houses were quite modest. Around 15 nuns, of peasant and artisan background, lived in Franciscan house in Kisslegg. These women did not live enclosed and survived by caring for the sick in the town, baking hosts, making candles, sewing linens for church use, and cleaning and repairing liturgical items for churches in the region. The convent had a bit of property and earned some money from the interest on small-scale loans.[128] The *Seelenschwestern* in Riedlingen were even poorer, surviving in the eighteenth century almost exclusively on alms. A 1765 report stated, "Originally there were only a few sisters, who cared for the poor and dressed the dead, therefore they are called to this day the *Seelschwestern* (sisters of the souls). For a residence they had only a normal house and a barn, which was once a tavern called the Owl."[129]

The Franciscan nuns in Munderkingen, by contrast, acquired considerable wealth in the seventeenth century, mostly property brought to the convent by wealthy nuns. The 12 nuns, mostly from local burgher families, had originally devoted themselves to caring for the sick and poor. After the enforcement of full enclosure in 1629, the nuns disappeared from the town's streets and devoted themselves to candle making and textiles. Despite its wealth, the convent was not a center of learning – in 1685 a papal *breve* had to be translated, since none of the nuns could read Latin.[130]

Female monasticism was very lively in the century after the Thirty Years' War. In southwest Germany, Franciscan and Dominican nuns were found in every city and most small towns. There was no shortage of women willing to enter the convents and most houses, even the smallest, acquired enough wealth to build new churches and residences in the early eighteenth century. Most nuns lived under some form of cloistering, but in many cases it was not strictly enforced. The Franciscan nuns in Saulgau, for example, brewed beer, distilled schnapps, sewed stockings, and made candles. When forbidden by the city to continue these activities because they competed with local artisans, the nuns opened a school and a hospital and supported themselves by farming.[131] These activities, together with the sewing of church linens, the baking of hosts, and the cleaning of liturgical items, were the common activities of nuns.

The active life of the tertiaries contrasted with the aristocratic lifestyle of the large Cistercian and Benedictine houses. These modest houses were closely integrated into the world of Catholic cities and small towns, and the nuns had families in the area. The great convents, like their male counterparts, created ties between different Catholic regions, since they often drew nuns from greater distances. Female monasticism remained very vital, despite the (not always successful) effort to enforce enclosure right up to the end of the eighteenth century.

The ubiquity of female Franciscan and Dominican houses in southwest Germany contrasts with the small number of houses of friars. Most male Dominican and Franciscan houses closed during the 1520s and 1530s, during the rise of Protestantism. Although the Franciscans made a modest comeback in the late seventeenth century, there were only about ten houses of friars in the region that constitutes modern

Württemberg, while there were about 30 houses of female Franciscans and Dominicans.

The Jesuits and the Capuchins

The Capuchins first came to Germany in the late sixteenth century, and their success during and after the Thirty Years' War explains some of the weakness of the older orders of friars. In many ways, the Capuchins exemplified the extravagant, public, and dynamic nature of Baroque Catholicism, supporting pilgrimages, processions, and the cult of the Virgin Mary and the saints. The Capuchins were also renowned for their commitment to pastoral work among the common folk, as preachers, military chaplains, missionaries, and pastors.

The Capuchins came to supplant the Jesuits as the leading "reformed" order after 1650, although the Jesuits remained important and influential. The Jesuits continued to dominate Catholic education right up to the dissolution of the order in 1773, holding important faculty positions in most universities. Most of the Catholic elite continued to be educated at Jesuit secondary schools, including many parish priests. As the episcopal administration of German dioceses finally founded seminaries in the early eighteenth century, they usually turned to the Jesuits to teach in them. Even Joseph II, the secularizing Emperor, praised Jesuit educators, saying in 1769 " the Jesuits of Germany behave very well there; they are learned and zealous – adding other praises – and concluding that what has happened to them elsewhere wouldn't happen in German." In 1773, Joseph feared that the abolition of the society would lead to a collapse of higher education in the Habsburg lands.[132]

Jesuit colleges across Germany settled into a routine of teaching and preaching.[133] Although some new houses were founded after 1650, the great era of expansion and building ended with the Peace of Westphalia. "Between about 1580 and 1650 the Jesuits built or renovated over thirty churches, as well as constructed or restored several chapels."[134] This building program meant that the Society's physical presence in the most important Catholic cities, secured by its impressive churches, complemented its domination of education. Furthermore, the support the Catholic elite gave to the Society meant that it continued to receive substantial financial donations. Thus, the small house in Ellwangen was completely rebuilt in the early eighteenth century following the gift of over 90,000 *Gulden* from the last surviving member of the Augsburg patrician family von Peutingen.[135] As a result, Jesuit colleges and churches were large and impressive (and provoked envy from other orders) and each house supported large numbers of Jesuits. Several hundred Jesuits resided at times in the Jesuit college in Dillingen, which supported a full university, while between 50 and 70 Jesuits lived in Munich, supporting a *Gymnasium* (secondary school) with 1000–1600 students.[136]

About 20–40 Jesuits lived in houses in smaller towns. The college in the Swabian town of Rottenburg, founded in 1649, was quite typical.[137] The fathers taught at the Latin School and the *Gymnasium* and served as preachers in both parish churches, where they also taught catechism classes. The Rottenburg Jesuits also did pastoral work at the pilgrimage shrine at Weggental and organized both a Marian sodality in the town and a second confraternity at the shrine. They were popular as missionaries in the villages of the region and also held retreats where priests from the area could undertake Loyola's *Spiritual Exercises*.

Relations between the Jesuits and the host towns could be difficult. In 1672, after 20 years in Rottweil, the Jesuits left the town, claiming a lack of financial support.[138] The Jesuits returned in 1692, but the town council accused them of being overly interested in money and of failing to provide sufficient teachers for the secondary school. The Dominicans, who also taught in the schools, organized the opposition. The author of the college's chronicle admitted that the Society had very little influence in the town in this period but claimed that a 1719 mission in the town brought the population over to their side. In the middle of the eighteenth century, the Rottweil College flourished and the Jesuits were apparently prized as teachers and developed a clientele among the parish clergy of the region, who often left the Jesuits books and property in their wills.[139]

If most of the Jesuits' work was focused on teaching and preaching in cities and towns, they did engage in a new wave of missionary work in the countryside. As Louis Châtellier has shown, starting in the late seventeenth century, the Jesuits came to emphasize expeditions to the countryside to evangelize the population.[140] These expeditions were well organized and involved an intensive program of sermons, prayer meetings, confession, and masses. The 1683 mission to the villages of the *Hochstift* Speyer by two Jesuit fathers must have been exhausting. "The fathers visited 150 parishes, gave communion to over 30,000 people, converted 100 Protestants, taught over 300 catechism lessons, and preached almost 500 sermons, all in a period of about ten months   [They] worked very hard, cramming several masses and sermons into each one- to two-day visit in a parish."[141]

In the middle of the eighteenth century, Jesuit missions began to provoke opposition from local officials and parish priests. In the 1760s and 1770s, priests in Austrian villages in Outer Austria stayed away from Jesuit missions and officials claimed that the Jesuits encouraged superstition and religious excess. Nevertheless, the same officials had to admit that the Jesuit missionaries were popular in the villages and that they encouraged the "devotion and dedication to prayer of the people."[142] Châtellier refers to the first half of the eighteenth century as the "golden age of missions," with the focus of this work being in Bavaria, the southwest, and the Rhineland.[143] The shifting emphasis of Jesuit work toward these "missions to the people" probably weakened the Society's influence with the Catholic elite, although, as we shall see, opposition to the Jesuits was not strong in the German-speaking lands, at least outside of Austria.

Perhaps because the order has not found its modern historian, the role of the Capuchins remains relatively unknown.[144] "Over against the dominance of the Jesuit order and its effective public activities at the focal point of confessional conflict in the *Erzstift* [Mainz], the work of the second important reform order [the Capuchins] was less conspicuous."[145] Yet the Capuchins were surely not inconspicuous in Catholic Germany. Founded in Italy in 1528 as a strictly reformed Franciscan order, the Capuchins expanded rapidly in the sixteenth century, coming to Germany in the 1580s from both Italy and the Netherlands. "They were impossible to overlook, marked by the [long] beard, the chestnut brown habit with the long pointed hood [*Kapuze*, or *Cappuccino* in Italian], the white corded belt with rosary beads, the short cape, and sandals."[146]

The Capuchins spread rapidly through Germany during the Thirty Years' War. In part, this was because of the friars' early attachment to the Catholic armies as military chaplains. The order also had a predilection for proselytizing in Protestant regions. Thus, the Capuchins came to the Protestant city of Hildesheim in 1631, in the wake of Tilly's victorious Catholic army.[147] In Bavaria and Franconia, 9 houses were established before 1618 and 16 during the war. The order continued to expand in this area after the war, adding 16 more houses between 1650 and 1700, and 22 in the eighteenth century. Fifteen Capuchin houses were founded in the Austrian province of Styria between 1600 and 1711.[148] The number of Capuchins working in the Outer Austrian Province of the order (southwest Germany) grew from about 300 in the 1660s to over 600 in 1775.[149] The Capuchins also earned a reputation for bravery during the war, for example remaining in the town of Coesfeld in Westphalia after the Jesuits fled the arrival of Protestant troops in 1633.[150]

In 1622, Fidelis of Sigmaringen, a Capuchin friar attached to a Habsburg regiment deployed in the Grisons (or Graubünden) region of

Switzerland, was killed by a band of rebellious Protestant peasants. Although he was only beatified in 1729 and canonized in 1745, the cult of Fidelis developed quickly after his death, spread of course by the Capuchins themselves.[151] Fidelis was a perfect martyr for the Thirty Years' War, a missionary killed for his faith by godless heretics. His cult was patronized by the Habsburgs (Fidelis had studied law in the Habsburg city of Freiburg), by the Hohenzollern family (he had been born in Hohenzollern lands), by soldiers (he had been an army chaplain), and by the common people in Catholic Switzerland and the southwest who lived along confessional boundaries and suffered during the war. The prestige of the saint helped the Capuchins establish a reputation as incorruptible and tireless servants of the faith and simple pastors of the common folk.

As preachers and pastors, the Capuchins focused their efforts in the countryside. Their pastoral work placed them at the center of Baroque religiosity. In the Archbishropric Mainz, for example, the Capuchins promoted the cult of the Eucharist and served as pastors at all the major pilgrimage shrines of the region.[152] During the Thirty Years' War, and in the decades after the war as well, the Capuchins also served as emergency parish priests, gaining considerable experience among the rural population. They enhanced this reputation as *Volksseelsorger*, that is "people's pastors," by appearing regularly in the countryside in order to help parish priests conduct services and hear confessions during the Easter and Christmas seasons.[153] The Capuchins helped provide pastoral services in more than 30 locations in the region around Münster in the eighteenth century.[154]

The Capuchins specialized in preaching and in pastoral work in shrines. The vast majority of the friars in the Hildesheim house were licensed as preachers. Interestingly, Capuchin preachers rarely provoked the hatred of Protestant pastors as the Jesuits did, even in confessionally mixed towns such as Hildesheim, despite the fact that Capuchin sermons were often anti-Protestant.[155] In the early seventeenth century, the town council in Freiburg complained that Capuchin sermons were overly dramatic and caused laughter among the audience. The councilors were also displeased that the friars had criticized the city government.[156]

The Capuchins were often the only monks or mendicants seen in villages. They traveled through the Breisgau and in the Black Forest villages around Freiburg collecting alms, and then appeared at Easter and Christmas to help priests hear confessions and say Mass.[157] Hillard von Thiessen argues that the popularity of the Capuchins in the villages came in great measure from the friars' *Gottesnähe*, their closeness to God. The Capuchins' reputation as holy men was maintained, he argues, by the order's careful balancing of the Franciscan contemplative tradition with the commitment to pastoral work. The contemplative tradition was preserved by enforcing the vow of poverty, by moving the friars from house to house, thus limiting their individual reputations, and by preserving communal practices within the Capuchin houses.

> Contemplativity and nearness to God were central pillars of the self-understanding of the order, its legitimacy, and its credibility. The contemplative achievements of its fathers, with effects right up to the blessing of miracle working, was considered, both within and outside the order, as a sign of God's approval.[158]

The Capuchins operated at the intersection of official Catholicism and popular religion. They demonstrated considerable sympathy for the religious needs of rural people, particularly in serving at pilgrimage shrines and providing people with access to sacramentals.[159] But there was a darker side to these "people's friars," for they were often active in witch hunts. The Capuchins were "a shadowy presence" in 1747 when several women were arrested for witchcraft, tortured, and executed in the district around Marchtal in Upper Swabia. A Capuchin from Biberach was an expert witness at the trial and attempted to exorcize one of the accused witches. Lyndal Roper argues,

> The Capuchins certainly contributed much to the reinvigoration of rural Catholicism, a genuinely popular religion by the eighteenth century; but as their role in these witchcraft cases suggests, their success may have owed more than a little to their intuitive grasp of suffering, especially of women's travails, and their ability to exploit their flock's fear of the Devil.[160]

Like the Jesuits, the Capuchins sometimes faced opposition from parish priests or from local officials, who felt they interfered with normal pastoral work.[161] In 1591, the city council in Freiburg, perhaps informed by complaints from Cologne that the Capuchins were overly aggressive and active in that city, opposed the foundation of a house. The Capuchins persisted and, with the support of the Austrian authorities and the bishop, settled in Freiburg in 1598.[162] These concerns increased in the eighteenth century, as secular priests gained self-confidence and increasingly internalized the model of the good pastor. By the middle of the century, criticisms of the Capuchin friar as the manipulative exploiter of the credulity of the common folk were common among the secular clergy and the episcopal hierarchy.

During the century after 1650, the Capuchins were essential for the functioning of Baroque Catholicism. In southwest Germany, Capuchin houses could be found in every small town. The houses were modest, with usually about a dozen resident friars, as were the churches. The population of Riedlingen, where the Capuchins first settled in 1645, supported the friars with alms, as did the town council, nearby noblemen, and neighboring monasteries.[163] The Capuchins in Rottweil performed many roles:

> The Capuchins acted as exorcists and as pastors to prisoners. They often helped in the rural parishes in the area or served the pilgrimage shrines of the region like Aggenhausen auf dem Heuberg. They appeared as military chaplains and at the blessings of cattle and fields. Their library was used by readers from outside the monastery.[164]

The Capuchins, perhaps more than any of the other orders, made possible the variety and extent of popular Baroque religiosity in the century after the Thirty Years War. As we will see, Baroque Catholicism in Germany depended on a network of churches, chapels, and shrines, with a fairly large clerical establishment to serve it. Because of the rigidity of the benefice system and the economic problems caused by ongoing warfare, there was a real need for inexpensive, flexible, popular preachers and pastors like the Capuchin friars.

Conclusion

The view of German Catholicism from the top-down – from the perspective of the Catholic elite and the point of view of those who held important positions in the German Church – was confident, even triumphant, during the century after 1650. This optimism and confidence can be seen most impressively in the building projects of the monasteries.

An important aspect of this new tone was a willingness to back away from the kinds of disciplinary measures that had often characterized Tridentine reform. After 1650 Catholic leaders, but also monks, nuns, Jesuit fathers, Capuchin friars, and, most importantly, parish priests, most often turned to persuasion and propaganda to promote Catholicism. This style left space for the diverse and varied religious practices of Baroque Catholicism – indeed the building of new churches and monasteries provided the spaces for those practices. The shift away from social discipline and militancy allowed for the accommodation of popular needs and a wide participation in the practices of Baroque Catholicism.

Chapter 5: Baroque Catholicism

Baroque Catholicism evolved continuously during the century after 1650, developing differently in the various regions of Germany. It is nevertheless possible to identify the practices and devotions that were characteristic of this period. Beyond these structures, what distinguished Baroque Catholicism was a dynamism characterized above all by the constant elaboration of religious practice at the local level.

Baroque Catholicism in Germany was, then, neither monolithic nor stagnant. Furthermore, the dynamism of Catholic practice was partly the result of more or less permanent tensions, especially those between the clergy and the laity, the elite and popular classes, and the Church and the state. These tensions were in a sense fruitful, in that they drew various social groups into active engagement with Catholicism and its practices, yet they were never serious enough to undermine the identification of all social groups with the Roman Catholic Church.

As was the case with all the established confessions in Germany, Catholicism experienced a conflict between the laity and the clergy. This conflict developed in part out of the clergy's increased effort to discipline the population, especially in the interconnected areas of sexuality and popular sociability. The Catholic Church, however, did not pursue this disciplinary agenda with any vigor after the Thirty Years' War, at least before the last decades of the eighteenth century. At the same time, the development of a kind of widespread clericalism, characterized by a respect for the necessary role of the priest in a wide range of religious services, is a sign of broadly positive clergy/lay relations.

Tensions in Catholic regions also included an element of popular-elite conflict, especially where increasingly educated and economically comfortable priests, monks, nuns, and other ecclesiastics interacted with the peasants and townspeople who paid the tithes that supported them. Conflicts about the economic power of the clergy were endemic, but they were somewhat mitigated by the paternalistic behavior of many ecclesiastical lords and by the (limited but real) opportunities for social advancement through positions in the Church. Most importantly, the Catholic parish clergy generally understood the importance of providing the services that were important in the day-to-day lives of the rural population. This accommodating attitude made the Church's economic and political power somewhat easier for the wider population to accept.

The constant expansion and elaboration of practice was the result of a number of other important factors. One was the interaction between the wide array of devotional opportunities and options offered by the Church and a kind of popular activism in seeking out and supporting "new" practices. This interplay was closely related to the way in which clergy and laity responded to the inherent tension between tradition and innovation. Wolfgang Brückner has used the phrase "renewal through selective tradition" to describe the way in which Catholics at all levels of society chose from the religious options available to them.[1]

Baroque Catholicism was the home of both active communal traditions and an intense individual religiosity. Although communal religion has often been identified with popular and traditional religion and individual devotions with elite and Tridentine practices, in fact Baroque Catholicism had room for both styles of piety. The same individual and the same community could embrace both communal and individual devotions. Most obviously, this mix of modes can be seen at pilgrimage shrines, which welcomed individual pilgrims and communal processions, and where individual prayers coexisted with dramatic services for hundreds or even thousands of believers. Furthermore, the dynamism of Baroque Catholicism affected both communal and individual practices, as many new devotions developed throughout the century and a half after 1650.

Baroque Catholicism was a religious revival that reached all levels of society in the century after 1650. Individuals and communities, laypeople and clergy, city dwellers and peasants, rich and poor, participated in an increasingly active and elaborate religiosity. This religiosity was, as we shall see, embedded in the rituals and ceremonies of the Roman Catholic Church, yet also closely linked to the experiences of everyday life. Here too, there was often friction, yet at least until the middle of the eighteenth century German Catholics experienced few serious conflicts between everyday life and their religious practice.

Structures of Baroque Religiosity

Churchliness

German Catholicism experienced a true period of revival in the century after 1650. The religious enthusiasm of this period was broadly shared across the population, although contemporaries were especially struck by the extent of peasant participation in Catholic religiosity. It is also apparent that Baroque Catholicism was one of a series of revivals – like that of the fifteenth century, or the Ultramontane revival of the nine-teenth century – that were a regular part of the history of German Catholicism.[2] Furthermore, while Baroque Catholicism owed much to the Jesuit-inspired Counter-Reformation era (1570–1620), the post-1650 period had its own character. "Only after 1660 then began a new boom, with a continuously growing intensity of an unfolding broad culture of piety."[3]

Evidence of this broad revival can be found in all regions of Germany. Pilgrims flocked to existing shrines in large numbers and made more, and more generous donations, than ever before, while many new shrines appeared and developed into important pilgrimage destinations.[4] New confraternities, especially confraternities of the Rosary, were organized in villages and towns, and promoted more frequent prayers and services. Townspeople and villagers, with and without the support of the clergy, organized new processions, endowed masses for the dead, built chapels and churches, and demanded more frequent church services. As we have seen, monasteries and other ecclesiastical organizations participated actively in this movement, promoting shrines, purchasing relics, building churches, and patronizing new devotions.

A reinvigorated popular engagement with Catholic practice had always been a goal of Church reformers. These ecclesiastics expected reforms to create a disciplined and educated clergy that would in turn guide and control popular practice. In one sense, this program succeeded. A deeply rooted clericalism came to characterize German Catholicism in the seventeenth and eighteenth centuries. Clericalism meant that all social classes, from princes down to the poorest peasant, generally accepted the indispensable role of the priest for all manner of Catholic services.[5] Clericalism was in turn closely linked to the strong churchliness (*Kirchlichkeit*) of

German Catholicism. People increasingly practiced their devotions within the (admittedly broad) framework of the Roman Catholic Church.

The characteristic structures and practices of Baroque Catholicism – pilgrimages and processions, confraternities, the cults of Mary and the Eucharist, the worship of saints, and so on – all exhibited aspects of clericalism and churchliness. At the same time, these practices were embedded in the everyday life of the population, especially the rural population. The give and take between the Church and its theologically oriented and educated leaders, and the needs of everyday life will provide the conceptual framework for much of the following discussion.

An older generation of Church historians insisted that Baroque Catholicism was a true reflection of the official religion of the Catholic Church. Ludwig Veit and Ludwig Lenhart's *Kirche und Volksfrömmigkeit im Zeitalter des Barocks* (*Church and Popular Religion in the Age of the Baroque*), published in 1956, but reflecting essentially the state of the field before World War II, insists that the hallmark of Baroque Catholicism was the renewed connection of the people with the liturgy of the Church.[6] Central to this connection were the sacraments, in particular baptism, confession, communion, and marriage, where "the Catholic Church remained in strong contact with the thinking and lifestyle of the people."[7]

Despite their desire to emphasize the churchliness of Baroque Catholicism, Veit and Lenhart recognized that the Catholic population did not always follow the Church's lead. In fact, two of the seven sacraments – confirmation and extreme unction – were widely ignored and even resisted. Another problem from the point of view of these Church historians was the widespread use of sacramentals, especially the blessings of land, cattle, and water, which they referred to as "religious trash."[8] Yet Veit and Lenhart also state that the sacramentals made Catholicism "a true people's church."[9] Churchliness, then, constituted only one aspect of the population's ties to Catholicism.

Wolfgang Brückner similarly emphasizes the churchliness and clericalism of Baroque Catholicism, but also points to the weight of tradition, emphasizing the revival of late medieval forms of piety.[10] Furthermore, Brückner has repeatedly argued that the Catholic population, the clergy, and the Church as an institution all resolved the inherent tension between tradition and innovation by operating on the basis of what he calls "renewal as selective tradition."[11]

The selective promotion and use of traditional devotions and forms of organization led, according to Brückner, to a more "uniform" and "widespread" religious practice than had ever existed before. This situation was the consequence of the reform of the clergy, which by the eighteenth century was educated, resident in the parishes, and engaged in pastoral work that allowed a "long-term catechizing of the laity of all classes and estates "[12] Brückner certainly accepts the dynamic nature of Baroque religiosity, but he also argues that religious practice was more tightly constrained by the institutional Church than it had been in earlier periods, especially the fifteenth century.

Churchliness was partly the consequence of what Robert Bireley calls "the evangelization of ordinary people," which was an effort aimed at "raising the level of religious knowledge and practice "[13] This was a program that included regular catechism lessons, rural missions, frequent preaching, and episcopal visitations and other methods of administrative oversight of parish life. Much of this work fell to the parish clergy and, as we have seen, after 1650 priests were generally equipped, by background and training, to provide these basic services.[14] The work of parish priests was supplemented by the more sporadic efforts of religious orders and ecclesiastical officials.

The Jesuits conducted missions to the German countryside right up until the abolition of the order in 1773. These missions were especially important in Bavaria, Austria, and southwest Germany and aimed to supplement and advance the work of the parish priests.[15] In Bavaria in the 1760s, reports of impending arrival of missionaries caused parents and children to study their catechisms with renewed vigor, in order to pass tests the Jesuit visitor would give. As Louis Châtellier says, "a strange time, when for several weeks a whole village lived in tune with the lessons of Peter Canisius' small catechism."[16] The missionaries' sermons, lessons, and ceremonies certainly emphasized the central role of the Church and the clergy in religious life and discouraged religious practices that took place outside the framework of official practice.

The cult the Eucharist provides the most obvious example of churchliness. Integral to the mass, part of most processions and pilgrimages, central to the sacraments of confession and communion, and present at each believer's deathbed, the blood and body of Christ were fundamental to Catholic practice. Furthermore, of course, the Catholic doctrine of transubstantiation came to distinguish Catholicism from the Protestant confessions, a distinction that mattered much in Germany.[17] Tridentine reformers thus sought to both enhance the stature of the sacrament and to prevent what they considered "superstitious abuses" of the Eucharist. Both efforts were quite successful; the Eucharist maintained its place at the center of the Catholic cult and Tridentine norms were generally followed across Germany.

Tridentine norms included the rejection of communion in both kinds, the suppression of private and frequent votive masses (the *Messreihen*), a reduction in the number of low masses, and the more careful and respectful treatment of the consecrated host. The shift to these norms was slow, as the reception of the Roman Missal of 1570 indicates. Many dioceses kept their own liturgical books, even publishing new ones in the early seventeenth century, as happened in Mainz in 1602. This missal was replaced in 1698 by the so-called *Missale Romano-Moguntinum*, which was based on the Roman book but contained local customs as well.[18] This somewhat reserved attitude toward Roman models was even more apparent when one looks at the publication of rituals, liturgical books that contained regulations for services that were not directly part of the mass, including sacraments and sacramentals. The *Rituale Romanum* of 1614 was not adopted in the Bishopric of Constance until 1766, and other dioceses continued to publish their own rituals into the eighteenth century.[19]

The *Messreihen*, that is the frequent celebration of votive masses, usually purchased for a particular purpose, were forbidden by the 22nd session of the Council of Trent.[20] These masses had been popular in Germany in the sixteenth century. In the diocese of Cologne, "complicated rituals developed, such as the seven-votive-masses series in honor of Saint Sophia and her daughters, Faith, Hope, and Charity, for freedom from distress."[21] In obedience to the Tridentine decrees, priests who came to the parishes after 1650 no longer celebrated such masses. This change may not have been good for levels of popular participation in church services, and it is probable that parishioners experienced the mass itself in an increasingly passive way by the eighteenth century.[22]

The population also responded to the Tridentine promotion of more frequent confession and communion hesitantly. Still, by the later seventeenth century, almost everyone fulfilled their annual obligation to confess and take communion at Easter, an obligation that was enforced by the use of certificates of confession (*Beichtzettel*) and recorded in parish registers.[23] The practice of frequent confession and communion remained uncommon in the countryside, although in some regions it was not unusual for rural people to confess three or four times a year. In one village in Westphalia, the villagers confessed, on average, three times a year around 1700 and between five and six times a year by the 1770s.[24] More frequent communion caught hold where it was encouraged by confraternities and in regions where Jesuit missionaries were active.[25]

Confessionals, which John Bossy has identified as important elements in (and symbols of) the Tridentine understanding of penance as highly individual, came late to Germany.[26] In the region around Bonn, about one-quarter of the churches had confessional boxes in the last decades of the seventeenth century, and only by the mid-eighteenth century did over 90% of churches have a confessional box, though few had more than one.[27] W. David Myers points out that "the enclosed confessional house" only became common after 1650 and that privacy was not the main purpose of these early boxes. Instead, argues Myers:

> the confessional served a vital function: it made confession a physically prominent element of Roman Catholicism. Always present to remind the faithful of their obligation, the structure also provided a constant opportunity for the repentant. Because it was situated permanently in the church, the confessional booth gave the sacrament a conspicuousness and dignity it had previously lacked   privacy in the modern sense was still absent, as the crowds waiting their turn took a great interest in the proceedings. The event, however, appears at least decorous, a highly formal ritual embodying all the solemnity and display of Baroque Catholicism.[28]

Some aspects of the cult of the Eucharist caught on particularly slowly. Although promoted by the Jesuits, the celebration of first communion was only widely adopted in the later eighteenth century. A first communion celebration, with all 10- to 12-year-old children dressed as angels, was held in the Duchy of Jülich-Berg in the 1720s, where the Jesuits had sent regular missions. In the neighboring Electorate of Cologne, where the Jesuits were not allowed to conduct missions, these ceremonies only became common after 1750.[29] It appears that first communion took hold even later in southern Germany.[30]

Even Veit and Lenhart, who were convinced that the Tridentine decrees had led to a "eucharistic renaissance" in German Catholicism, recognized that this revival "expressed itself more strongly in forms of devotion than in a substantial increase in the frequency of taking communion."[31] The most popular eucharistic devotions all dated from the fifteenth century and before, for example the Corpus Christi celebrations and the Holy Week festivities. In Bavaria, the elaboration of the Holy Week celebrations began even before the Thirty Years' War, especially in the university towns of Dillingen and Ingolstadt where the Jesuits were active. By the eighteenth century, elaborate Good Friday processions incorporated many theatrical elements, while passion plays also became more common, including the famous Oberammergau passion play.[32]

Fronleichnam, or Corpus Christi, was of course the primary eucharistic feast day. This event became, as Wolfgang Brückner emphasizes, "the great public ceremony of homage to the divine ruler of the world   " and clearly pedagogical and dogmatic in its purpose.[33] In Bavaria, Corpus Christi celebrations became more dramatic during the Baroque period, with increasingly elaborate processions.[34] In Westphalia, Corpus Christi processions became regular events after 1650 in towns and in most villages in the first decade of the 1700s.[35] The elaboration of Corpus Christi did not however mean transforming the rituals, but rather adding new ceremonies to the many communal/traditional features of this celebration. John Bossy has even argued that that "the socially integrative powers of the host," which became less important in the mass, were incorporated into the feast of Corpus Christi in post-Tridentine Catholicism.[36]

Finally, the centrality of the cult of the Eucharist can be seen in the decoration of churches and altars. Altars received particular attention and were renovated in all Catholic regions in the Baroque period, often at the initiative of the parishioners. In Alsace, hundreds of new altarpieces were installed in parish churches in the eighteenth century, often decorated by well-known artists from south Germany and paid for by the community.[37] In the diocese of Münster, many new Baroque altars were built into the Gothic churches of the countryside. The new altars emphasized the centrality of the Eucharist. Significantly, the consecrated host now resided in the tabernacle on or hanging next to the altar, instead of in the *Sakramentshäuschen,* a cupboard in the wall of the choir.[38] The same trend occurred in the Rhineland, where by 1743 only nine of the dozens of churches examined still had "wall tabernacles."[39]

We have to be careful, however, not to overemphasize the central place of the Eucharist, and of Christocentric devotions more generally, in Baroque Catholicism. Louis Châtellier's study of Catholic Alsace shows a growth in Christocentric devotions, for example through confraternities, but also a continued strong attachment to traditional saints and to the Virgin Mary. Altars renovated in Alsace in the eighteenth century had a complex and multilayered iconography, with the patron saint of the parish remaining on the high altar, the Holy Family frequently on the altar to the right, and the Mary on the left. Images of Christ appear in about 80% of the altars, but Châtellier emphasizes that "one should not forget the loyalty the people in the countryside maintained for the patron saint and the mother of God."[40]

The churchliness, vitality, and popular character of Baroque Catholicism can all be seen in the cult of the Virgin Mary.[41] The reform orders and the Church certainly promoted Marian religiosity, with the aim of emphasizing that Mary represented the Church itself. The ubiquitous statues and images of Mary on pillars, towers, and houses "demonstrated the true Church and right belief" and the feasts of the Virgin were important events in the liturgical year.[42] Devotion to the Virgin was further reinforced and adapted in popular religious practice, where it was the primary mode in pilgrimage practice, confraternities, and in the cult of the Rosary.

Mary also protected good Catholics, and this role became even more important in the aftermath of the Thirty Years' War. An example: the inhabitants of the Habsburg city of Constance credited the Virgin with saving the city during a Swedish siege in 1633. After the Peace of Westphalia, the 1633 siege was commemorated by a communal procession to a Loreto Chapel on the outskirts of the city, and by other processions, especially in times of plague or military threat. The construction of a Marian column in 1683, at the time of the Turkish siege of Vienna, sealed the central place of Mary in the identity of the inhabitants of the city of Constance. In 1698, the city council ordered the restoration of the inscription over the Kreuzlingen Gate, where the Swedes had attacked in 1633. The inscription showed Mary and read: "*Praesidium civibus, terror hostibus* (the protector of the citizens, the terror of enemies)."[43] Constance's loyalty to Marian devotions was also part of the city's incorporation into the Austrian state, as the Habsburgs gave special attention to the cult of the Virgin Mary.[44]

The Council of Trent also maintained the cult of saints against the Protestant critique, but in practice many Church leaders feared that these devotions could easily get out of their control and did little to support them. After 1650, however, some elements within the Church promoted devotion to saints within a framework that was supposed to prevent "excesses" and "superstitions."

The movement to reinvigorate the cult of the saints certainly took hold in southern Germany, where monasteries decided to import relics of "catacomb saints." With the discovery of previously unknown catacombs in Rome in 1578, a large number of bodies of saints now became available.[45] Between 1670 and 1700, Bavarian monasteries brought dozens of bodies to Germany, and the numbers increased further in the first decades of the eighteenth century. Obviously, many abbots and abbesses procured these relics in order to enhance the prestige of their abbeys, often in competition with neighboring houses. In upper Swabia in 1727, the Abbey of Ochsenhausen made its catacomb saints, Maximus,

Innocence, and Emerentiana, the centerpieces of a major renovation of the interior of the monastery church, with paintings, a new altar, and new reliquaries.[46] In 1750, when popular interest in these saints had apparently died down, the monks organized a new "entry" of the saints into the monastery, because, as one monk wrote, "the believers measure true worth also from outward ornamentation, [so] we decorated the bodies expensively and celebrated their return."[47]

The catacomb saints provided monasteries with prestige and with the opportunity to propagate the faith in grand Baroque style. Some of the relics also became the centerpieces of pilgrimage shrines of some importance, especially in Bavaria. The appeal of these relics may be related to the completeness of many of the saints' skeletons and the fact that most were preserved behind glass, which made them visually accessible to the devout.[48] To this day, one can see the bodies of the catacomb saints of the Abbey of Ottobeuren (Bonifatius, Benedictus, and Victoria), behind glass imbedded in three heavily decorated altars in the monastery church.

The relics of the catacomb saints came to symbolize the deeply visual and tactile aspects of Baroque Catholicism. Yet they also represent the ongoing interplay of Church and people, the role of institutions like monasteries, and the constant elaboration of religious practice. However, the Catholic people could be fickle too; by the 1760s, despite all their efforts, the monks at Ochsenhausen found that the devout would no longer come to worship the catacomb saints so expensively housed in their church.[49]

Liturgical year

Pilgrimages and processions, together with church feasts, formed the liturgical year, which structured the daily lives of the population. The Catholic Church's commitment to retaining the cult of the saints, while strengthening both Christocentric and Marian devotions, meant that the liturgical year of the late seventeenth century kept most of its medieval characteristics. As described by Robert Scribner, the liturgical year was a "ritual cycle   constituted by the great feasts which re-enacted liturgically the major mysteries of Christian belief, the Incarnation and the saving Death and Resurrection of the Lord." Scribner emphasizes that the liturgical year was uneven, with a majority of the most important feasts occurring between Christmas and June, centering on Easter.[50]

The development of the liturgical year reflected broader trends within Baroque Catholicism. As in other areas, the liturgical year became more elaborate, it reflected the interplay of popular and clerical desires, and it remained closely linked with everyday life while also increasingly being practiced within the framework of official rites. All these elements could be found in the development of communal pilgrimages, which became the most visible aspect of the liturgical year piety. Confraternities also contributed to the elaboration of the liturgical year by sponsoring services and particular holidays, responding to a mix of lay and clerical initiatives.

The liturgical year in most places consisted of many layers of holidays.[51] In 1642, Pope Urban VIII prescribed 34 feast days for the whole Church. To this list were added celebrations of national, regional, and diocesan saints. In cities, confraternities organized feast days in honor of the patron saints of various monastic orders. In the countryside, the hail holidays (*Hagelfeiertage*) had great importance. These holidays consisted of a mass of petition, usually followed by a procession, in which the community asked for divine protection against bad weather and disease. Many communities celebrated votive holidays as well, as thanks for divine assistance at the time of an earlier plague or other natural disaster. To this list must be added the annual parish festival, the *Kirchweih*. Contemporary officials and modern scholars have estimated that in cities between 40 and 50 and in the countryside between 60 and 80 obligatory feasts were celebrated annually. This experience clearly distinguished Catholic from Protestant Germany and was a major feature of Catholic culture.

Both the clergy and the population encouraged the introduction of new feasts and the elaboration of older ones. Some new holidays, for example those dedicated to the Immaculate Conception of Mary, or to the Jesuit saints, were added to the calendar at the initiative of Church and state authorities.[52] Local initiatives, particularly in the form of votive holidays, added another layer of church feasts to each village or town calendar. Thus the residents of the village of Bettmaringen, in the Black Forest, celebrated St Anthony's Day, St Margaret's Day, and the Purification of the Virgin, all holidays not celebrated fully in neighboring parishes.[53]

In Bavaria, "in the Baroque, much of the practice of the liturgical year increased [to a level] of great festivity, where in the sixteenth century it had taken place in relatively reserved form." Beginning in Munich, and spreading to other towns, Bavarians enhanced Lenten celebrations with passion plays and by a new element, the *Ölbergandachten*, that is scenes from Christ's last days, either presented as set pieces or as short plays. On Good Friday, the traditional sacred performance of laying a crucifix in a "Holy Sepulchre" built into the church was celebrated in increasingly detailed style. Representations of Christ's grave became bigger and fancier, sometimes taking up the whole of the church choir.[54]

It was also at this time that Munich burghers started putting up crèches in their homes at Christmas, copying from monastic models.[55] Other aspects of Christmas celebrations were added in this period as well. Abraham à Sancta Clara, the renowned Augustinian preacher, promoted the celebration of St Nicholas Day (December 6) as a preparation for Christmas, during which a figure dressed as Bishop Nicholas distributed gifts to children, while also questioning them about their behavior.[56]

In the Rhineland, episcopal authorities lamented that on the evening of Pentecost young people in the villages engaged in "excessive eating and drinking, also dancing and jumping, rejoicing and lewd singing, and whatever else in the way of immorality and stimulation this causes."[57] On this holiday, unmarried young people apparently gathered in village inns, with the young women providing the food and the men the drink. Several episcopal ordinances in the 1660s appear to have failed to prevent this less than devout addition to an important religious holiday.

Many of the less somber practices associated with the liturgical year were primarily the result of popular initiatives, although churchmen encouraged the carrying of flags and crosses during processions until the eighteenth century.[58] Official Church efforts to promote more sober and respectful celebration of holidays had limited resonance. In the countryside outside Cologne, processions on church feasts often featured music, especially drumming, as well as "noisy stage scenes with comical sidebars."[59] Once a month in some Austrian villages in Upper Swabia the villagers concluded church services with processions in which they carried statues of the saints out of the church and through the village.[60]

There were close and obvious links between the elements of the liturgical year and the everyday life of the rural population. The church festivals of the "Lord's season" (Herrenjahr), those running from Christmas to Pentecost, mostly fell during the less busy parts of the agricultural year. Many feasts including opportunities for priests to bless fields and animals and some saints' days had particular purposes. In the Black Forest, for example, peasants celebrated Saints Fabian and Sebastian for protection against the plague, and St Agatha against fire.[61] As Hermann Hörger emphasizes, in reference to Bavaria:

Thus it is almost inevitable that the liturgical celebrations centered on Christ should coincide with the natural turning-points of the solar year, and that a ritual of procreation, representing new life in God, should be built into the celebration of Easter night: the Easter candle, signifying the risen Christ, is immersed in the baptismal font, the womb of the church, to invest the church with divine life.[62]

None of this is surprising as historians and anthropologists have long understood the ways in which traditional Christianity came to be integrated into rural society. The complex place of what Andreas Holzem calls "the religious experience" of Baroque Catholicism is not complete, however, without a discussion of the role of religion in the rites of passage: birth, marriage, and death.[63]

The rites of passage

There is surprisingly little written about the place of birth, marriage, and death rituals in Baroque Catholicism. Veit and Lenhart's massive study emphasizes that Baroque piety was firmly based in the sacramental life of the Catholic Church. At the same time, however, the authors recognize that popular traditions were a major part of all these rites. Veit and Lenhart suggestively state that "the Catholic Church remained in strong contact with the thought patterns and way of life of the people   [and] the religious ways of the people often came fully and in an undiluted way to expression."[64]

The interplay between popular traditions and the ceremonies of the official Church around baptism, marriage, and death was not unproblematic in the Baroque period, but it was also not a source of extensive conflict. Some of the developments of the decades around 1600, in particular the introduction of parish registers, were reinforced and made routine after 1650. Church and state officials in most places backed off from some other Tridentine reforms, such as the effort to control the size and expense of the celebrations around baptisms, weddings, and funerals. At the same time two central tendencies of Baroque Catholicism, the elaboration of ceremonies and a basic churchliness of religious practices can be found in these rites as well.

John Bossy, in a famous article, has argued that the reforms of the Council of Trent aimed at clearing away many secular aspects of the sacraments, particularly baptism. In particular, Tridentine decrees ordered that baptisms take place within three days of birth and that the number of godparents be restricted to one or two.[65] Evidence from the seventeenth and eighteenth century indicates that these regulations were generally obeyed in the German-speaking lands. In a group of Austrian villages, babies were baptized within a day of birth and there was only one godparent, of the same sex as the baby.[66]

In Westphalia, lay people recognized the need for quick baptisms and very few babies died unbaptized.[67] On the other hand, regulations here were somewhat more flexible than Bossy found for Italy and France, and parents were allowed up to 15 days before bringing newborn babies to church. The popular view was that baptism was "nothing more than a rite and a reason for a celebration," and a longer waiting period meant that families could organize larger parties. In the countryside, the festivities were organized by neighboring women, who often went to the inn for libations before going to church for the baptism. In the villages in northern Westphalia studied by Werner Freitag, Tridentine reforms succeeded in reducing the number of godparents from three to two and reducing the wait before the baptism to a maximum of eight days.[68]

In the Rhineland, regional differences in baptismal rites developed. In the Mosel valley, baptisms were purely women's events from which men were expressly excluded. In the region around Bonn, the baptism in the church included family members and invited guests of both genders, but a separate women's ritual took place that included the purification of the mother. A 1665 decree of the Archbishop of Cologne attempted to limit these ceremonies, though it did not outlaw them. The same decree ordered parents to limit the number of godparents to one woman and one man, indicating that the Tridentine regulations had yet to change popular practice in this part of Germany.[69]

The clerical effort to cleanse baptism of profane elements, such as multiple godparents and rowdy celebrations, proceeded moderately in comparison to Italy and France; at the same time, the trend of moving rites more within the official Catholic framework progressed steadily. The effort to regulate the work of midwives constituted one aspect of this development. Regulations in the Bishopric of Münster required that midwives be good Catholics and that they present documentation attesting to their good moral character. Most importantly, midwives were expected to learn the proper formula for an emergency baptism from the parish priest.[70]

Andreas Holzem points out that this system led to tensions between clerical and lay understandings of baptism in the Münster countryside. One problem involved the traditional forms of the emergency baptism performed by many midwives, which included "incantations against devils, demons, and other dark forces."[71] Priests and episcopal officials sometimes did not recognize such baptisms as valid. Increasingly, villagers were themselves unsure of the validity of emergency baptisms and often had a child rebaptized in such circumstances. Even in 1750 there was considerable uncertainty about emergency baptisms, as this priest's report indicates:

> Since there is no proper and approved midwife to be found in this parish, thus it has happened recently, that one or several children died without holy baptism, or [died] in such a way that one can not really know if they had received the emergency baptism or not.[72]

The fact that both the clergy and laypeople were concerned about the proper form of emergency baptisms indicates the importance of this rite for everyone involved, especially parents of course. In southwest Germany, rural communities complained vociferously about priests who were too slow in baptizing newborns. Indeed, baptism was clearly considered one of a parish priest's most important duties. Villagers always deployed stories of priests "allowing" babies to die unbaptized in letters of complaint about their pastors.[73] This focus on baptism shows the importance people attached to the rite and the sense that a priest's failure in this area of pastoral work would be taken seriously by higher authorities.

As we have seen, the Council of Trent, in the *Tametsi* decree, reaffirmed traditional Catholic marriage theology, but effectively outlawed "clandestine marriages" by requiring the publishing of banns and the solemnization of weddings in the presence of witnesses and a priest.[74] Unlike for Protestants, marriage remained a sacrament of the Catholic Church, and one development in the Baroque era was that the "churchly" elements of weddings – especially the service in the church – developed a stronger place among the many rituals around marriage.[75]

The increased churchliness of weddings did not mean that wedding feasts and other rituals were curtailed, perhaps since church and state recognized the central importance of such secular rituals to marriages.[76] Nevertheless, marriage developed a stronger Catholic flavor. In Bavaria, and it seems elsewhere, the actual exchange of rings and the blessing of the couple by the priest had traditionally taken place in the church portal.[77] After 1650, the ceremony gradually moved into the church and became more elaborate, combining the blessing of the bride, the exchange of vows and rings, followed by a wedding mass. Although much of this ritual followed the prescripts of the Roman Missal of 1570, a wide variety of practices were found within the various Bavarian dioceses.[78]

The Catholic Church gained only partial control of marriage in the Rhineland. A 1747 decree of the Archbishop of Cologne lamented the fact that young people were marrying without parental permission, but with the approval of parish priests. According to Thomas Paul Becker, "before 1747, the efforts of Church and state had not been able to achieve anything more than the formal assimilation of the marriage rituals to the ecclesiastical norms."[79]

Church and state officials were more interested in regulating premarital and extra marital sexual activity, than in sanitizing marriage rituals. The *Sendgerichte*, the local ecclesiastical courts in Westphalia and the Rhineland, regularly punished women, and to a lesser extent men, for illegal sexual activity. The majority of these courts' cases in the Bishopric of Münster (60%) were cases of illegitimate birth, while 26% of the cases involved premarital conception.[80] It is an indication of popular acceptance of official teaching about marriage and sex that the incidence of such cases fell in the late seventeenth century and remained at low levels until after 1750.

Another indication of the churchliness of marriage rites is the very low incidence of Protestant–Catholic marriages in biconfessional (or multiconfessional) cities. In Oppenheim, a small city in the Rhine valley near Mainz, 94.6% of Catholics married other Catholics in the seventeenth and eighteenth centuries.[81] Intermarriage was also almost unknown in Augsburg, the largest biconfessional city, after the Thirty Years' War.[82] The same was true in Colmar, in Alsace, where an influx of Catholic immigrants from the countryside in the decades around 1700 tipped the demographic balance in favor of the Catholic community, but did not lead to more Protestant–Catholic marriages.[83]

There were conflicts and tensions between the population and the Church, over, for example the appropriateness of premarital sexual relations, but there were few conflicts over the nature of the rites of passage. Indeed, marriage rituals in Baroque Catholicism were increasingly overseen by the parish priest, brought into the parish church, and folded into the officially approved rites, which, at the same time, remained flexible enough to incorporate a range of local and regional peculiarities.

The rituals that accompanied death, like the other rites of passage, became more elaborate in the Baroque period, while also gradually coming to conform more closely to the precepts of the Council of Trent. The effort to institute the sacrament of extreme unction, however, proceeded slowly. Parish priests regularly reported that people refused this sacrament, claiming it would lead to their immediate death.[84] In some areas, at least, this sacrament nevertheless became part of death rituals in the second half of the seventeenth century. In Westphalia, extreme unction was common by 1660s and 1670s, though some dying people still refused the sacrament.[85]

Deathbed confession and communion, the *viaticum*, was universally practiced and became the defining moment in the ritual of dying. By the late seventeenth century, it became widespread practice that church bells were rung when the priest left the church with the Eucharist, that neighbors were expected to pray and follow the priest in procession to the home of the sick person. In southwest Germany, priests who failed to perform these services were severely reprimanded by their parishioners, who considered it one of the most important duties of a pastor.[86] It was apparently difficult to get neighbors to accompany the priest, who often proceeded alone or in the company of just the sacristan through the village or town. "The attempt to give the procession to the dying ritual publicity generally failed."[87] Once at the bedside of the sick person, the priest heard a confession, gave communion, and then administered extreme unction.

In Bavaria, each diocese produced its own liturgical regulations. Over the century after 1650, the death rituals gradually came to more closely mirror the structure laid out in the 1614 *Rituale Romanum*. Thus the traditional order of the rituals – confession, followed by extreme unction, then communion – shifted to confession, then communion, with extreme unction coming last. Clearly the latter sacrament had acquired a new stature. Despite the acceptance of Roman models, Bavarian ritual books also contained descriptions of local practices and German prayers, part of the ongoing importance of popular traditions.[88]

Other aspects of death rituals were intensified in this period. The funeral mass, still uncommon before the Thirty Years' War, was an integral part of most funerals by 1700. Still, there were considerable local variations about funerals. In one village in Westphalia in the 1680s, funeral masses were universal, while in a nearby village few villagers requested them.[89] The close interplay of religious concerns and secular interest – honor, social rank, inheritance – was of course natural at funerals and wakes. Funeral feasts and wakes with drinking and dancing, all remained common, though Church regulations often required that funerals take place in the morning, in order to maintain decorum among the participants.[90]

In the case of all these rituals, there was no clear conflict between the regulations of the official Church and the needs and desires of the population. The Council of Trent certainly aimed at a separation of the sacred and the profane and sought to impose a greater solemnity on these rites, but in Baroque Germany this tendency was counteracted by the trend toward ritual elaboration and the clergy's willingness to accommodate popular demands. As with many other aspects of Baroque Catholicism, these rituals came to be practiced more often than not within the framework of official approved rites. This shift toward churchliness was primarily the result of a convergence of popular/lay needs and the program of the Catholic Church, rather than the imposition of new practices from above. Finally, this shift was never complete and rituals continued to vary from place to place.

Weekly and daily religious practice

The cults of the Eucharist, the saints, and the Virgin Mary were also essential to the development of daily and weekly practices. These services also became increasingly elaborate.

Attendance at weekly services, required by law, was almost universal, and the behavior of the common people during church services increasingly reflected the norms found in Church statutes. Parishioners were, for the most part, "devout and reverential," as the 1655 church ordinance in the Bishopric of Münster required.[91] Still, as everywhere in Catholic Germany, in Westphalia in the seventeenth century "a large portion of the community, especially the men, stood (outside) in front of the church, talking, gambling, sometimes making noise and fighting."[92] Beginning around 1700, Andreas Holzem identifies a decline in such "excesses," and by the 1740s everyone considered such behavior to be exceptional.[93] "Humble and reverential participation" were the norm during services in country parishes in the eighteenth century.[94]

In the Rhineland, priests and episcopal visitors reported that about 15% of parishioners arrived late for services or left early. In the seventeenth century, priests sometimes identified such behavior as a form of protest, but after 1700 parishioners more often missed parish services in order to attend mass at nearby monastic churches, chapels, or Jesuit services. Some villagers may not have been committed to parish conformity, but they had internalized the value of the mass. Indeed, one can safely assume that it was the more religiously engaged who traveled outside the parish to find more interesting or demanding services.[95]

In southwest Germany, the population not only attended services, but also sought to increase the number of masses available each week by pressuring priests to offer more services.[96] In the eighteenth century, town councils and village communes across the region pressed bishops and princes to create more parishes and hire more priests. These demands certainly reflected a need to accommodate a growing population, but they also came out of a popular commitment to regular and frequent services.[97] The villagers in Seebronn, an Austrian village in Swabia, supported their request for a resident priest by pointing to the very active worship of the Eucharist in the village church.[98]

The structures of Baroque Catholicism owed much to traditions inherited from medieval Christianity; after all, there was nothing new about the cults of the Eucharist, the Virgin, and the saints. At the same time, the effect of Tridentine reforms can be seen in the increasing churchliness and clericalism of religious practice. Finally, the sometimes dour and disciplined Counter-Reformation piety, as practiced for example at the Wittelsbach court in Munich, failed to penetrate into the countryside and declined in influence. Instead, an increasingly visual, tactile, and above all elaborate religiosity came to dominate all Catholic practice.

A Religious Revival

To understand Baroque Catholicism, one must examine the institutions and the practices that made it such a dynamic religious system. Confraternities were particularly important institutions, since they provided the organization for some of the central features of the post 1650 period: the extension of the sacral landscape, and the rise of communal pilgrimages and processions.

Confraternities

Confraternities became an important aspect of Baroque religiosity, initially in towns and, after 1700, in the countryside as well. Confraternities also embodied many of the apparent tensions with Catholicism. Confraternities had been important in late medieval Christianity and most had disappeared or fallen into disuse in the sixteenth century. Some of the confraternities of the post-1650 period were revivals of ancient brotherhoods, but many were new creations, like the ubiquitous Rosary confraternities, the Holy Family confraternities, and the Marian sodalities organized by the Jesuits. Not only could confraternities be traditional or Tridentine, some were clearly promoted by the clergy (like the Marian sodalities), while others were organized and funded by local communities with minimal clerical participation. The Rosary confraternities were a mix of these two forms. They were often organized by parish priests and linked to regional archconfraternities affiliated with the Dominicans. At the same time, many village communes initiated and funded the process of creating new Rosary confraternities.[99]

The confraternity was clearly a very flexible organizational form. Broadly speaking, there were two kinds of confraternities. One type, generally more traditional, was organized for the purpose of providing funerals, burials, and masses for deceased members. The second type, which included many of the confraternities founded after 1650, were devotional, in that they provided a framework for members to practice more intensive devotions. Many confraternities were in fact a mix of these forms. The St Sebastian Confraternity in the southwest German village of Wurmlingen, for example, required that members come together for regular prayers and special services, and that they confess and take communion at least five times a year. As the same time, the confraternity paid for funeral processions and indulgences for deceased members.[100]

Confraternities contributed to the churchliness of Baroque Catholicism. The devotional fraternities founded in the seventeenth century in cities and towns and villages in the first half of the eighteenth century, were Christocentric or Marian. The Jesuit Marian sodalities, for example, experienced renewed support after 1700. According to Louis Châtellier, "more than one in two Munich families were involved with the congregations at the end of the eighteenth century." The Jesuits' Marian brotherhood in Colmar in Alsace, a small town with 8000 inhabitants, had 250 members in 1748 and 650 in the 1760s.[101] There were other new-style confraternities that enjoyed considerable popularity in cities and towns. The Confraternities of the Agony of Christ, aimed at helping members "obtain a good death," attracted many members along the Rhine, for example in Cologne and in the smaller towns in Alsace and Baden.[102]

The spread of the cult of the Sacred Heart from France, where it developed in the late seventeenth century after visions experienced by a nun, Margaret Mary Alacoque, to the German-speaking lands, was a project led by churchmen. Two short books were published in 1695 describing the new devotion to the Sacred Heart and its popularity in France.[103] One of these books, written by a Jesuit, P. Bernhard Sonnenberg, a preacher in Munich, became especially influential in Vienna. In 1698, a confraternity was founded there to promote this eucharistic devotion. Affiliated with the Ursuline convent, the program of the confraternity emphasized frequent prayer, monthly communion, and of course the special celebration of the feast of the Sacred Heart.[104] This confraternity, and the devotion it promoted, was strongly tied to the institution of the Catholic Church; it was also a devotion popular with educated circles in Vienna, Innsbruck, and Munich, and had little resonance in the countryside.[105]

Marian and eucharistic confraternities did come to the countryside, especially in the eighteenth century, but villagers also continued to establish more traditional brotherhoods. In the Rhineland, Sebastian and Matthias brotherhoods, which organized prayers, processions, and pilgrimages to ward off the plague, remained common and active.[106] In other places, for example southwest Germany, the eighteenth century was the century of the Rosary confraternities, which were founded in dozens of parishes between 1650 and 1750.[107] The same is true in Bavaria, although there appears to have been a wider variety of confraternities there, from Jesus-Mary-Joseph brotherhoods, to Scapular confraternities, to the Brotherhood of the Five Sacred Wounds.[108]

The increased activity of confraternities in the countryside became "a danger for the religious-churchly life of the parish."[109] Confraternities often organized processions around the fields, or blessings of the crops, or other ceremonies frowned on by reformed churchmen.[110] Despite regular lamentations from officials, these ceremonies continued until they were attacked by enlightened reformers from the 1770s on. Could it be that the confraternities provided the kind of institutional structure that could contain the tension between clergy-dominated churchliness and a popular practice embedded in the needs of an agricultural world?

The elaboration of the sacral landscape

> Outside France, post-Tridentine Catholicism took on a primarily Baroque imprint. The love of sensuality of Baroque Catholicism found its obvious and spoken expression in the worship of the saints (especially in the form of the cult of the Virgin Mary), in the enthusiasm for church buildings, in processions, in sacred theater and much more. These all demonstrate forcefully how much everyday life was religiously stamped; indeed [daily life was] shot through with religiosity.[111]

Many of the practices and much of the style of Baroque Catholicism reflected its close links with everyday life in the countryside. The elaboration of the sacred landscape, as more churches, chapels, shrines, roadside crosses, and other structures were built, responded to a widespread desire for more holy sites and places to worship. Processions and pilgrimages brought groups of people to these sites and moved them through the countryside, often in order to bless fields and livestock or to seek divine protection from disease or bad weather. Although they reinforced the churchliness of religious practice, the feasts and holidays of the liturgical year were also tied to the changing seasons. Finally, as historians and anthropologists have long recognized, church services were an increasingly important part of the rites of passage – birth, marriage, death – in Catholic communities. Yet priests could not ignore the needs of families and communities as they officiated at baptisms, weddings, and funerals, and they adapted official rites to the needs of villagers and townspeople.

Southern Germany, Austria, and Franconia were the heartlands of Baroque sacred architecture. By 1750, many newly built or rebuilt monasteries, churches, and chapels dotted the countryside. In addition, Stations of the Cross, Mount Calvary statues, roadside crosses, and bridge statues were built in increasing numbers.[112] The number of new churches is quite striking. According to art historians, over 200 churches "of some artistic significance" were built in this period in Bavaria, Swabia, and Franconia.[113] During the episcopate of Friedrich Karl von Schönborn between 1729 and 1746, 150 churches were renovated or newly built in the dioceses of Würzburg and Bamberg. Many of these churches were designed by the renowned rococo architect Balthasar Neumann, known for designing the episcopal palaces at Würzburg and Bruchsal, as well as the great Franconian pilgrimage church at Vierzehnheiligen.[114]

Neumann's work for the Schönborn bishops, for whom he constructed rural churches as well as great palaces, was not unusual. Other renowned architects and decorators – the Asam brothers, the Zimmermann brothers, the Feichtmayrs, and others – worked for a range of patrons, often monasteries who built churches in the villages they controlled. The monastery of Ochsenhausen, for example, built several pilgrimage churches in the early eighteenth century, as well as four large parish churches, all in the latest style.[115] At the same time, as we have seen, almost all south German and Austrian monasteries built new monastic complexes in the century after 1650, and these buildings dominated the landscape.

Churches and chapels, especially those at pilgrimage shrines, were imbedded in the landscape and part of everyday life. Thomas DaCosta Kaufmann makes the point well:

A typical location for many of these monuments [pilgrimage churches] sets them picturesquely in nature; in one famous example, the church of Wies is literally set in the meadows after which it is named. A rustic setting also brings the church closer to the peasant population.[116]

Monastic complexes (where many local people worked, worshipped, paid taxes, or attended law court) and even well-known shrines like the Wieskirche (Bavaria), Einsiedeln (Switzerland), or Walldürn (Franconia) were places familiar to the rural population. Local churches and chapels, roadside shrines and crucifixes, and other small sites, many of which were paid for and maintained by local communities, were even more familiar. At the regional level, important patrons, like monasteries, nobles, and princes, created areas where holy images from regional shrines could be found in churches, on roadside crosses, and at pilgrimage way stations.[117] The omnipresence of sacred images, buildings, and spaces played an important role in making Catholicism part of everyday life.

The Rhineland and Westphalia did not become "Baroque landscapes" as did southern Germany. There were no Baroque churches in the villages of the diocese of Münster; instead the late Gothic parish churches built in the fifteenth century were repaired and sometimes enlarged after the Thirty Years' War. In the eighteenth century, the limited resources available for building were used to redo the interior of village churches.[118] A similar development took place in the Rhineland, where the traditional parish churches (dating from the fifteenth and early sixteenth centuries) were thick-walled, with three aisles, and often looked like (and sometimes served as) fortresses. Here too, the interiors of the churches were extensively rebuilt in the eighteenth century.[119] New high altars, statues, and decoration did not perhaps bring about as extensive an elaboration of the wider landscape as in southern Germany, but the new decor did widen the impact of Catholicism in everyday life. The new decoration also complemented and reinforced the new more reverential attitude toward church services.[120]

Pilgrimages and processions

Pilgrimage became the dominant style or mode of Baroque Catholicism after 1650 as more and more people participated in large communal processions to a growing number of shrines. The expansion, even explosion, of pilgrimage piety was the result of both clerical promotion of new shrines and popular discovery and support of both new and older sites. Pilgrimage piety was flexible enough to function in a variety of ways. Shrines strengthened Catholic identity and were centers of new devotional practices, but they were also places where peasants could access supernatural power to protect crops or cure disease. Pilgrimage piety reinforced the churchliness of popular Catholicism by incorporating the practical piety of the wider population.[121]

It is often difficult to distinguish pilgrimages from processions in the Baroque period. Regular (annual or monthly) community processions often traveled to local shrines, while more extensive pilgrimages, which could be either extraordinary events in response to a crisis or regular rituals, usually took the form of communal processions with flags, crosses, banners, and music. Indeed, the German word *Wallfahrt*, for which there is no direct English translation, refers to the kind of communal pilgrimage procession that was so common in the Baroque period.[122] Together, processions and pilgrimages brought life and movement into the sacral landscape. In southern Germany, especially Bavaria and Swabia, processions and pilgrimages filled a landscape that was densely furnished with sacred sites, and the popularity of pilgrimage piety further enhanced the number of sites. There were a smaller number of sites in Westphalia and the Rhineland, but these were intensively visited by the population, especially in the first half of the eighteenth century.

There was nothing archaic about Baroque processions and pilgrimages. As Wolfgang Brückner says, these were *actiones sacrae*, moments when the clergy and the laity together put Catholicism into practice. These expeditions drew on late medieval traditions, but there were also very modern.

> Processions were   at the very least used in a targeted way, in which [were found] modern forms of mass communication, of group cohesion, of communal identification through the common completion of ritual action, which won great prestige for the individuals and for the involved institutions, for example confraternities and village communes.[123]

Important regional shrines were widely promoted, by clergymen in pamphlets and learned books, and by the common people in woodcuts and roadside crosses. Roadside crosses marking the route to the important shrine of Dettelbach sprung up in large numbers across Franconia. Pilgrims stopped at them, or in small field chapels, to rest and pray, aided by a reproduction of the *Gnadenbild*, the miraculous statue at the shrine.[124] Images of the statue, in this case a 40-centimeter high wooden Pietà carved in the fourteenth century, were ubiquitous in the region around the shrine. Woodcuts and engravings circulated in large numbers, often produced by village craftsmen who copied from other engravings or from plaster statues brought from the shrine itself.[125] The fame of the Dettelbach shrine was further enhanced by the mass production of prayer sheets, short prayers dedicated to the "Mary at the holy shrine at Dettelbach," which were found in many households.[126] All major shrines produced and benefited from this kind of multimedia publicity, which was a significant aspect of the elaboration of Baroque religiosity.[127]

The growth in the number of shrines after 1650 was remarkable. In southwest Germany, dozens of new shrines appeared and many late medieval pilgrimage destinations experienced a revival.[128] In Alsace after 1680, over 75 new local shrines supplemented the small number of regional shrines that had existed before the Thirty Years' War. Louis Châtellier estimates that by the middle of the eighteenth century there was a pilgrimage center for every 3.5 parishes.[129] People used shrines more frequently and more intensely as well. The number of communicants at the Bavarian shrine of Altötting rose from about 120,000 a year at the end of the seventeenth century to over 200,000 a year in the first decades of the next century.[130] The shrine of Hohenspießberg (Bavaria) also peaked in popularity between 1700 and 1750. In this period, over 80 communal pilgrimages came annually to the shrine, with most villages making about six such *Wallfahrten* a year, but some making as many as 18.[131] People also used small shrines more intensively. Money offerings at the shrine of Engelwies (in the Black Forest) tripled between 1714 and 1728, peaked in the 1730s, and remained at high levels until the 1770s.[132]

The great pilgrimage shrines, like Altötting (Bavaria), Maria Zell (Austria), Einsiedeln (Switzerland), Vierzehnheiligen (Franconia), and Kevelaer (Rhineland) – all in a sense "national shrines" – were only one part of the network of pilgrimage sites that covered Catholic regions. There were also shrines of regional importance that attracted pilgrims from maybe 20 surrounding villages, along with thousands of local sites known only to the inhabitants of nearby towns and villages. One catalogue of shrines lists over 800 sites for southwest Germany alone, and the majority of those sites were active in the century after 1650.[133] Regional shrines included places like Triberg in the Black Forest. This shrine first attracted pilgrims in the 1640s, when an image of Mary was found in a tree, and then exploded into popularity again between 1690 and 1750 after a number of miraculous cures occurred at the shrine.[134] Small shrines often started as local initiatives and functioned without official approval. A new site at Wagenhart in southwest Germany attracted pilgrims without any official support in the years after 1700 and another site in the same region, called "Mintzlings," drew pilgrims away from an established shrine nearby.[135] In Bavaria a dense network of "secondary shrines" evolved, the great majority of them dedicated to the Virgin Mary and revolving around a sacred image.[136]

By the eighteenth century, each parish sent at least four to six processions to pilgrimage shrines each year. Many processions were annual events, the result of vows taken at a time of crisis. The parishioners of Dingolfing (Bavaria) went, for example, to shrines on the Bogenberg, at Altenkirchen, Frauenbiburg, Haindling, and on the Dreifaltigkeitsberg each year. They also organized further communal pilgrimages for special purposes, for example in 1649 and 1749 to Altötting, one assumes to celebrate the end of the Thirty Years' War.[137] The inhabitants of the village of Fischbach, on Lake Constance, made 11 different processions in 1698, including a procession around the fields on Ascension Day and a procession to the St George chapel on the *Hagelfeier*, the hail festival.[138]

Pilgrimage and processional piety were characteristic of German Catholicism everywhere, but the density of the network of shrines and the extent of the elaboration of practice varied from region to region. Southern Germany (Bavaria, Swabia, Austria) as well as Franconia developed the most elaborate rites (and have attracted the most historical and folkloric studies). The development of processions and pilgrimages in the Rhineland was slower and less intense. In this long-settled region, local shrines dating from the medieval period were mostly abandoned and forgotten in the sixteenth century, but many revived after 1650 alongside new Marian and Christocentric sites. "Thus, for example, those with painful leg injuries went not only to the blessed image of the Luxemberg Madonna at the [well-known shrine of] Kevelaer, but also to the bones of St Wendelin in Meckenheim."[139] There were even fewer shrines in Westphalia, and most were newer Marian sites. Nevertheless, the population used these shrines intensely, despite the comparatively small number of local sites.[140] Throughout Germany, confessional boundaries tended to limit the size of the Catholic population living near shrines, making them what became known as *Peregrinatio der Landschaft*, that is regional pilgrimages.[141]

Shrines had a range of functions in German society, but most primarily served what Werner Freitag has called a "practically oriented piety."[142] Pilgrims sought divine assistance in the form of protective magic, such as protection or relief from drought, hailstorms, and disease and they sought cures for a wide range of physical ailments and difficulties. As in other parts of Catholic Europe, communities and individuals made vows to perform pilgrimages to particular shrines, which could then become regular obligations. Some shrines evolved particular specializations, like the Marian shrine at Bergatreute, where grieving parents brought babies that had died unbaptized, seeking a miraculous cure that would bring the baby back to life long enough to be baptized.[143]

Gender and generational differences reflected the everyday nature of pilgrimage piety. Women under 40 were apparently overrepresented at shrines, particularly Marian shrines. Not surprisingly, the Virgin Mary had a special interest in helping and protecting expecting mothers and women in childbirth. Furthermore, shrines and the sacred power they possessed could be accessed by women as well as men, making them important centers of female religiosity. The shrine of Maria Steinbach, founded in the 1730s in Upper Swabia, was responsible for a range of miracles, but the majority involved the cure or rescue of children, the special interest of this Mary.[144] The Bavarian shrine of Hohenspeißenberg, by contrast, was favored by men, who made vows for protection from accidents, illness, and animal disease.[145]

Votive gifts and votive images given to shrines also show close links between pilgrimage piety and agricultural society. Many of the votive paintings found at the St Leonard Shrine at Siegartsbrunn (Bavaria) represent vows made in response to cattle epidemics. One of them, from 1732, shows a group of cattle processing around the shrine, underneath representations of Saints Leonard and Valentine offering cows and horses to the Virgin Mary and Baby Jesus.[146] Similarly, the text that accompanies a complex 1743 votive painting at Allerheiligen (Bavaria) reflects the importance of cattle.

> Paul Gärner from Sollä and his wife Maria took refuge in the Holy Trinity and all of God's powers in great fear of a [cattle] epidemic. They were protected from all misfortune. Had the painting made. Thank God and Mary and all the saints.[147]

Baroque shrines were almost all oriented around a sacred image, the *Gnadenbild*. This too was a new phenomenon, and even shrines, like the Holy Blood shrine at Walldürn, that had existed without such an image before the Reformation, acquired a sacred image sometime after the 1580s. Brückner emphasizes that the sacred image provided a focus for the cult at Walldürn, by illustrating the founding legend of the shrine, serving as a concrete location within the shrine for popular devotions, and providing an easily reproduced image for pamphlets, roadside crosses, and devotional literature.[148] Sacred images also acquired many of the characteristics of relics, becoming "miraculous images" that were credited with powers of their own, that could be accessed through physical contact with the picture or statue or even by holding or worshipping reproductions of the image. Pilgrims often sought to touch the images, or at least approach them and pray on the steps to their altars.[149]

The highly visual character of pilgrimage piety can been seen in the nature of many of the miracles associated with shrines. Holy Blood images, for example, were seen to bleed. More common were images of Mary where the Virgin was seen to shed tears, move her eyes, or change her coloring. In 1690, a ten-year-old girl saw the eyes of a figure of Mary move to look around the Herzogsspitalkirche in Munich during services. This miracle was soon accredited by the Bishop of Freising and gave rise to a lively pilgrimage in the heart of Munich. In other places, Mary was seen to cry, for example at the elevation of the host at the shrine at Steinbach, grieving the suffering of her son.[150] There was something concrete, but also very intimate and personal, about the two-way gaze exchanged between Mary and the devout in these highly decorated Baroque shrines. Brückner reminds us that a shrine became a major pilgrimage center "when a cult image had evolved, that could fulfill [the needs of] popular devotional styles in form and usefulness."[151] Visuality, was one such form.

The interplay of elite and clerical sponsorship and promotion and popular support and initiative determined the nature of the development of all individual shrines and the rise of pilgrimage and processional piety more generally. After 1650, this interplay shifted clearly toward popular initiative. Indeed the popular character of Baroque processions and pilgrimages has even led some historians to assume that these events were purely popular. Thomas Paul Becker calls the rise of pilgrimage in the Cologne region a "popular movement" (*Volksbewegung*) and Walter Pötzel argues that pilgrimage piety in Bavaria developed under the leadership of the "little man."[152]

Detailed studies of individual shrines show that clerical promotion was almost always part of the development of new shrines and pilgrimages.[153] Rebekka Habermas argues that the Bavarian shrine at Hohenspeißenberg, although initially founded by the monastery of Rottenbuch, owed its popularity to the "dynamic exchange between state and church pilgrimage policies on the one hand and the logic of miracles of the common folk on the other."[154] In the first decades of the eighteenth century, the popular search for miraculous assistance came to dominate the discourse at Hohenspeißenberg, as elsewhere, and elite notions of deploying shrines to encourage sober devotion and strengthen popular ties to the Church faded into the background.

All shrines required popular support to succeed, even when their origins lay with monasteries, convents, princes, or bishops. Some shrines, like the one at Peiting near Hohenspeißenberg, were primary popular creations.[155] Miracles began to occur around a Marian image there in the 1640s. Soon crowds gathered at an unconsecrated chapel to pray and seek divine assistance, though no services were held. Local officials, especially from nearby villages, appealed to the local priest, the bishop, and the Elector for assistance. In 1670, the village commune of Peiting funded an expansion of the chapel, a commitment that seems have forced the bishop to consecrate the church and accept this new site. Habermas argues that the shrine at Peiting received more popular support in the later seventeenth century than Hohenspeißenberg, for the population was somewhat hesitant to respond to the massive elite support for the latter shrine.[156]

The important shrines of Dettelbach and Walldürn in Franconia both benefited from clerical promotion, especially before the Thirty Years' War, but both thrived most dramatically after 1700.[157] In this period, the balance of clerical promotion and what Brückner calls "thronging folk" shifted in favor of the latter. Still, in this region the large and fairly well organized Catholic states did not allow shrines to experience "wild growth" as occurred in some other regions.

In southwest Germany, some shrines did grow rapidly and primarily as a result of popular enthusiasm. Although a nearby monastery was willing to profit from its popularity, the shrine at Steinbach (Upper Swabia) developed around 1730 because many peasants and artisans saw the eyes of a Marian statue move and there soon followed a large number of miraculous cures.[158] Large numbers of pilgrims forced a skeptical episcopal hierarchy to investigate the miracles credited to Maria Steinbach. After an exhaustive investigation, which produced reams of documents, the investigators accepted the reports of miracles and the Bishop approved the new pilgrimage. Here the initiative belonged to the local population and the clerical authorities followed the lead of the faithful.

The officials of the Bishop of Constance who investigated the miracles at Steinbach worried that too much discussion of miracles would bring down the derision of their Protestant neighbors. Yet in the end, they were convinced that the miracles the peasants reported had taken place. This was not unusual. Werner Freitag has shown how monks and nuns in Westphalia increasingly accepted popular reports of miracles in the century after 1650. Indeed, reports of more and more miracles required the Church leaders to accept the vast majority of them if they were to keep any oversight over pilgrimage piety.[159] Until the later eighteenth century, popular confidence in miracles forced the clergy and lay elite to accept their reality of divine intervention in everyday affairs. Cultural influences within Baroque Catholicism could and did move in many different directions.

The Role of the Laity

The dynamism of Baroque Catholicism was the consequence of the fact that a variety of social groups, institutions, and cultural traditions were able to contribute to the development of religious practices. Clerical initiatives were many and varied and included the Jesuit promotion of the cult of the Eucharist and the Marian devotions, monastic support of pilgrimages and shrines, and the parish clergy's encouragement of the Rosary. We have also seen how the laity, including the peasantry, took a major role in developing new devotions. The fact that laypeople were far from passive recipients of religion imposed from above had two central origins. On the one hand, rural communal institutions and town councils played the important role in organizing local religion. On the other hand, religion continued to be vital in helping people and communities understand and overcome the difficulties of everyday life.

Local church, communal church

It should not surprise historians that town councils took a strong role in organizing Catholic religious life. The urban elite in Imperial cities such as Cologne and Aachen, in territorial cities such as Munich and Münster, and in small cities like Rottweil (Swabia) or Überlingen (Lake Constance) had identified themselves with the forces of Catholic Reform already before the Thirty Years' War. In adopting Tridentine models, especially under the influence of the Jesuits, urban elites did not, however, turn over control of the local religious life to church authorities. Traditions of resistance to the authority of bishops were powerful in all episcopal cities. In Speyer, for example, the bishop was only allowed to enter the city with permission of the City Council.[160] In all cities, councils continued to play an important role in appointing clergy, organizing processions and church holidays, constructing churches, and founding monasteries and convents, as they had since at least the fifteenth century.

Of course city governments had less control of religious life in court cities like Munich, than they did in independent cities like Cologne. Still, even in Munich, where the active and notoriously pious Wittelsbach princes intervened continuously in local Catholic life, the local elite was able to put its stamp on religious practice. From the 1620s on, for example, the Wittelsbachs ordered the cloistering of all of Munich's nuns, ending a long-standing tradition whereby some convents had played a major role in the funerals of leading burghers. Elements in the city elite, however, supported the nuns in developing new ways of helping the souls of local people, who were often their kin. By the later decades of the seventeenth century, the Ridler and Pütrich convents became what Ulrike Strasser calls "prayer and purgation factories," providing frequent prayers to save Munich residents from the perils of purgatory.[161]

In the small imperial city of Überlingen, the city council controlled the whole ecclesiastical establishment of the city. Already in the years around 1600 the Council had organized the city's clergy into a collegiate chapter (*Stift*), over which the council had full control. The Überlingen City Council used this control to demand better education and proper behavior from parish priests, while at the same time reserving these fairly well paid positions for the sons of the local elite.[162] The town's elite played a major role in founding new confraternities, organizing processions, and funding additional religious practices. Catholic cities, then, provide important examples of local, lay influence over religious life.

Peasant communes (the *Gemeinden*), the local governments of villages, were also actively engaged in local religious life. Village leaders exerted considerable influence over the appointment and removal of the parish clergy, they often controlled parish finances, and they took a leading role in organizing local devotions. This "communal church" came out of the late medieval tradition so well described in the work of Peter Blickle and his students.[163] The popular notion that the parish should be managed by local institutions was closely linked to the conviction that parish resources, especially the tithes paid by peasants, should be used to provide services to the residents of the parish. The communal church remained an important force in rural Catholicism after the sixteenth century, even in the face of more efficient state structures and reformist ecclesiastical institutions.

It appears that this communal church was strongest in southwest Germany and along the Rhine, in part because of the absence of a strong centralizing state in this part of Germany. However, communal institutions and the practices of local government have been less studied in other Catholic regions and there are indications that the communal church existed in some form in most rural regions. In the politically fragmented region of southwest Germany, communes administered parishes, oversaw the work of the parish priest, and organized devotional life.[164] In most parishes, the churchwardens were appointed by the village officials and submitted their accounts to them. Village officials and parish priests often fought over possession of the keys to offerings boxes, with the most frequent solution being that each kept a key. Tellingly, when Austrian officials attempted in the 1770s and 1780s to ascertain the value of ecclesiastical property holdings and endowments, they sent requests for information to monasteries and other ecclesiastical institutions, but often received reports back from village officials.[165]

Communal influence was often informal. Unlike in parts of Switzerland, few communes in the southwest or in the Rhine valley possessed the formal right to appoint parish priests.[166] By the later seventeenth century, however, communes could and did recommend priests for benefices, recommendations that were taken seriously by episcopal officials, and they could, of course, orchestrate effective campaigns to drive unpopular priests from a village. Communes possessed even more influence over secondary benefices that supported chaplains and other kinds of assistant priests, as these had often been endowed by rural communities.

Werner Freitag, in his study of a group of villages in northern Westphalia, emphasizes another aspect of communalism.[167] In these villages, religious life remained deeply communal, in contrast to an increasingly oligarchical political system. Poorer villagers, more and more cut out of political decision-making, remained active in the church community. At the same time, parish priests, all of them local men, were well integrated into village life. "In this context, pastoral work meant religious services, the provision of sacraments, preaching, but also celebrating together.[168] Priests were treated with special respect and honor, and they in turn were expected to behave with a certain modesty, which meant that they were to respect local norms and traditions and not flaunt their education or status in the parish. Here, communalism included the incorporation of the priest into the local rural community.

Louis Châtellier's study of Alsace emphasizes further characteristics of communalism.[169] Especially in the first half of the eighteenth century, communes were instrumental in organizing the ubiquitous processions and pilgrimages, founding confraternities, building stations of the cross and roadside crucifixes, and redecorating parish churches. Châtellier argues that these efforts had the effect of concentrating religious life in the parish, something that Tridentine reformers wanted, but which only succeeded because it received the support of village communes.

All this communal engagement with the local church provided an important way for the rural population to influence the nature of Baroque Catholicism. One should not forget, however, that rural communes were the power bases for the rural elite, especially the land-owning big farmers, the *Bauer*. Nevertheless, communal institutions, although they were increasingly incorporated into state administrative structures in many places, remained quite receptive to popular demands in religious matters. Popular influence over Baroque religiosity was exerted in the hurly-burly of daily life as well as through the communal institutions.

Baroque Catholicism and everyday life

Kaspar von Greyerz points to the features of religious life that were intimately tied to rural life.[170] There were close connections between the rhythm of the liturgical year and the structure of the agricultural calendar. Miracles were a common part of daily life and were usually linked to aspects of official Catholic practice, especially the Eucharist. Pilgrimage shrines were almost always the sites of miraculous cures, the majority of which benefited the rural population. *Ex voto* images from shrines "document many typical peasant work accidents."[171] Finally, peasants were very attached to the sacramentals – objects, such as candles, amulets, water, that had been blessed by a priest – and they also expected and demanded that priests bless fields, farm animals, wells, houses, and wedding beds.

Hermann Hörger, in his study of religion in a group of Bavarian villages, argues that a kind of traditional Catholicism continued to be the dominant religion in the countryside after 1650. This religion was a communal religion that helped peasants overcome, or at least accept, the insecurities of pre-modern life.[172] In this functional interpretation, traditional Catholicism was rooted in the daily life of agricultural populations and could not survive the development of rural industry and other changes of the eighteenth century. Beginning the later seventeenth century, says Hörger, this religious system was starting to change, challenged by a Tridentine Catholicism that emphasized the salvation of the individual.

Although he highlights a link that should not be forgotten, Hörger overstates the case when he presents traditional Catholicism as essentially a religion aimed at meeting the needs of a pre-modern agricultural society. Baroque Catholicism, as presented here, was something distinct from traditional Christianity; it was a complex set of practices and beliefs, responding frequently to the desires of rural people, but also framed by the theology and priorities of the international Catholic Church. Andreas Holzem seeks to find a middle position that accommodates the reciprocal influence of religion "imposed" from above and religious ideas that develop out of everyday life.

> The "didactic campaign" of Tridentine influenced piety created examples/models, which were then available as a form of expression for religious needs, if one might use this modern idiom in a modified sense. This embeddedness and reciprocal permeation therefore continually left open a variety of religious-social "plausibilities" which had developed out of everyday culture and experience.[173]

Holzem's point fits well for what we know about Baroque Catholicism in Germany. Efforts to forcefully regulate popular religious practice in the decades around 1600 gave way to what Holzem calls "soft disciplining" between 1650 and the middle of the eighteenth century. As we have seen, the development of pilgrimage piety, the increase in the number of weekly services, the growing number of confraternities, and the elaboration of the sacral landscape were all the result of both clerical promotion and popular demands, which frequently reflected the needs of an agricultural society. Some other practices, such as the continued use of sacramentals or the blessings of animals, fields, and buildings, made the clergy uncomfortable and declined drastically in cities, but such practices proved to be too important for the rural population to be worth attacking. In this context, Richard van Dülmen is certainly correct: "[The Catholic Church] skillfully understood how to speak to and integrate the various interests of even the common man."[174]

Regional Variety in Baroque Catholicism

The number of local studies does not really allow for anything more than an impressionistic and somewhat speculative categorization of regional varieties of Baroque Catholicism.[175] Furthermore, even within these regions, it is possible to identify sub-regions, or *Landschaften*, that shared a similar religious culture. Finally, as should be clear by now, conditions within German Catholicism allowed each community – each city, town, village, and hamlet – to maintain its own set of traditions.

A number of factors can be examined to create regional "types." The first of these would be what we might call the structures and traditions of religious practice. Some practices, such as the cults of the Virgin Mary and the Eucharist, were quite similar across Germany. The resonance of some other practices varied considerably. These included the number and types of confraternities, the intensity of pilgrimage and processional piety, the density of the sacral landscape, and the place of the cult of the saints.

The role of the clergy also varied. Regions where the Jesuits were particularly influential developed differently from areas where the Capuchins set the tone, or where the Jesuits were not a presence. Some regions, especially in southern Germany, were densely furnished with monastic institutions, while large stretches of Westphalia were without monasteries or convents. Episcopal power varied in its importance and influence as well. Of great importance was the character of the secular clergy. Were parish priests local men? What were the social origins of the local clergy? How, where, and by whom were they trained? How much of a clerical culture existed and to what extent did parish priests participate in local sociability and local politics?

Political and institutional factors also influenced regional religious styles. There was rather more uniformity in Catholic practice where one found large, organized states. This uniformity was especially obvious in Bavaria and Austria, but also characterized the culture of the larger ecclesiastical territories like Mainz and Würzburg. Secular states also had somewhat different religious priorities than did ecclesiastical principalities. Political fragmentation, as was so pervasive in southwest Germany and the Rhineland, and the presence of Protestant neighbors, seems to have led to a wider variety of practices and stronger local traditions.

The greatest difficulty in developing such an analysis lies in weighing the different factors. If one examines, for example, the density of the sacral landscape and the pervasiveness of pilgrimage piety, then southern Germany (including Austria and Bavaria) and the Rhineland formed a region well furnished with such sacred sites and activities. Franconia and Westphalia, by contrast, had fewer shrines and fewer local pilgrimage sites, though several regional pilgrimages (Walldürn, Vierzehnheiligen) were very important. On the other hand, Bavarians and Austrians, residents of large secular states, faced different pressures than the subjects of smaller princes, imperials knights, abbots, and bishops in the southwest and the Rhineland.

Southwest Germany

This region was characterized by a dense sacral landscape, a vibrant pilgrimage piety, many confraternities, and an active cult of the saints. The Jesuits continued to influence clerical culture, though this influence declined after 1700 in favor of the Capuchins. This was a region of wealthy monasteries and military orders, many with secular power, and they marked the sacral landscape with huge building projects in the early eighteenth century. The most important bishop in this region, the Bishop of Constance, gained some influence after 1650, but episcopal structures were not strong. The clergy was mostly local, recruited from small towns, of burgher and artisan background. Only after 1750 does one find priests of peasant origin.

The political fragmentation of the region contributed to the localization of Catholicism, as did the presence of Protestants, especially in the Duchy of Württemberg. There were some important Habsburg territories, in the Breisgau and around Lake Constance, but the Catholic secular states were otherwise small and weak. Communal institutions in the towns and in the villages were important and active in religious life.

Rhineland and Alsace

This region resembled southwest Germany in its religious traditions. There may have been somewhat fewer shrines and pilgrimages here, perhaps due to a somewhat smaller number of monasteries. Saints' cults were perhaps more deeply imbedded in local religion than anywhere else in Germany. Jesuit influence was quite limited after 1650 and the number of monastic institutions fairly small. Episcopal power varied considerable, from the small and weak Bishoprics of Speyer and Worms, to the important and wealthy sees of Mainz, Trier, and Cologne. This was also the heartland of the aristocratic Imperial Church and few higher churchmen demonstrated much concern with pastoral issues. Parish priests often immigrated to the Rhine Valley from other regions, partly because seminaries and other Catholic educational institutions were underdeveloped in the west.

The rise of French power in Alsace meant that the Catholic Church received considerable state support in that region. Further north, the larger ecclesiastical states (Mainz, Trier, Cologne) seemed to grow more confident of their stability and, as a result, complacent in terms of Church reform. Cologne, the largest Catholic city in the Empire, exerted important influence over Catholic culture in the Rhineland, especially as a publishing center. Protestant influence was important in the middle Rhine valley, but confessional conflict declined in importance after 1650, particularly as the Electoral Palatinate abandoned confessional confrontation and then in the early eighteenth century came to be ruled by Catholic princes.

Franconia

Catholicism in Franconia centered on the two large Prince-Bishoprics of Würzburg and Bamberg. This region had fewer pilgrimage shrines than in the west and south, though several large shrines drew many pilgrims. The cult of the saints was relatively unimportant and in the Baroque period this was a deeply Marian region.

There are indications that the clergy in Franconia was quite homogeneous. The region inherited a strongly Jesuit-dominated educational establishment from the pre-Thirty Years' War period, especially in Würzburg, as well as a tradition of activist bishops. There were also fewer monasteries and convents relative to southern Germany and the biggest city, Nuremberg, was Lutheran. As a result, bishops and the noblemen dominated Franconian Catholicism.

Politically, communal institutions were weaker here, while quite a large number of Catholic Imperial knights governed small territories. Franconia also straddled the confessional frontier that ran through Germany and Catholics here continued to be concerned with threats from powerful Protestant neighbors, like Hessia, Saxony, and Nuremberg.

Westphalia

Institutionally and politically, Westphalia shared many characteristics with Franconia. This was also a region of large ecclesiastical principalities, it was on the confessional frontier, and it was politically and culturally dominated by the local nobility. Surrounded by Protestant regions, Westphalian Catholics may have become more militant than in some other places. Westphalia was rather more isolated from the southern German Catholic centers than Franconia and it did not have the density of seminaries and educational institutions found further south.

Jesuit influence was important in Münster, the largest Catholic center, and the Jesuits continued to educate most priests into the eighteenth century. At the same time, parish priests seem to have been recruited from nearby towns and remained local in outlook, especially in the more isolated regions north of Osnabrück. There were few pilgrimage shrines in Westphalia, though pilgrims used the smaller number of shrines intensely. Finally, the sacral landscape was underdeveloped here, compared to the south. There were few monasteries and convents and village churches remained simple on the exterior, though most were outfitted with Baroque interiors after about 1700.[176]

Bavaria

Bavaria was one of the heartlands of Baroque Catholicism. *Bavaria Sancta* was a land of many shrines, an ever more elaborate sacral landscape, and a large number of well-populated convents and monasteries. Confraternities may have been somewhat less common than in the southwest and in Alsace, but religious life was dense and very vibrant.

The Jesuits remained very active in Bavaria until the suppression of the order in the 1770s, conducting missions and visitations. The Capuchins, however, were also active, along with a number of other orders, for example the Franciscan orders in Munich. The parish clergy was of local origin, trained at Jesuit secondary schools, seminaries, and at the Jesuit run Catholic universities at Ingolstadt and Dillingen. Oversight of the parish clergy was probably stronger in Bavaria than anywhere else, so Bavarian priests came perhaps the closest to being representatives of official Roman Catholic piety in the countryside.

Much of the institutional strength of Bavarian Catholicism came, as we have seen, from the active role the Bavarian state took in religious affairs. Communes were less influential than in some other regions and local officials enforced obedience to ducal edicts. Popular initiative, however, remained important, for example in the development of pilgrimages and in the elaboration of services, so that, even in Bavaria, Baroque religiosity was not a mirror of elite or state desires.

Austria

Austrian Catholicism owed much to the Bavarian model, though it developed in its own directions after 1650. The Habsburgs certainly instrumentalized Catholicism, making it the cultural glue of their multinational empire and stamping elite religiosity with the personal style of the ruling family, the *Pietas Austriaca*. At the popular level, shrines and pilgrimages were very important, though the network of shrines and other sacred sites are less dense than further west.

Monasteries and episcopal institutions were increasingly dominated by the state after the 1620s, making for more uniformity in liturgical traditions and in the training of the clergy. The Austrian nobility, having almost all converted to Catholicism during the Thirty Years' War, dominated the upper levels of the Church. Less is known about the parish clergy, though they were generally local men, at least in the Tyrol and in other parts of Inner Austria, and these regions even exported priests. Finally, the defeat of Austrian Protestantism in the Thirty Years' War increased the confidence of the Catholic elite, while the ongoing wars with the Turks maintained the level of militancy much longer than in other German-speaking Catholic regions.

Taken together, this survey indicates several different clusters of regions. If one examines Catholic Germany in light of the experience of the Protestant Reformation, one can contrast the regions that were seriously threatened by Protestantism – Austria, Franconia, and Westphalia – with those where Protestantism never gained a strong foothold. From the perspective of state power, Bavaria and Austria represent one extreme, with the southwest and the Rhineland constituting the other end of the spectrum. Communal control of the local church was strong in the southwest and West, weaker in Bavaria, Austria, and Franconia.

More speculatively, it appears that Baroque Catholicism flowered most completely and most elaborately in what we might call the "old Christian" regions.[177] Christianity had been planted in the late Roman period west of the Rhine and south of the Danube. When the parish structure was put in place during the Middle Ages, parish churches in these areas were dedicated to many obscure local saints, giving them a link to the landscape that did not exist in the regions, like Franconia and Westphalia, conquered and converted after the Carolingian period. The density of the sacral landscape in southwest Germany, the Rhineland, and Bavaria, certainly owes much to the length of Christian history in these regions. The same can be said about the large numbers of monasteries and convents, particularly of the older orders (Benedictines and Cistercians), many of which were very ancient and well endowed with lands and incorporated parishes.

Conclusion

Baroque Catholicism flourished in Germany for about 100 years, from the end of the Thirty Years' War until the Enlightenment began to draw the Catholic elite away from the religiosity of the Baroque. The convergence of lay and clerical, elite and popular, urban and rural religiosity in this period was both unusual and far from accidental. The leaders of the Church chose to avoid conflict and accommodate popular, especially peasant, demands for a religion that engaged the needs of an agricultural world. Operating at the intersection of institutional priorities and everyday life, parish priests generally adopted a pastoral mode that met the requirements of their parishioners. The people, of all social classes, engaged Catholicism actively, seeking out new devotions, revitalizing traditional practices, and critiquing the work of the clergy. Together, these elements created a dynamic and mostly successful religious system.

One must, however, be careful to avoid romanticizing the Baroque period. German peasants were never happy about the wealth and power of the monasteries, in particular, and the secular power wielded by all manner ecclesiastical institutions was an ongoing source of conflict and discontent. The elite, in turn, were always uncomfortable with what they considered the "superstitious practices" of the population, a skepticism that turned into a full-scale campaign to eradicate such practices in the later eighteenth century. The benefice system, which provided the material basis for pastoral work, was deeply flawed, and undermined both the material comfort of the parish clergy and their relationship with their parishioners. Finally, could it be that by 1750 or so the ongoing elaboration of religious practice and institutions had reached a kind of saturation point that demanded some sort of realignment, even for people in the countryside?

Chapter 6: German Catholicism in the Late Eighteenth Century

As the eighteenth century progressed, educated Catholics, laypeople, and clergymen became increasingly uncomfortable with certain aspects of Catholic practice. Pilgrimages and shrines, processions and confraternities, the proliferation of church services and holidays all came under criticism. After about 1750, this reformist tendency, which was firmly in the tradition of clerical attacks on popular "superstition and excess," was reinforced by a broader and more radical Enlightenment attack on Catholic institutions, particularly the ecclesiastical states and the monasteries. This movement began with widespread attacks on the Jesuits, leading to the dissolution of the Society in 1773. Finally, in the 1770s and 1780s, the Habsburg state, under the Emperor Joseph II, undertook a massive reform of Catholicism in the Habsburg lands, abolishing monasteries and confraternities, outlawing most pilgrimages and processions and dramatically curtailing the number of church holidays. In 1803, the *Reichskirche* itself was destroyed, with the large secular states taking over all the ecclesiastical states that had survived French invasion and other secularizations.

One way to frame the history of German Catholicism in the second half of the eighteenth century, then, is to trace the assault on the institutions and practices that has characterized the Baroque synthesis. The most radical attack was led by Emperor Joseph II and peaked the 1780s. Another related but distinct trend was the effort by the Catholic elite to reform Catholicism, under the banner of enlightened Catholicism. This tendency included the episcopalist movement (Febronianism), which aimed at creating a national Catholic Church dominated by the bishops and freed from Papal and state influence. Like the Josephine reformers, enlightened Catholics deplored the excesses of Baroque practices and moved to reform or eliminate them. Unlike much of the French

Enlightenment, German Catholic *Aufklärer* were not anticlerical, indeed many were clergymen themselves, and they aimed above all at creating a simpler, less elaborate form of Catholicism.

Baroque Catholicism was also undermined by the withdrawal of elements of the urban population from participation in its most characteristic practices, such as pilgrimages, processions, and confraternities. Traditionally referred to by historians as the "secularizing" of the elite, the movement of elements of the Catholic elite toward a more simple, internalized religious practice had more in common with many aspects of Tridentine reform than with the more radical dechristianization found in some other places in Europe.[1] By 1800, the consequence of these developments was a rural and artisan population that remained committed to much of Baroque Catholicism, now increasingly considered "traditional," and an urban elite, strongly represented in state structures and among much of the clergy, that supported "enlightened" or "reformed" Catholicism. If this division undermined Catholic unity, it did not necessarily mean a decline in Catholic identity among most people.

Continuities

One aspect of German Catholicism in the later eighteenth century was the recommitment on the part of both the Church and the state to the effort to create a strong parish-oriented rural religion. This movement was a continuation of the reforms of the Tridentine period and built on the clericalization of Baroque Catholicism. What distinguished late-eighteenth-century developments were two somewhat contradictory trends. On the one hand, influenced by broad intellectual developments of the times, the Catholic clergy increasingly sympathized with the social and economic problems of the people, and increasingly oriented pastoral work toward the common people. On the other hand, this effort also had the marks of a paternalistic program aimed at disciplining the population "for their own good."

Louis Châtellier has pointed to the development of a "religion of the poor" within Catholicism. Initially promoted by missionaries to rural parishes, this perspective attracted support from clergymen who found themselves in direct contact with rural people. Châtellier argues that these clergymen began to understand that poverty might make it difficult for poor people to achieve salvation, as it led to "a hardness of the heart."[2] As a result, and in keeping with Enlightenment ideas, charity and almsgiving took on a new importance in many places, including at monasteries.[3]

Some priests took their parishioners' side against landlords. In 1768, *Pfarrer* Flach, in the upper Swabian village of Mainwangen, incited his parishioners to protest against taxes and rents imposed by their (and his) lords, the Cistercian monks of the abbey of Salem.[4]

More common among that Catholic elite was a broad sympathy for the common people or the poor couched in a paternalistic promotion of a less elaborate and (in their view) "wasteful" religiosity. Ludovico Antonio Muratori, the Italian historian, librarian, and church reformer, was very influential in southern Germany and especially Austria, as well as in Italy. In the 1740s, a group of Muratori supporters at the Benedictine University in Salzburg organized to promote his ideas. Muratori favored a kind of "anti-Baroque Catholicism" and in his *On Well-Ordered Catholic Devotion* advocated a simplified parish-based religion that used the vernacular in services.[5] In this "practical Christianity," the common people should learn their catechism, take the sacraments, and understand the Ten Commandments. "As for the ignorant people, they ought to at least know the Apostle's Creed, and this not in Latin but taught to them in the vernacular, so that the mind understands what the tongue is saying."[6] Muratori also argued that pilgrimages, processions, and many other practices were "excrescences" that should be abolished and that a drastic reduction in the numbers of monks and nuns was necessary.[7]

Johann Michael Sailer, most famous for his work as professor of pastoral theology and ethics at the University of Dillingen in Bavaria, also advocated a rapprochement between Enlightenment ideas and Christianity. His pastoral theology was heavily Christocentric and he favored a simplified parish life, in which well-trained priests would preach the gospel and promote practical good works and charity.[8] His widely read *Complete Prayer-Book for Catholic Christians* (1803) aimed at "guiding ordinary believers in the various stages of their existence" and emphasized one's duties to less fortunate neighbors.[9] Sailer's theology told priests to concern themselves with their less fortunate parishioners – and is thus firmly in the tradition of the *pastor bonus* of the previous century – but his emphasis on *Glückseligkeit* (blessedness or felicity) echoed terms used by non-Catholic writers like Moses Mendelsson and Immanuel Kant.[10] Finally, as Châtellier points out, Sailer's theology was a "message of hope addressed to all men" and thus an aspect of a "religion of the poor."[11]

The pastoral letters (*Hirtenbriefe*) of German bishops in the eighteenth century reflect both a concern with the economic well-being of believers and a paternalistic critique of their religiosity. These letters openly attacked Baroque practices, as a 1767 letter from Augsburg states, "It is purity

(*Reinlichkeit*) that we are advocating. We do not favor splendor (*Glanz*) and dazzling externals. Only those things that are proper and beneficial should be cared for." Priests were admonished to remove images and votive paintings from churches and to refrain from setting out reliquaries for viewing. Instead, they were told to encourage their parishioners to take frequent communion.[12] These letters reflect an attitude within the episcopal bureaucracy that closely resembles that of Tridentine reformers in the decades around 1600. Indeed, influential writers like Muratori frequently cited the decrees of the council and the writing of Carlo Borromeo.[13]

New Developments

The Catholic reform movements of the eighteenth century also reflected the influence of Jansenism, especially in Austria.[14] There were personal ties between leading Jansenists in France and the Austrian Netherlands and members of the German Catholic elite and Jansenist books were widely read.[15] Jansenist ideas did much to reinforce the general elite discomfort with Baroque Catholicism and contributed to the strong emphasis on a more personal and internal religion promoted by Muratori and his followers. This discomfort was not new. Beginning around 1700, officials of the Bishop of Constance, for example, expressed concern that people were too willing to believe in miracles and that there were too many new shrines. In the early 1730s, the episcopal commission investigating a popular new shrine at Steinbach (Upper Swabia) struggled manfully against a flood of reports of miraculous cures before giving official recognition to the shrine.[16] By the later eighteenth century, official discomfort moved beyond skepticism to an outright attack on the central practices of Baroque Catholicism.

Jansenist influence can be seen most importantly in the anti-Jesuit campaign that led to the dissolution of the Society in 1773. This campaign was strongest in Austria. The Empress Maria Theresa's "personal religious attitudes have been described as Jansenist," and she gradually developed a critical, if not hostile, attitude toward the Jesuits. In 1767, she ceased confessing to her long-time Jesuit confessor.[17] Already in 1751, the Jesuits lost control of censorship in the Habsburg monarchy. In the 1750s and 1760s, the Austrian government steadily reduced the influence of the Jesuits in the educational system.

Elsewhere in the German-speaking lands, for example in Bavaria and in the Franconian bishoprics, hostility to the Jesuits grew in the eighteenth century.[18] Critics of the Jesuits aggressively attacked them for their loyalty to the Papacy, their adherence to traditional theology, and their commitment to casuistry in pastoral care. Criticism of the Jesuits' pastoral theology was part of the effort to simplify Catholic practice and led, especially in secular Catholic states, to an attack on the Jesuit monopoly of the training of priests. Many state officials, episcopal leaders, and secular clergy came to see the Jesuits as an obstacle in their project of creating a simpler, more enlightened Catholicism.[19] Still, we should not overestimate the influence of Jansenist elements outside Austria, and the Society of Jesus remained powerful across Catholic Germany until the suppression.

Jansenism was much less important in the Catholic Enlightenment in Germany than was what historians have come to call Episcopalism, or Febronianism. Febronianism was an ecclesiastical and political movement precipitated by the 1763 publication of *de Statu Ecclesiae* (*on the State of the Church*) by Nikolaus von Hontheim, the Auxiliary Bishop of Trier, writing under the pseudonym Justinus Febronius. Hontheim's 600-page Latin work of theology, canon law, and ecclesiastical history vigorously attacked the development of papal monarchy within the Catholic Church, while advocating a strong episcopal system of Church government and a central role for secular rulers in Church affairs.[20]

In *de Statu Ecclesiae*, Hontheim outlined the historical origins of papal authority, tracing it to the successes of the papal court system and the University of Bologna law school in the Middle Ages and to falsified scholarly works such as the ninth-century forged decretals of Isidore Mercator (known as the pseudo-Isidore). Hontheim supported his historical arguments with a theological position advocating the independence of the bishops from the Pope. He did not deny the primacy of the Bishop of Rome, but argued that neither scripture nor tradition grants the Pope legal or political jurisdiction over the bishops. He insisted that many papal prerogatives – such as the right to confirm episcopal elections, grant dispensations, or hear legal appeals from episcopal courts – were usurpations. *De Statu Ecclesiae* even argued that some of the decrees of the Council of Trent illegally increased papal control over local churches. Hontheim was a conciliarist, for he considered Church councils the ultimate source of authority in the Church. Pope Clement XIII formally condemned the work in 1764 and a number of refutations were published, mostly in Italy.

Hontheim's work was well received in Germany, particularly in the Rhenish bishoprics, because it drew on a number of traditions. Hontheim refers regularly to Gallicanism, with the aim of bringing "the liberties of the French Church" to Germany. The popularity of

Febronianism among educated Catholics in Germany, however, has to be traced to several specifically German traditions. The first of these was the sentiment, strong in Germany for centuries, that the Italians who dominated the Papacy did not understand conditions in Germany. This view often coincided with anti-Jesuit feeling after the Thirty Years' War, because many Catholics blamed the Jesuits, papal nuncios, and Rome for the confessional extremism that contributed to the length and destruction of the war. Furthermore, aristocratic prince-bishops and cathedral canons remained committed to the mix of secular and ecclesiastical powers that characterized the Imperial Church (*Reichskirche*), and Febronianism seemed to provide intellectual support for their position at a time when they were under increasing attack for their aristocratic lifestyle and lack of religious training and commitment.[21]

However, Febronianism was not really a defense of the aristocratic *Reichskirche*, even if it tapped into the traditionalist dislike of Roman interference in German affairs. Hontheim's treatise can be considered part of the Catholic Enlightenment in Germany, especially in its non-Austrian, non-Bavarian form. Much of the appeal of his work came from the fact that he gave a strong role within the Church to the very public who read the work: clerics, scholars, and canon lawyers. Febronianism was also strongly episcopalist, giving bishops extensive powers, and German, in advocating national and provincial synods as ultimate sources of authority. This episcopalism peaked with the Emser Congress of 1786, when reform-minded bishops combined an attack on the Papacy with a call for major reforms of popular religion.[22]

Joseph II and Josephinism

Ultimately, Febronianism lost much of its vitality by the 1780s as the Josephine reforms in Austria accelerated. The story of Joseph II's policies and their reception is fairly well known but when placed in the context of the wider history of Catholicism in Germany gains considerable complexity. Joseph's policies in the 1770s and 1780s, and the similar ones pursued by the Bavarian state in this period, certainly owed much to the venerable tradition of *Staatskirchentum*, that is state control of the Church.[23] The attacks on the elaborate Church calendar and on popular religious practices such as pilgrimage reflected the importance of the reforming ideas that came out of ecclesiastical and Jansenist circles. Joseph's goal of redeploying resources from monasteries, confraternities, and other church endowments for educational and pastoral purposes also reflected the emphasis on pastoral work that dated back to the Council of Trent.

Perhaps the most visible Josephine reform was the drastic reduction in the number of feast days. The effort to reduce the large number of church holidays went back, however, to at least the 1750s, before Joseph came to power. In 1754, the Austrian state ordered the abolition of 20 feast days, leaving only 15 in place.[24] Bishops and ecclesiastical officials in other regions were also interested in reducing the number of holidays. In fact, "not a single large state and hardly any middle-sized states neglected to institute a policy of feast day reduction."[25] A 1770 decree of the Bishop of Bamberg expressed one kind of ecclesiastical concern clearly.

> Feast day devotions are generally quickly taken care of and most people spent the rest of the day in sinful idleness, indulging in drinking (*Zechen*), gambling, and all kinds of merrymaking, so that these days, which were created by our ancestors in order to honor God through his saints, have been, by this impious behavior, turned into days of insulting God and reviling his saints.[26]

Bishops were also secular princes and, like the Austrian emperors and the Bavarian electors, were interested in a more disciplined and productive population. Cameralist officials and enlightened intellectuals believed that a reduction in the number of *Feiertage* would bring considerable economic benefit. The influential cameralist writer Johann Heinrich Gottlob von Justi wrote in 1761:

> Good policy should not allow any superfluous feast days and the economy (*Nahrungsstand*) suffers greatly from them   It has been calculated that neglected work on one single feast day in such a big empire (as Germany) causes a loss of a million [*Gülden?*]; and this is in fact not the biggest loss. Everyone wants to live better on a feast day; everyone uses up at least twice as much as on a workday. It is not an exaggeration if one estimates that another two million is wasted on a feast day.[27]

Educated Catholics came to accept the argument that the apparent economic backwardness of Catholic Germany could be traced to the large number of holidays. Peter Hersche has estimated that in Catholic cities people celebrated between 40 and 50 *Feiertage* and in the countryside between 60 and 80. To these numbers must be added all Sundays, as well as the days before many feast days, when peasants and artisans stopped work early to attend services. There can be no question that the number and importance of feast days was one of the salient differences between Catholic and Protestant culture in Germany. In the wave of reductions in the 1780s, between one-third and one-half of all feast days were outlawed.[28] Local feast days and votive holidays, like the *Hagelfeiertage* ("hail holidays") aimed at seeking supernatural protection for crops, were the first ones to be abolished.

Pilgrimages and processions, as well as confraternities, which organized much of the extra-parochial religious practice, came under attack for the same reasons as feast days. First, extended pilgrimages also took peasants away from their work. Secondly, pilgrimages and processions gave opportunity for drinking, illicit sexual activity, and all sorts of undisciplined behavior. Finally, these practices were not conducive to the kind of sober, even somber, style of religious services many priests came to favor in the later eighteenth century. Here again, we see the interplay of secular and religious concerns so characteristic of the Catholic Enlightenment in Germany.[29]

Joseph's policies were, then, neither new nor unique. What was unprecedented was the vigor and consistency with which they were instituted. Furthermore, Joseph and his officials were open and explicit about their goals. The resources of the Church should be redeployed to improve education and pastoral care. Joseph viewed it as his personal duty, and the duty of the state, to provide the people with more and more effective education and pastoral care.[30]

Next to the reduction in the number of feast days, the abolition of monasteries became the policy most identified with the Josephine reforms. As we have seen, the suppression of the Society of Jesus constituted the first major destruction of an important religious order.[31] The Jesuits, however, had little in common with the contemplative and mendicant orders that became the targets of Enlightenment attacks and secularization policies of princes. These monasteries were attacked for absorbing resources and providing few practical benefits in return and for allowing a luxurious lifestyle for their inhabitants. Joseph and his officials focused on suppressing the contemplative orders and moving the monks into either teaching or pastoral work. Despite some resistance from monasteries and, especially, convents, about a third of all monasteries were closed by 1790.

The Austrian government used the property of the suppressed Austrian monasteries to create a Religious Fund. This fund paid out pensions to those former monks and nuns who could not find other gainful employment. What was left over was to be used to create new parishes, dioceses, seminaries, and schools. This ambitious program turned out to be difficult to institute. The cost of pensions for retired regular clergy put a larger burden on the Religious Fund than officials had expected.[32] At the same time, local officials and parish communities submitted a large number of requests for new parishes, and it soon became clear that the resources freed up by the abolition of monasteries, even when supplemented by the endowments from abolished confraternities and other small institutions, did not come close to meeting the demand for new parishes.[33]

The popular reaction to Joseph's policies is quite well known. Peasants and artisans often refused to work during the abolished feast days, maintained their devotions to the saints, and continued to go on processions and pilgrimages. Much of the resistance was passive. In many places, local people continued to celebrate the old saints' days well into the middle of the nineteenth century. In other places, they continued to honor the traditional holidays with prayer meetings and went on processions without the parish priest if he was unwilling to participate.[34]

Peter Hersche has shown that at times the opposition to these reforms could become violent, particularly "where communal autonomy (as in Switzerland and in Vorarlberg) was well developed." Young people tore the mandates abolishing holidays down from church doors and forced sacristans to announce illegal processions and holidays. In the Austrian Vorarlberg in 1789, people broke into closed churches and chapels and openly held processions.[35] Servants and farmhands in the countryside and journeymen in the towns tended to be the leaders of opposition, both because much of the weight of more working days fell on them and as young people, they tended to be the most active in the celebrations held on feast days.[36]

Opponents of the reduction in saints' days and processions accused the reforming Catholic authorities of forcing them to become Lutherans. A song from Bavaria made this point explicitly:

> Saint Benno the patron of our land
> We call to you for help
> Make the request in heaven for Bavaria
> That it not become Lutheran
> The feast days have now been abolished
> Only the calendar has it right
> and one saint after the other
> has been eliminated, and is leaving here.[37]

A priest reported on the reaction in 1770 in the *Hochstift* Bamberg to an ordinance abolishing a large number of saints' days:

> Herr Kailing [the parish priest]   read out on Sunday   the *Feyertags-patent.* You should have heard the first noise, the whole church moved, women and men stood up in full fury, they muttered loudly: one should shoot the priests (*Pfaffen*) in the head for what they are saying from the pulpit. Soon the seven sacraments will be abolished [they said], and in this state of anger they left the church   saying: the Bishop of Bamberg can give us orders, but the Pope is a heretic, yes an arch-heretic, the devil has given him to us, not a good spirit, and we will [have to] become Lutheran [38]

The popular accusation that enlightened Catholic authorities wanted to turn the people into Lutherans was widespread. Bavarian and Franconian peasants used the term frequently. Perhaps because the new regulations were only sporadically enforced in these regions, people felt a certain freedom to express their disdain. Educational reforms, new hymn books (*Kirchengesangsbücher*), liturgical changes, and the redecoration of churches all led to the accusation that the reformers were Lutherans. For example, the 1763 ordinance eliminating some feast days in Canton Luzern was called the "Lutheran Mandate," while a "cleaned-up" church in Salzburg came to be called the "Protestant church."[39] Such strong language demonstrates both the strength of popular Catholic identity and the extent to which they considered the enlightened reforms a threat to core elements of that identity.

Rural communities did not reject all aspects of the Josephine program. The goal of putting more resources into pastoral care, particularly by providing more and better paid secular priests and creating new parishes, was widely popular. Peasants favored, for example, the idea of paying priests a proper salary so that they would not expect fees for benedictions and other "extra" services.[40] Peasant communities in the Habsburg territories in southwest Germany were quick to submit requests for new parishes, outlining in detail the size of the proposed congregation, the distance from existing churches, and the problems caused by absentee or distant parish priests. Here traditions of communal management of the local church, combined with the clericalization of Catholic practice, meant that communities were eager to acquire more effective local pastoral care.[41] There were two sides to this issue as well, however – Josephine reformers moved to close chapels, shrines, and other holy sites, at the same time as they built new parish churches.[42]

Secularization and the End of the Imperial Church

The Catholic Enlightenment had a great impact on the Catholic elite. The clergy, especially in the hierarchy, but also many parish priests, came to question the practices of Baroque Catholicism and the traditional institutions of the Church, particularly the monasteries. Furthermore, in the second half of the eighteenth century, educated laypeople and even artisans withdrew from the "expressive piety" of Baroque Catholicism.[43]

The same people supported the abolition of the monasteries and, ultimately, the secularization of the ecclesiastical estates in the Napoleonic period. Recent research has made it clear that the Imperial Church was not destroyed by Protestant princes, and not even really by Napoleon, but was allowed to disappear by the Catholic elite itself.[44]

The failure of the Catholic elite to defend Catholic institutions reflects, of course, what Derek Beales calls "a fundamental change of attitudes," a tendency among the middle class to move away from the beliefs and practices of Baroque Catholicism, some that occurred throughout eighteenth century Europe.[45] At its most simple, this viewpoint included the view that resources should be used to improve this world, rather than preparing people for the next world, that religious uniformity was unnecessary and toleration preferable, and that all institutions, especially religious institutions, should be examined in the light of reason. In Germany, enlightened Catholic laypeople experienced a decline in churchliness and drifted away from church services. Piety became more internalized and individualized, practiced in a family setting rather than in a communal framework.

As we have seen, the Enlightenment ideas in Catholic Germany began to affect rulers and government officials first. The result was "enlightened absolutism" in which the state, like the Austrian state of Joseph II, undertook to reform society. The close ties between enlightened intellectuals and the state had much to do with the support those intellectuals gave to the ultimate absorption of the Catholic ecclesiastical states by the larger territories. At the same time, Enlightenment ideas in southern Germany, particularly scientific research and historical work, also began as an intellectual revival in the monasteries, preventing any clear anti-clerical perspective from developing.

By the last decades of the eighteenth century, however, new ideas began to spread beyond the courts, the bureaucracy, and the monasteries, although perhaps somewhat slower and later than in Protestant areas.

Reading clubs (*Lesegesellschaften*) were one of the most obvious examples of the growing engagement of the public with new ideas. The club at Mainz was very active, with over 200 members reading a wide range of newspapers and periodicals. Catholic universities, particularly the new university at Bonn and the University of Mainz, became centers of Enlightenment thought. Studies of membership in the Freemasons and the *Illuminati* show that the Catholic Enlightenment was "the achievement of a socially mixed intelligentsia, both lay and clerical, noble and bourgeois."[46]

There is important evidence of a "secularization" of particular groups in society during the last decades of the eighteenth century, or at least their movement away from traditional Catholicism. Rudolf Schlögl has studied the middle classes of the Catholic cities of Aachen, Cologne, and Münster from the 1770s to the 1820s.[47] Schlögl argues that his study of wills and death inventories, combined with an analysis of sermons and devotional literature, indicate a clear mental shift away from Baroque Catholicism. By the end of the eighteenth century, for example, middle class Catholic wills no longer included endowments for masses and in many cases contained absolutely no references to God or the saints. These developments reflected a new theological focus among literate Catholics: "a change from an angry, vengeful God to a distant, but loving, God the father."[48] This "mental shift" also included a tendency toward internalizing religion, understood as a person moral system, more detached from daily life than had traditionally been the case. Schlögl pushes his analysis even a step further, arguing that the Enlightenment "should be understood as a movement of adaptation to massively changed lay piety in the cities."[49] These changes included a male withdrawal from the Church and a resulting feminization of Catholic practice. Elements of the Catholic bourgeoisie rejecting Baroque Catholicism in favor of a more personal religion, one that "formed a personality made up of a conglomerate of various roles, among which the believing, Catholic Christian was only one of many."[50]

Michael Pammer, in his study of Catholic practice in Upper Austria, also argues that people from many social groups moved away from Baroque Catholicism in the last decades of the eighteenth century.[51] This was particularly true for the parish clergy, which was strongly influenced by Jansenism. Pammer identifies new forms of piety as "Reformed Catholicism." Adherents of this "religious type" were

> friends of a modest liturgy and did not really like pilgrimages, processions, and non-sacramental church feasts because of their uselessness for

the economy or for moral education; they appreciated religious orders only insofar as they justified themselves by caring for the sick or with pedagogical activities; they considered masses for the soul as useful only in a limited way and they considered confraternities expendable[52]

Pammer's research indicates that this kind of Catholicism coexisted with traditional Baroque Catholicism in the period 1750–1780 and then came to dominate Catholic religiosity in Upper Austria after 1780. This was not just an elite movement, despite its intellectual debt to Jansenism, and Reformed Catholicism was important within society before it became the official religion of the Josephine state. The decline of Baroque Catholicism meant that a "plurality of opinions" about religion existed in the later eighteenth century and that individuals had considerable freedom to choose the kind of Catholicism they preferred.[53]

The work of Pammer and Schlögl suggests that, at the very least, the literate urban population embraced changes in religious practices in the later eighteenth century, changes that might be called secularizing tendencies. The extent of these tendencies is impossible to measure – perhaps strongest in Austria, weaker in the Southwest and West. One consequence was surely skepticism about many of the central practices of Baroque Catholicism – processions, pilgrimages, confraternities – and a rejection of some of the key institutions of the Church, particularly monasteries and, to a lesser extent, the ecclesiastical states. This trend reinforced the critique of Catholic Enlightenment and contributed to the Josephine reforms and together these movements left the Baroque synthesis in shambles.

Secularizing trends within Catholic society thus pre-dated the secularization of the monasteries (which began in Austria in the 1780s) and the final destruction of the Imperial Church in 1803.[54] "Secularizing"and "secularization" are, however, somewhat misnomers. Just as the Enlightenment in Catholic Germany was not anti-clerical in the same way as it was in France, there is little evidence of dechristianization in Catholic Germany. Here we return to the notion that many Catholics in the later eighteenth century, among the clergy and the laity, developed a critique of Baroque Catholicism that undermined the institutions and practices that underpinned it. They did not reject Catholicism, but rather sought a new religious style and a new set of pious practices.

Church historians have often presented the secularization of the Imperial Church in the Napoleonic era as the destruction of a vibrant Catholic world by an (unholy) alliance of French secularists and

Protestant princes. Indeed, the Catholic hierarchy actively promoted this view in the nineteenth century in order to strengthen Catholic identity. Matthias Erzberger's widely read *Die Säkularisation in Württemberg* (1902), for example, referred to the "expropriation" and the "robbery of the Catholic Church," while blaming the secularizers for any Catholic economic or educational backwardness.[55] This perspective was useful for the Ultramontane leadership in the nineteenth century, but the secularization of 1803–1806 was really the culmination of a process that began in the middle of the previous century. By 1800, much of the Catholic elite agreed that ecclesiastical states were not an appropriate part of the modern world.[56]

Conclusion

Baroque Catholicism came under attack during the second half of the eighteenth century from Catholics themselves. Most of the critics considered themselves "enlightened" in some sense. As we have seen, however, enlightened Catholicism was a diverse movement. One important strand owed much to the tradition of church reform that went back to the Council of Trent and before, and which aimed at cleaning up popular superstitions and simplifying religious practice. The Jansenist movement often dovetailed with the reformist tendency, particularly in promoting a more personal and individual religiosity. The diversity of these attacks did not necessarily make them more successful, as the experience of the Josephine reforms makes clear.

Josephinism drew on all these "enlightened tendencies," but emphasized the role of the state in reforming Catholicism. This of course led to direct conflicts with Church institutions, even when the Papacy and many bishops were willing to accept Joseph's program. The strong popular resistance to this program led Joseph's successors to back away from many reforms, although the reduction in the number of feast days and the abolition of monasteries were never completely reversed.

Even when one looks at Josephinism – certainly the most radical of the anti-Baroque programs of the eighteenth century – one finds elements that the rural population could support. The plan to improve pastoral care by creating more parishes and hiring more priests was widely popular. German Catholic peasants considered an active parish clergy that responded to the demands and needs of their parishioners an integral part of the religiosity – Baroque Catholicism – that was part of their everyday world. Those groups in society that moved decisively away from

Baroque Catholicism in the late eighteenth century, particularly the urban middle class studied by Schlögl, also wanted an active secular clergy that would teach religion and morals to the common people.

A careful analysis of the decline of Baroque Catholicism has to begin with a nuanced understanding of what Baroque Catholicism really was like. Yes, it was a religion of many saints' days, pilgrimages, processions, the widespread use of sacramentals, and, as Erik Midelfort has reminded us, a belief in demons and exorcism. It was also a communal and clericalized religion that depended on the pastoral care of a clergy that accepted, in general, the notion of the *pastor bonus*, the good shepherd. This later aspect of German Catholicism was compatible with the simpler, reformed religion advocated by the enlightened elite. It should surprise no one that studies of nineteenth century German Catholicism show that elements of both Baroque and enlightened religiosity were important in the new Ultramontane synthesis that developed in the first half of the nineteenth century.

Conclusion

Baroque Catholicism was one phase in the ebb and flow of the history of Christianity in Central Europe. The fifteenth century was a time of religious enthusiasm characterized by a popular passion for pilgrimages, relics, the cult of the saints and the Eucharist, as well as a social and institutional crisis of the Church. The sixteenth century was the century of the Reformation and the Council of Trent, a period of retrenchment within German Catholicism, and a time when the elite pushed for a more somber religious style. As we have seen, Baroque Catholicism harkened back to many elements of late medieval religiosity, but should also be considered as a synthesis of elements from the previous two periods. Enlightened Catholicism of the period 1750–1840 was a critique of that synthesis, with an emphasis on the internalization and privatization of religious practice, an emphasis that owed much to Tridentine tradition. From the 1830s until the First World War, an Ultramontane hierarchy and clergy dominated German Catholicism and supported a renewal of pilgrimage piety and other elements of the "Baroque" religiosity so reviled by enlightened reformers and Protestants.

It is overly simplistic, but nevertheless useful, to see this grand chronology in terms of a series of dichotomies. These dualities include the contrast between elite and popular religiosity, the push for "reform" and the appeal to tradition, the emphasis on individual/private/internal religion and communal/external religiosity, and the focus on (self-) discipline against the preference for dramatic, even uncontrolled, appeals to the sacred. Thus the pendulum swung back and forth between periods when the elite pushed for a more disciplined, private, internal, and individual religion – the sixteenth century and the Enlightenment, and the periods when popular preference for a more communal and dramatic religious practice dominated, as was the case in the fifteenth century, the period from 1650 to 1750, and much of the nineteenth century.

This study has emphasized the religious practice of people in their daily lives. This perspective perhaps courts the danger of underplaying the importance of the Catholic Church as a powerful institution or of downplaying the role of religion in supporting the development of the modern state and modern social forms. Certainly one of the important achievements of the confessionalization thesis has been to give Catholicism a role in the process of modernization. Perhaps now it is possible, even in the land of Luther, to move beyond the age-old debate about the "progressive" character of Protestantism and the "reactionary" character of Catholicism, in order to examine what religion meant to the people who practiced it, taught it, preached it, and believed it.

Historians of modern Europe have rediscovered the role of religion in the founding of the modern world, whether in the origins and progress of the French Revolution, in the motivations and ideology of the founders of the United States, or in the culture of the European and American middle classes. German historians have shared this interest, noting the important role of Catholicism (in particular) in the development of nineteenth-century society and politics. The creation of strong Catholic milieus in the early 1800s highlights the continued confessional fragmentation of German society and culture, while the importance of Catholic political organization in the creation of parliamentary democracy in Bismarck's empire shows the adaptability of Catholicism in the modern world.[1]

Of course Reformation scholars have always insisted on the centrality of religion in the development of the modern West. However, as historians have moved to consideration of the period after 1550, the rise of the state has taken central stage in the historical narrative and religion has often been reduced to a tool of state-builders.[2] This book seeks to remind us that religion – as an important part of everyday life – remained central throughout the early modern period, not just in the sixteenth century. Understanding the nature of Catholic identity and culture provides depth and nuance to our understanding of both the consequences of the Reformation/Counter-Reformation and the origins of modern society.

The heart of this book remains the description and interpretation of Baroque Catholicism in the German-speaking lands. This is in one sense a historiographical project, an outline of what historians, theologians, anthropologists, and folklorists have said and thought about these issues.

This is also a presentation of how the Catholic Church and the people who held positions within it interacted with the society around them. Most of all, it is an interpretation of what Catholicism meant to the peasants, craftsmen, shopkeepers, merchants, priests, monks, and nuns who practiced it and lived it.

Notes

Introduction

1. See for example the best recent history of Early Modern Germany: Peter Wilson, *From Reich to Revolution: German History, 1558–1806* (London, 2004).
2. This has much to do with the importance of Reformation Studies in the United States.
3. R. Po-chia Hsia, *The World of Catholic Renewal. 1540–1770* (Cambridge, 1998) and Robert Bireley, *The Refashioning of Catholicism, 1450–1700. A Reassessment of the Counter-Reformation* (Basingstoke, 1999), both written by historians of Germany, are exceptions to this tendency.
4. The focus on German-speaking regions means that Bohemia and the Spanish/Austrian Netherlands are excluded. Excursions will be made to Catholic Switzerland and Alsace, regions whose ties to the Empire were tenuous after 1648.
5. The concept of the "invisible boundary" comes from Etienne François, *Die unsichtbare Grenze. Protestanten und Katholiken in Augsburg, 1648–1806* (Sigmaringen, 1991).
6. Wolfgang Reinhard and Heinz Schilling, eds. *Die katholische Konfessionalisierung* (Heidelberg, 1995). For an overview, with bibliography, see Joel F. Harrington and Helmut Walser Smith, "Confessionalization, Community, and State Building in Germany, 1555–1870" *The Journal of Modern History* 69 (1997): 77–101; Marc R. Forster, "With and Without Confessionalization: Varieties of Early Modern German Catholicism" *Journal of Early Modern History* 1 (1998): 315–343.

Chapter 1: Catholic Germany before Trent

1. Gerald Strauss, *Manifestations of Discontent* (Bloomington, 1971).
2. Felipe Fernández-Armesto and Derek Wilson, *Reformations: A Radical Interpretation of Christianity and the World, 1500–2000* (New York, 1996).
3. Lionel Rothkrug, "German Holiness and Western Sanctity in Medieval and Modern History" *Historical Reflections/Réflexions Historiques* 15 (1988): 161–249; Lionel Rothkrug, "Holy Shrines, Religious Dissonance, and Satan in the Origins of the German Reformation" *Historical Reflections/Réflexions Historiques* 14 (1987): 143–286; Lionel Rothkrug, "Popular Religion and Holy Shrines. Their Influence on the Origins of the German Reformation and their Role in German Cultural Development" in James Obelkevich, ed. *Religion and the People, 800–1700* (Chapel Hill, 1979).
4. Good overviews of Christianity around 1500, with bibliography, can be found in Robert Scribner, *The German Reformation* (Atlantic Highlands, 1996), chap. 2 and Euan Cameron, *The European Reformation* (Oxford, 1991), chaps 1–6.
5. Eike Wolgast, *Hochstift und Reformation. Studien zur Geschichte der Reichskirche zwischen 1517 und 1648* (Beiträge zur Geschichte der Reichskirche in der Neuzeit; Bd. 10), (Stuttgart, 1995); Marc R. Forster, "The Elite and Popular Foundations of German Catholicism in the Age of Confessionalism: The Reichskirche" *Central European History* 26 (1994): 311–325.
6. The latter were also known as the *Johanniter* or the Knights of Malta. Forster, "With and Without Confessionalization."
7. Ecclesiastical jurisdiction included the right of church courts to try cases involving marriage, some morals regulations such as blasphemy, and any cases involving the clergy and church property.
8. Walter Ziegler, "Altbayern, 1517–1648" in Walter Brandmüller, ed. *Handbuch der bayerischen Kirchengeschichte*, Vol. II (St Ottilien, 1993), p. 5.
9. Bernd Moeller, *Imperial Cities in the Reformation. Three Essays* (Original 1962, Durham, 1982).
10. Gerald Strauss, *Nuremberg in the 16th Century* (New York, 1966), chap. 4.
11. Miriam Chrisman, *Strasbourg and the Reform. A Study in the Process of Change* (New Haven, 1967), chap. 3.
12. Peter Blickle, *Communal Reformation. The Quest for Salvation in Sixteenth-Century Germany* (New Jersey, 1992); Rosi Fuhrmann, "Die

Kirche im Dorf. Kommunale Initiativen zur Organisation von Seelsorge vor der Reformation" in Peter Blickle, ed. *Zugänge zur bäuerlichen Reformation* (Zürich, 1987), pp. 147–186. Rosi Fuhrmann, *Kirche und Dorf: Religiöse Bedürfnisse und kirchliche Stiftung auf dem Lande vor der Reformation* (Stuttgart, 1995); Robert W. Scribner, "Communalism: Universal Category or Ideological Construct? A Debate in the Historiography of Early Modern Germany and Switzerland" *Historical Journal* 37, no. 1 (1994): 199–207.

13. Blickle, *Communal Reformation*, p. 25.

14. Fuhrmann, *Kirche und Dorf.*

15. Fuhrmann, *Kirche und Dorf,* p. 12.

16. Pilgrimages: Philip Soergel, *Wondrous in His Saints. Counter-Reformation Propaganda in Bavaria* (Berkeley, 1993); Lionel Rothkrug, see note 3; Hans Dünninger, *Maria siegt in Franken. Die Wallfahrt nach Dettelbach als Bekenntnis* (Würzburg, 1979); Wolfgang Brückner, *Die Verehrung des Heiligen Blutes in Walldürn* (Aschaffenburg, 1958). Confraternities: Ludwig Remling, *Bruderschaften in Franken. Kirchen- und Sozialgeschichliche Untersuchung zum spätmittelalterlichen und frühneuzeitlichen Bruderschaftswesen* (Würzburg, 1986). Processions: Charles Zika, "Hosts, Processions and Pilgrimages: Controlling the Sacred in Fifteenth-Century Germany" *Past and Present* 118 (1988): 25–64.

17. Werner Freitag, *Pfarrer, Kirche, und ländliche Gemeinschaft. Das Dekanat Vechta 1400–1803* (Bielefeld, 1983).

18. Michael Mullett, *The Catholic Reformation* (London, 1999), chap. 1; Bireley, *The Refashioning of Catholicism*, pp. 21–23; Hajo Holborn, *A History of Modern Germany. The Reformation* (New York, 1959), pp. 110–116; Cameron, *The European Reformation*, chap. 3; Walter Ziegler, "Altgläubige Territorien im Konfessionalisierungsprozess" in Anton Schindling and Walter Ziegler, eds. *Die Territorien des Reichs im Zeitalter der Reformation und Konfessionalisierung. Land und Konfession* (Münster, 1989–1999), Vol. 7 (hereafter   *Territorien*).

19. Gérald Chaix, *Réforme et contre-réforme catholiques. Recherches sur la Chartreuse de Cologne au XVIe siècle* (Salzburg, 1981).

20. Mullett, *The Catholic Reformation*, p. 2.

21. *Versorgungsinstitut,* crudely translated as "a provisioning institution," captures the idea that many noble families considered ecclesiastical institutions appropriate and comfortable places to put unmarried sons and daughters and that the resources of these institutions should be reserved for the offspring of noble families.

22. Wolgast, *Hochstift und Reformation*, pp. 19–27.
23. Marc R. Forster, *The Counter-Reformation in the Villages. Religion and Reform in the Bishopric of Speyer, 1560–1720* (Ithaca and London, 1992), pp. 32–36.
24. Hauptstaatsarchiv Stuttgart B466a/356; Marc R. Forster, *Catholic Revival in the Age of the Baroque. Religious Identity in Southwest Germany, 1550–1750* (Cambridge, 2001), chap. 1; Engelbert Buxbaum, *Petrus Canisius und die kirchliche Erneuerung des Herzogtum Bayern, 1549–1556* (Rome, 1973), p. 47.
25. Francis Rapp, *Réformes et Réformation à Strasbourg. Eglise et société dans le Diocèse de Strasbourg (1450–1525)* (Paris, 1974), Livre III, chap. 2.
26. Freitag, *Pfarrer, Kirche, und ländliche Gemeinschaft*, esp. pp. 86–104.
27. Rapp, *Réformes et Reformation à Strasbourg*, Livre III, chap. 2.
28. Rapp, *Réformes et Reformation à Strasbourg*, Livre III, chap. 2. See also Lawrence Duggan, "The Unresponsiveness of the Late Medieval Church: A Reconsideration" *Sixteenth Century Journal* 9 (1978): 3–26.
29. Duggan, "The Unresponsiveness of the Late Medieval Church" *Sixteenth Century Journal* 9 (1978): 19–21. See also Simone Laqua, "Concubinage and the Church in Early Modern Münster" *Past and Present* 1, Supplement 1 (2006): 72–100; Forster, *Catholic Revival*, p. 31; Freitag, *Pfarrer, Kirche und ländliche Gemeinschaft*, chap. 2; Forster, *Counter-Reformation in the Villages*, esp. chaps 2 and 3; Alexander Jendorff, *Reformatio Catholica. Gesellschaftliche Handlungsspielräume kirchlichen Wandels im Erzstift Mainz: 1514–1630* (Münster, 2000), pp. 304–306. See below, Chapter 2, for a further discussion of concubinage.
30. Forster, *The Counter-Reformation in the Villages*; Freitag, *Pfarrer, Kirche, und ländliche Gemeinschaft*, esp. p. 128.
31. Cameron, *The European Reformation*, p. 36.
32. Robert James Bast, *Honor your Fathers. Catechisms and the Emergence of a Patriarchal Ideology in Germany, 1400–1600* (Leiden, 1997), chap. 3, esp. pp. 118–119.
33. Bast, *Honor your Fathers*, esp. chap. 3.
34. Cameron, *The European Reformation*, p. 46.
35. Robert Scribner, "Ritual and Popular Religion in Catholic Germany at the Time of the Reformation" in *Popular Culture and Popular Movements in the Reformation* (London, 1987).
36. Bernd Moeller, "Piety in Germany Around 1500" in Steven Ozment, ed. *The Reformation in Medieval Perspective* (Chicago, 1971), pp. 50–75. Also published as Bernd Moeller, "Religious Life in Germany on the

Eve of the Reformation" in Gerald Strauss, ed. *Pre-Reformation Germany* (London, 1972), pp. 13–42.

37. Susan Karant-Nunn, *The Reformation of Ritual. An Interpretation of Early Modern Germany* (New York and London, 1997).

38. Philip Soergel, *Wondrous in His Saints. Counter-Reformation Propaganda in Bavaria* (Berkeley, 1993), p. 27.

39. Cameron, *The European Reformation*, p. 17.

40. Berndt Hamm, *Reformation of Faith in the Context of Late Medieval Theology and Piety. Essays by Berndt Hamm* (Leiden, 2003), chap. 2.

41. Berndt Hamm, "Normative Centering in the Fifteenth and Sixteenth Centuries: Observations of Religiosity, Theology, and Iconography" *Journal of Early Modern History* 3 (1999): 307–354, quote p. 327. See also Hamm, *The Reformation of Faith* (Leiden, 2004), esp. chap 3.

42. Robert Scribner, *The German Reformation* (Atlantic Highlands, 1996), chap. 2.

43. Thomas A. Brady Jr., "Settlements: The Holy Roman Empire" in Brady et al., eds. *Handbook of European History, 1450–1600. Late Middle Ages, Renaissance, and Reformation* (Leiden and New York, 1994–1995), pp. 349–352.

44. Scribner, *The German Reformation*, p. 28.

45. Amy Leonard estimates that about half of all convents survived the Reformation, as opposed to about 20% of male monasteries. Amy Leonard, *Nails in the Wall. Catholic Nuns in Reformation Germany* (Chicago, 2005), pp. 4–5.

46. Scribner, *The German Reformation*, p. 28; Susan Karant-Nunn, *Luther's Pastors: The Reformation in the Ernestine Countryside* (Philadelphia, 1979).

47. Blickle, *Communal Reformation*; Peter Blickle, The *Revolution of 1525. The German Peasants' War from a New Perspective* (Baltimore, 1981); Franziska Conrad, *Reformation in der bäuerlichen Gesellschaft: Zur Rezeption reformatorischer Theologie im Elsass* (Stuttgart, 1984).

48. Steven Ozment, *The Age of Reform. An Intellectual and Religious History of Late Medieval and Reformation Europe* (New Haven, 1980), pp. 280–289.

49. Scribner, *The German Reformation*, p. 34.

50. Brady, "Settlements: The Holy Roman Empire" in *Handbook of European History*, pp. 349–352.

51. Holborn, *A History of Modern Germany. The Reformation*, p. 233.

52. Tracy, *Europe's Reformations, 1450–1650. Doctrine, Politics, and Community* (Lanham, MD, 2006), p. 92; Cameron, *The European Reformation*, pp. 347–348.

53. Walter Ziegler, "Bayern" in *Territorien*, Vol. 1, p. 74.
54. Ziegler, "Bayern" in *Territorien*, Vol. 1, p. 74. See also Ziegler, "Altbayern 1517–1648" in Brandmüller, ed. *Handbuch der bayerischen Kirchengeschichte*, pp. 17–18.
55. Ziegler, "Bayern" in *Territorien*, Vol. 1, p. 75.
56. Ziegler, "Bayern" in *Territorien*, Vol. 1, pp. 59–60. See also Ziegler, "Altbayern" in Brandmüller, ed. *Handbuch der bayerischen Kirchengeschichte*, pp. 18–21.
57. Ernst W. Zeeden, "Salzburg" in *Territorien*, Vol. 1, p. 82.
58. Ziegler, "Bayern" in *Territorien*, Vol. 1, pp. 59–60. See also Ziegler, "Altbayern" in Brandmüller, ed. *Handbuch der bayerischen Kirchengeschichte*, pp. 18–21.
59. Soergel, *Wondrous in his Saints*, chap. 1: Rothkrug, see note 3.
60. Franz Bosbach, "Köln" in *Territorien*, Vol. 3, pp. 64–68; Brigitte Garbe, "Reformmaßnahmen und Formen der katholischen Erneuerung in der Erzdiözese Köln (1555–1648)" *Jahrbuch des kölnischen Geschichtsverein* 47 (1976): esp. pp. 137–142.
61. Franz Bosbach, "Köln" in *Territorien*, Vol. 3, p. 67. Chaix, *Réforme et Contre-Réforme Catholiques*, pp. 121–122.
62. Robert Scribner, "Why Was There No Reformation in Cologne?" *Bulletin of the Institute of Historical Research* 49 (1976).
63. Chaix, *Réforme et Contre-Réforme Catholiques*, pp. 105–122.
64. Compare Nuremberg, with three parishes and Strasbourg with nine.
65. Chaix, *Réforme et Contre-Réforme Catholiques*.
66. Scribner, "Why Was There No Reformation in Cologne?".
67. Bernhard Sicken, "Franken 1517–1648" in Brandmüller, ed. *Handbuch der bayerischen Kirchengeschichte*; Walter Ziegler, "Würzburg" in *Territorien*, Vol. 4, pp. 106–109.
68. Bernhard Sicken, "Franken 1517–1648" in *Handbuch der bayerischen Kirchengeschichte*; Günter Christ, "Bamberg" in *Territorien*, Vol. 4, pp. 149–154.
69. Zeissner, quoted in Christ, "Bamberg" in *Territorien*, Vol. 4, p. 153.
70. Günter Dippold, *Konfessionalisierung am Obermain. Reformation und Gegenreformation in den Pfarrsprengeln von Baunach bis Markgraitz* (Staffelstein, 1996), p. 119.
71. Rudolfine Freiin von Oer, "Münster" in *Territorien*, Vol. 3; Johannes Meier, "Paderborn" in *Territorien*, Vol. 3; Thomas Rohm, "Osnabrück" in *Territorien*, Vol. 3; Alois Schröer, *Die Kirche in Westfalen im Zeichen der Erneuerung* (Münster, 1986). See also Freitag, *Pfarrer, Kirche und ländliche Gemeinschaft*.

72. As above. See also R. Po-chia Hsia, *Society and Religion in Münster, 1535–1618* (New Haven, 1984).
73. Johannes Meier, "Paderborn" in *Territorien*, Vol. 3, p. 153.
74. Schröer, *Die Kirche in Westfalen*, p. 134.
75. Cameron, *The European Reformation*, pp. 344–345; Mullett, *The Catholic Reformation*, pp. 33–34, 56–57.
76. Tracy, *Europe's Reformations*, pp. 89–92; Mullett, *The Catholic Reformation*, pp. 36–37.
77. Ozment, *The Age of Reform*, p. 406.
78. Ziegler, "Altbayern 1517–1648" in Brandmüller, ed. *Handbuch der bayerischen Kirchengeschichte*, pp. 33–38.
79. R.J.W. Evans, *The Making of the Habsburg Monarchy, 1550–1700* (Oxford, 1979), chap. 1.
80. Forster, *The Counter-Reformation in the Villages*, pp. 42–49.
81. Forster, *The Counter-Reformation in the Villages*; Bernhard Vogler, *La vie religieuse en Pays-Rhénan dans la seconde moitié du XVIe siècle (1556–1619)* (Lille, 1974); Karant-Nunn, *Luther's Pastors*.
82. John Bossy, *Peace in the Post-reformation* (Cambridge, 1998), esp. chap. 3.
83. See discussion of concubinage in Forster, *The Counter-Reformation in the Villages* and in Freitag, *Pfarrer, Kirche und ländliche Gemeinschaft*, p. 128 and whole chap. 2.
84. Erwin Iserloh, "Johannes Eck (1486–1583)" in Iserloh, ed. *Katholische Theologen der Reformationszeit*, Vol. 1 (Münster, 1984), pp. 65–71; Erwin Iserloh, *Johannes Eck (1486–1583). Scholastiker, Humanist, Kontroverstheologe* (Münster, 1981).
85. Eck's pastoral writings emphasized lay obedience of the clergy: Bast, *Honor your Fathers*, pp. 142–143.
86. Herbert Immenkötter, "Johan Fabri (1478–1541)" in Iserloh, ed. *Katholische Theologen*, Vol. 1, pp. 90–97.
87. Quoted in Immenkötter, "Johan Fabri" in Iserloh, ed. *Katholische Theologen*, Vol. 1, p. 90.
88. Immenkötter, "Johan Fabri" in Iserloh, ed. *Katholische Theologen*, Vol. 1, p. 93; Robert Scribner, *For the Sake of Simple Folk* (Cambridge, 1981), p. 239.
89. Scribner, *For the Sake of Simple Folk*, pp. 232–233. Remigius Bäumer, "Johannes Cochleus (1479–1552)" in Iserloh, ed. *Katholische Theologen*, Vol. 1, pp. 73–80.
90. Robert Scribner, *For the Sake of Simple Folk*, pp. 235–239; Erwin Iserloh, "Thomas Murner (1475–1537)" in Iserloh, ed. *Katholische*

Theologen, Vol. 3, pp. 19–32; Paul Merker, ed. *Thomas Murner. Von dem großen Lutherischen Narren* (Straßburg, Karl J. Trübner, 1918).

91. Remigius Bäumer, "Johannes Hoffmeister OESA (1509/10–1547)" in Iserloh, ed. *Katholische Theologen*, Vol. 4, pp. 43–57.
92. Johannes Meier, "Die katholische Erneuerung des Würzburger Landkapitels Karlstadt im Speigel der Landkapitelsversammlungen und Pfarreivisitationen, 1549 bis 1624" *Würzburger Diözesansgeschichtsblätter* 33 (1971): 91.
93. Paraphrased in Bäumer, "Johannes Hoffmeister OESA (1509/10–1547)" in Iserloh, ed. *Katholische Theologen,*Vol. 4, p. 53.
94. The Carthusians at Cologne experience the same shift in the 1540s and 1550s. See Chaix, *Réforme et contre-réforme catholiques*.
95. Schröer, *Die Kirche in Westfalen*, pp. 31–32.
96. Buxbaum, *Petrus Canisius*, p. 55.
97. Soergel, *Wondrous in His Saints*.
98. John W. O'Malley, *Trent and All That. Renaming Catholicism in the Early Modern Era* (Cambridge, MA, and London, 2000), esp. p. 59.

Chapter 2: The Counter-Reformation Episode: 1570s–1620s

1. On the use of these concepts, see O'Malley, *Trent and All That*.
2. Wolgast, *Hochstift und Reformation*, p. 308.
3. Martin Heckel, *Deutschland im konfessionellen Zeitalter* (Göttingen, 1983); Brady, "Settlements: The Holy Roman Empire" in *Handbook of European History, 1400–1600*, pp. 353–355.
4. H.R. Schmidt, *Konfessionalisierung im 16. Jahrhundert* (Munich, 1992), p. 41.
5. Ziegler, "Würzburg" in *Territorien*, Vol. 4; Sicken, "Franken 1517–1648" in Brandmüller, ed. *Handbuch der bayerischen Kirchengeschichte*, pp. 183–200; Meier, "Die katholische Erneuerung des Würzburger Landkapitels Karlstadt" *Würzburger Diözesangeschichtsblätter* 33 (1971): 51–125.
6. Johannes Merz, "Fulda" in *Territorien*, Vol. 4, pp. 139–141. See below for more on Fulda.
7. Ziegler, "Würzburg" in *Territorien*, Vol. 4, p. 119. *Die Gesamtlösung der Religionsfrage im Hochstift.*
8. Ziegler, "Würzburg" in *Territorien*, Vol. 4, pp. 119–120; Sicken, "Franken 1517–1648" in Brandmüller, ed. *Handbuch der bayerischen Kirchengeschichte*, p. 194.

9. Wolfgang Brückner, *Die Verehrung des Heiligen Blutes in Walldürn* (Aschaffenburg, 1958).
10. Sicken, "Franken 1517–1648" in Brandmüller, ed. *Handbuch der bayerischen Kirchengeschichte*, p. 194.
11. On Speyer: Forster, *The Counter-Reformation in the Villages.*
12. GLAK (Generallandesarchiv Karlsruhe) 229/57524, 1588, December 2, p. 2.
13. GLAK 229/79260.
14. GLAK 229/57524, 1589, March 28.
15. GLAK 229/57523, 1589, May 25, GLAK 229/57524, 1589, "Bericht der Bauern."
16. GLAK 229/57524, 1588, December 2, pp. 5–7.
17. ARSJ (Archivum Romanum Societas Jesu), Rh. Inf. 48, p. 104v.
18. GLAK 94/392.
19. GLAK 229/79260.
20. Franz Xavier Remling, *Geschichte der Bischöfe zu Speyer* (Mainz, 1854), pp. 452–454.
21. Friedhelm Jürgensmeier, "Kurmainz" in *Territorien*, Vol. 4, pp. 83–87. See also Andreas Ludwig Veit, *Kirche und Kirchenreform in der Erzdiözese Mainz im Zeitalter der Glaubensspaltung und der beginnenden tridentinischen Reformation* (Freiburg, 1920); Jendorff, *Reformatio Catholica.*
22. Jürgensmeier, "Kurmainz" in *Territorien*, Vol. 4, p. 84.
23. Jürgensmeier, "Kurmainz" in *Territorien*, Vol. 4, p. 84.
24. Evans, *The Making of the Habsburg Monarchy*, chap. 1.
25. Evans, *The Making of the Habsburg Monarchy*, p. 20.
26. *Vorderösterreich*, Outer Austria or Further Austria was a scattered complex of territories in present-day southwest Germany and Alsace. See Forster, *Catholic Revival* and Dieter Stievermann, "Österreichische Vorlände" in *Territorien*, Vol. 5, pp. 256–277.
27. Heinz Noflatscher, "Tirol, Brixen, Trient" in *Territorien*, Vol. 1, pp. 86–101; Jürgen Bücking, *Frühabsolutismus und Kirchenreform in Tirol (1565–1665). Ein Beitrag zum Ringen zwischen "Staat" und "Kirche" in der frühen Neuzeit* (Wiesbaden, 1972).
28. Tyrol: Bücking, *Frühabsolutismus und Kirchenreform in Tirol*, pp. 62–77. Outer Austria: Forster, *Catholic Revival*, pp. 26–30.
29. Inner Austria consisted of the Duchies of Carinthia, Steiermark, and Krajina, and parts of Friulia and Istria. Karl Amon, "Innerösterreich" in *Territorien*, Vol. 1, pp. 103–116.

30. Evans, *The Making of the Habsburg Monarchy*, p. 45; Regina Pörtner, *The Counter-Reformation in Central Europe. Styria 1580–1630* (Oxford, 2001), esp. chaps 3–5.

31. Walter Ziegler, "Nieder- und Oberösterreich" in *Territorien*, Vol. 1, pp. 118–133; Joseph F. Patrouch, *A Negotiated Settlement. The Counter-Reformation in Upper Austria under the Habsburgs* (Boston, Leiden, Cologne, 2000).

32. Ziegler, "Nieder- und Oberösterreich" in *Territorien*, Vol. 1, pp. 126–127.

33. Patrouch, *A Negotiated Settlement*, pp. 71–86.

34. Ziegler, "Nieder- und Oberösterreich" in *Territorien*, Vol. 1, p. 129.

35. Ziegler, "Altbayern 1517–1648" in Brandmüller, ed. *Handbuch der bayerischen Kirchengeschichte*; Walter Ziegler, "Bayern" in *Territorien*, Vol. 1, pp. 62–68.

36. See above, Chapter 1.

37. Ziegler, "Altbayern 1517–1648" in Brandmüller, ed. *Handbuch der bayerischen Kirchengeschichte*, p. 44.

38. John O'Malley, *The First Jesuits* (Cambridge, MA, and London, 1993); R. Po-chia Hsia, *The World of Catholic Renewal, 1540–1770* (Cambridge, 1998), pp. 31–33.

39. Quoted in Forster, *The Counter-Reformation in the Villages*, p. 69.

40. See, for example, Stadtarchiv Mainz 15/400, 15/401, Archivum Romanum Societas Jésu, Rh. Inf. 48, Historia, pp. 4v, 27v, 32v, 42r, 58r, 74r, 115v–116r.

41. John O'Malley, "The Historiography of the Society of Jesus" in O'Malley et al., eds. *The Jesuits. Cultures, Sciences, and the Arts, 1540–1773* (Toronto, 1999), pp. 24–25.

42. Bireley, *The Refashioning of Catholicism*, pp. 137–139.

43. Hansgeorg Molitor, *Kirchliche Reformversuche der Kurfürsten und Erzbischöfe von Trier im Zeitalter der Gegenreformation* (Wiesbaden, 1967), chap. 2.

44. Peter Schmidt, *Das Collegium Germanicum in Rom und die Germaniker. Zur Funktion eines römischen Ausländerseminars (1552–1914)* (Tübingen, 1984).

45. Molitor, *Kirchliche Reformversuche*.

46. Peter Rummel, "Jesuiten" in Brandmüller, ed. *Handbuch der bayerischen Kirchengeschichte*, p. 844.

47. Anton Schindling, "Schulen und Universitäten im 16. und 17. Jahrhundert" in Walter Brandmüller, et al., eds. *Ecclesia Militans. Studien zur Konzilien- und Reformationsgeschichte. Remigius Bäumer*

zum 70. Geburtstag gewidmet, Vol. I, *Zur Konziliengeschichte* (Paderborn, 1988), pp. 564–565.

48. Forster, *Counter-Reformation in the Villages,* pp. 69–72.
49. Bireley, *The Refashioning of Catholicism,* p. 138.
50. Georg Föllinger, "Zur Priesterausbildung in den Bistümer Köln, Paderborn und Konstanz nach dem Tridentinum" in Brandmüller et al., eds. *Ecclesia Militans,* p. 385; Freitag, *Pfarrer, Kirche und ländliche Gemeinschaft,* pp. 163–168.
51. Buxbaum, *Petrus Canisius;* Rummel, "Jesuiten" in Brandmüller, ed. *Handbuch der bayerischen Kirchengeschichte,* pp. 842–843.
52. Ziegler, "Würzburg" in *Territorien,* Vol. 4, pp. 118–119.
53. Karl Hengst, *Jesuiten an Universitäten und Jesuitenuniversitäten* (Paderborn, 1981) esp. pp. 162, 298.
54. Rudolf Reinhardt, *Restauration, Visitation, Inspiration. Die Reformbestrebungen in der Benediktinerabtei Weingarten von 1567 bis 1627* (Stuttgart, 1960); Forster, *Catholic Revival;* Rummel, "Jesuiten" in Brandmüller, ed. *Handbuch der bayerische Kirchengeschichte,* p. 855.
55. Louis Châtellier, *Europe of the Devout. The Catholic Reformation and the Formation of a New Society* (Cambridge, 1989); Rummel, "Jesuiten" in Brandmüller, ed. *Handbuch der bayerische Kirchengeschichte,* pp. 855–856.
56. Châtellier, *Europe of the Devout,* p. 14.
57. Châtellier, *Europe of the Devout,* p. 24.
58. Châtellier, *Europe of the Devout,* p. 65.
59. Châtellier, *Europe of the Devout,* chap. 5.
60. Jeffrey Chipps Smith, *Sensuous Worship. Jesuits and the Art of the Early Counter-Reformation in Germany* (Princeton, 2002).
61. Smith, *Sensuous Worship,* p. 80.
62. Smith, *Sensuous Worship,* p. 35.
63. Smith, *Sensuous Worship,* p. 81.
64. Smith, *Sensuous Worship,* pp. 90–91.
65. Smith, *Sensuous Worship,* p. 200. IHS stood for *Ihsus,* the Greek for Jesus.
66. Smith, *Sensuous Worship,* pp. 4–5.
67. Hansgeorg Molitor, "Die untridentinische Reform. Anfänge katholischer Erneuerung in der Reichskirche" in Brandmüller et al., eds. *Ecclesia Militans,* pp. 399–491.
68. Molitor, "Die untridentinische Reform" in Brandmüller et al., eds. *Ecclesia Militans,* pp. 413–414.
69. Jendorff, *Reformatio Catholica,* pp. 140–141. Jendorff states that "Confessionalization in the sense of Catholicization took place along Mainz, not Roman-Tridentine lines."

70. Forster, "The Elite and Popular Foundations of German Catholicism" *Central European History* 26 (1994): 311–325.
71. Forster, *The Counter-Reformation in the Villages.*
72. Sicken, "Franken" in Brandmüller, ed. *Handbuch der bayerischen Kirchengeschichte*, p. 183.
73. Schröer, *Die Kirche in Westfalen*, Vol. 1, pp. 441–444.
74. Schröer, *Die Kirche in Westfalen*, Vol. 1, p. 32.
75. Josef Krasenbrink, *Die Congregatio Germanica und die katholische Reform in Deutschland nach dem Tridentinum* (Münster, 1972).
76. Bireley, *The Refashioning of Catholicism*, p. 62.
77. For example in the city of Münster: Hsia, *Society and Religion in Münster.*
78. On Fulda, see the brilliant study of Gerritt Walther, *Abt Balthasars Mission. Politische Mentalitäten, Gegenreformation und eine Adelsverschwörung im Hochstift Fulda* (Göttingen, 2002).
79. Walther, *Abt Balthasars Mission*, p. 692.
80. Jendorff, *Reformatio Catholica*, pp. 118–119.
81. Ziegler, "Bayern" in *Territorien*, Vol. 1, p. 665.
82. Wolfgang Wüst, "Schwaben" in Brandmüller, ed. *Handbuch der bayerischen Kirchengeschichte*, pp. 110–111.
83. Forster, *Catholic Revival*, pp. 38–40.
84. Franz Ortner, *Reformation, katholische Reform, und Gegenreformation im Erzstift Salzburg* (Salzburg, 1981), pp. 89–90; Zeeden, "Salzburg" in *Territorien*, Vol. 1, p. 82.
85. Molitor, *Kirchliche Reformversuche Trier* (Wiesbaden, 1967), Part III, chap. 1.
86. Georg Föllinger, "Zur Priesterausbildung in den Bistümer Köln, Paderborn und Konstanz nach dem Tridentinum" in Brandmüller et al., eds. *Ecclesia Militans*, pp. 370–378.
87. Franz Bosbach, "Köln" in *Territorien*, Vol. 3, p. 78; Thomas Paul Becker, *Konfessionalisierung in Kurköln. Untersuchungen zu Durchsetzung der katholischen Reform in den Dekanaten Ahrgau und Bonn anhand von Visitationsprotokollen 1583–1761* (Bonn, 1989), pp. 88–89.
88. Bosbach, "Köln" in *Territorien*, Vol. 3, pp. 78–79.
89. Forster, *Counter-Reformation in the Villages*, pp. 64–74.
90. On visitations: Gerald Strauss, *Luther's House of Learning: Indoctrination of the Young in the German Reformation* (Baltimore, 1978); Ernst W. Zeeden and Hansgeorg Molitor, *Die Visitation im Dienst der Kirchlichen Reform* (Münster, 1967); Forster, *Counter-Reformation in the Villages*; Forster, *Catholic Revival.*

91. Meier, "Die katholische Erneuerung des Würzburger Landkapitels Karlstadt" *Würzburger Diözesangeschichtsblätter* 33 (1971), section III.
92. Meier, "Die katholische Erneuerung des Würzburger Landkapitels Karlstadt" *Würzburger Diözesangeschichtsblätter* 33 (1971): 78–82.
93. Meier, "Die katholische Erneuerung des Würzburger Landkapitels Karlstadt" *Würzburger Diözesangeschichtsblätter* 33 (1971): 78–82, 69–71.
94. Peter Thaddäus Lang, "Reform im Wandel. Die Visitationsinterrogatorien des 16 und 17. Jahrhunderts" in Peter Lang and Ernst W. Zeeden, eds. *Kirche und Visitation. Beiträge zur Erforschung des frühneuzeitlichen Visitationswesens in Europa*, pp. 145–146.
95. Forster, *Catholic Revival*, pp. 41–47.
96. Peter Thaddäus Lang, "Die Erforschung der frühneuzeitlichen Kirchenvisitationen. Neue Veröffentlichungen in Deutschland" *Rottenburg Jahrbuch für Kirchengeschichte*, p. 193.
97. Forster, *Counter-Reformation in the Villages*; Hans Ammerich, "Formen und Wege der katholischen Reform in den Diözesan Speyer und Straßburg. Klerusreform und Seelsorgereform" in Volker Press et al., eds. *Barock am Oberrhein* (Karlsruhe, 1985), pp. 290–327; Paul Warmbrunn, "Konfessionalisierung im Spiegel der Visitationsprotokolle" *Jahrbuch für westdeutsche Landesgeschichte* 19 (1993).
98. Sicken, "Franken" in Brandmüller, ed. *Handbuch der bayerischen Kirchengeschichte*, pp. 183–184, 195–196.
99. Molitor, *Kirchliche Reformversuche*; Molitor, "Kurtrier" in *Territorien*, Vol. 5, pp. 61–65.
100. Molitor, *Kirchliche Reformversuche*, Part II, chap. 5, Part III, chap. 2.
101. Bosbach, "Köln" in *Territorien*, Vol. 3, p. 78; Becker, *Konfessionalisierung in Kurköln*, pp. 94–97. Becker and Bosbach seem to disagree about the power of the archdeacons, especially in the later seventeenth century.
102. Forster, *Catholic Revival*, pp. 48–50.
103. Rona Johnston, "The Implementation of Tridentine Reform: The Passau Official and the Parish Clergy of Lower Austria, 1563–1637" in Andrew Pettegree, ed. *The Reformation of the Parishes. The Ministry and the Reformation in Town and Country* (Manchester and New York, 1993).
104. John Headley, "Borromean Reform in the Empire? *La Strada Rigorosa* of Giovanni Francesco Bonomi" in *Church, Empire and World. The Quest for Universal Order, 1520–1640* (Variorum Collected Studies Series, 1997). See also, Johan Georg Mayer, *Das*

Konzil von Trent und die Gegenreformation in der Schweiz (Stans, 1901) and Hans Berner, Ulrich Gäbler, and Hans Rudolf Guggisberg, "Schweiz" in *Territorien*, Vol. 5, pp. 278–323, esp. pp. 313–317.

105. Headley, "Borromean Reform in the Empire?," p. 233.

106. Berner, Gäbler, and Guggisberg, "Schweiz" in *Territorien*, Vol. 5, p. 314.

107. Lang, "Reform im Wandel" and Heinrich R. Schmidt, *Konfessionalisierung im 16. Jahrhunderts* (Munich, 1992), pp. 68–75.

108. Jendorff, *Reformatio Catholica*, pp. 304–305.

109. Forster, *Catholic Revival*, p. 31.

110. Headley, "Borromean Reform in the Empire?," p. 233.

111. Simone Laqua, "Concubinage and the Church in Early Modern Münster" *Past and Present* Supplement 1 (2006): 72–100.

112. See Freitag, *Pfarrer, Kirche und ländliche Gemeinschaft*, chap. 2; Forster, *Counter-Reformation in the Villages*, esp. chaps 2 and 3; Jendorff, *Reformatio Catholica*, pp. 304–306.

113. Alois Hahn study as presented in H.R. Schmidt, *Konfessionalisierung im 16. Jahrhunderts*, pp. 69–71.

114. Forster, *Counter-Reformation in the Villages*; Forster, *Catholic Revival*.

115. The same laments are still echoed by modern Church historians. See, for example, Herbert Immenkötter und Wolfgang Wüst, "Augsburg – Freie Reichstadt und Hochstift" in *Territorien*, Vol. 6, p. 26.

116. Becker, *Konfessionalisierung in Kurköln*, chap. 2.2.

117. Schmidt, *Konfessionalisierung im 16. Jahrhunderts*, p. 74.

118. Meier, "Die katholische Erneuerung des Würzburger Landkapitels Karlstadt" *Würzburger Diözesangeschichtsblätter* 33 (1971): 84.

119. Meier, "Die katholische Erneuerung des Würzburger Landkapitels Karlstadt" *Würzburger Diözesangeschichtsblätter* 33 (1971): 89–90.

120. Schröer, *Die Kirche in Westfalen*, p. 465; Freitag, *Pfarrer, Kirche und ländliche Gemeinschaft*, pp. 104–119.

121. Freitag, *Pfarrer, Kirche, und ländliche Gemeinschaft*, p. 118.

122. Forster, *Catholic Revival*, pp. 51–53; Enderle, *Konfessionsbildung und Ratsregiment*; Enderle, "Rottweil und die katholischen Reichstätte im Südwesten" *Territorien*, Vol. 5, pp. 215–230.

123. Bosbach, "Die katholische Reform in der Stadt Köln" *Römische Quartalschrift für christliche Altertumskunde und Kirchengeschichte* 84 (1989): pp. 120–159.

124. Bosbach, "Die katholische Reform in der Stadt Köln," pp. 138–139.

125. Bosbach, "Die katholische Reform in der Stadt Köln," p. 148.

126. Sicken, "Franken" in Brandmüller, ed. *Handbuch der bayerischen Kirchengeschichte*, p. 223.

127. Forster, *Counter-Reformation in the Villages*, p. 56.

128. Forster, *Catholic Revival*, pp. 53–57.

129. Reinhardt, *Restauration, Visitation, Inspiration*, p. 23.

130. Peter Schmid, "Regensburg – Freie Reichsstadt, Hochstift und Reichsklöster" in *Territorien*, Vol. 6, p. 49.

131. Hugo Ott, "Die Benedictinerabtei St. Blasien in den Reformbestrebungen seit 1567, besonders unter Abt Kaspar II (1571–1596)" *Freiburger Diözesan Archiv* 84 (1964): 156.

132. Schmid, "Regensburg – Freie Reichsstadt, Hochstift und Reichsklöster" in *Territorien*, Vol. 6, p. 49.

133. Reinhardt, *Restauration, Visitation, Inspiration*, pp. 11–12.

134. Headley, "Borromean Reform in the Empire?," pp. 235–236.

135. Sicken, "Franken" in Brandmüller, ed. *Handbuch der bayerischen Kirchengeschichte*, pp. 197–198.

136. Forster, "The Elite and Popular Foundations of German Catholicism: The *Reichskirche*" *Central European History* 26 (1993).

137. Schmid, "Regensburg – Freie Reichsstadt, Hochstift und Reichsklöster" in *Territorien*, Vol. 6, p. 49.

138. Reinhardt, *Restauration, Visitation, Inspiration*, esp. pp. 20–30.

139. O'Malley, *Trent and All That*, chap. 2.

140. Schmidt, *Konfessionalisierung im 16. Jahrhundert*, pp. 76–77. See also Schilling and Reinhard, *Die katholische Konfessionalisierung*.

141. Forster, "With and Without Confessionalization"; Harrington and Smith, "Confessionalization, Community, and State Building in Germany, 1555–1870."

142. Bast, *Honor Your Fathers*, pp. 141–142.

143. Bast, *Honor Your Fathers*, pp. 230–231.

144. Bast, *Honor Your Fathers*, pp. 196–197; Bireley, *The Refashioning of Catholicism*, pp. 101–104.

145. Catechism instruction was an important part of rural missions in the century after 1650. See below, chap. 5.

146. Peter Thaddäus Lang, "Reform im Wandel" in Zeeden und Lang, eds. *Kirche und Visitation*, pp. 131–190; Lang, "Die Erforschung der frühneuzeitlichen Kirchenvisitationen" *Rottenburger Jahrbuch für Kirchengeschichte* 16 (1997): 185–193.

147. See, for example, Paul Warmbrunn, "Konfessionalisierung im Spiegel der Visitationsprotokolle" *Jahrbuch für westdeutsche Landesgeschichte* 19 (1993): 350–351.

148. Becker, *Konfessionalisierung in Kurköln*, p. 157.
149. Forster, *Counter-Reformation in the Villages*, p. 115.
150. Becker, *Konfessionalisierung in Kurköln*, p. 157; Warmbrunn, "Konfessionalisierung im Spiegel der Visitationsprotokolle," pp. 353–354.
151. Lang, "Reform im Wandel" in Zeeden und Lang, eds. *Kirche und Visitation*, p. 142; Warmbrunn, "Konfessionalisierung im Spiegel der Visitationsprotokolle," p. 342.
152. Becker, *Konfessionalisierung in Kurköln*, pp. 317–318.
153. Bosbach, "Die katholische Reform in der Stadt Köln" *Römische Quartalschrift für christliche Altertumskunde und Kirchengeschichte* 84 (1989): 146.
154. Enderle, "Rottweil und die katholische Reichstädte im Südwesten" in *Territorien*, Vol. 5, pp. 227–229.
155. Forster, *Counter-Reformation in the Villages*; Forster, *Catholic Revival*; Heribert Raab, "Gegenreformation und katholische Reform im Erzbistum und Erzstift Trier (1567–1711)" *Römische Quartalschrift für christliche Altertumskunde und Kirchengeschichte* 84 (1989): 184.
156. Raab, "Gegenreformation und katholische Reform im Erzbistum und Erzstift Trier (1567–1711)" *Römische Quartalschrift für christliche Altertumskunde und Kirchengeschichte* 84 (1989): 184.
157. Bosbach, "Die katholische Reform in der Stadt Köln" *Römische Quartalschrift für christliche Altertumskunde und Kirchengeschichte* 84 (1989): 147.
158. Soergel, *Wondrous in His Saints*.
159. Dünninger, *Maria siegt in Franken*.
160. Dünninger, *Maria siegt in Franken*. pp. 59–63.
161. Bossy, "The Counter-Reformation and the People of Catholic Europe" *Past and Present* 47 (1970): 51–70.
162. H.J. Schroeder, *Canons and Decrees of the Council of Trent* (St Louis and London, 1941), p. 204.
163. Chaix, "Die schwierige Schule der Sitten" in Heinz Schilling, ed. *Kirchenzucht und Sozialdisziplinierung* (*Zeitschrift für historische Forschung*, Beiheft 16), p. 211, see also pp. 200–201.
164. Schmidt, *Konfessionalisierung im 16. Jahrhundert*, pp. 76–78, with full bibliography.
165. Thomas Max Safely, *Let No Man Put Asunder. The Control of Marriage in the German Southwest. A Comparative Study, 1550–1600* (Kirksville, 1984); Joel Harrington, *Reordering Marriage and Society in Reformation Germany* (Cambridge, 1995).

166. Bossy, "The Counter-Reformation and the People of Catholic Europe."
167. Veit, *Kirche und Kirchenreform in der Erzdiözese Mainz*, pp. 81–83.
168. Becker, *Konfessionalisierung in Kurköln*, pp. 279–291; Schmidt, *Konfessionalisierung im 16. Jahrhundert*, p. 77.
169. The following section is based on Chaix, "Die schwierige Schule der Sitten" in Heinz Schilling, ed. *Kirchenzucht und Sozialdisziplinierung im frühneuzeitlichen Europa*, pp. 199–217.
170. Here Chaix is drawing on a study by Gerd Schwerhoff, *Köln in Kreuzverhör. Kriminalität, Herrschaft und Gesellschaft in einer frühneuzeitlichen Stadt* (Bonn, 1991).
171. Veit, *Kirche und Kirchenreform in der Erzdiözese Mainz*, p. 88.
172. For a discussion of *Leichtfertigkeit*: Ulrike Strasser, "Vom 'Fall der Ehre' zum 'Fall der Leichtfertigkeit.' Geschlechtsspezifische Aspekte der Konfessionalisierung am Beispiel Münchner Eheversprechens- und Alimentationsklagen (1592–1649)" in Peer Frieß and Rolf Kießling, eds. *Konfessionalisierung und Region* (Constance, 1999), esp. pp. 230–233.
173. Veit, *Kirche und Kirchenreform in der Erzdiözese Mainz*, pp. 87–90; Friedhelm Jürgensmeier, *Das Bistum Mainz. Von der Römerzeit bis zum II. Vatikanischen Konzil* (Frankfurt, 1988), p. 211.
174. Peter Burke, *Popular Culture in Early Modern Europe* (New York, 1978).
175. Jürgensmeier, *Das Bistum Mainz*, pp. 211–213.
176. Jürgensmeier, *Das Bistum Mainz*, p. 211.
177. Otto Feldbauer refers to the end of "classical concubinage," in which the priest lived openly and continuously with a woman in a marriage-like relationship. Feldbauer, "Der Priester als Vorbild und Spiegel. Die Konfessionalisierung des Pfarrklerus im Herzogtum/ Kurfürstentum Bayern, am Beispiel der bayerischen Teile des Bistums Freising 1560–1625" in Peer Frieß and Rolf Kießling, eds. *Konfessionalisierung und Region*, esp. pp. 257–263.
178. Schmidt, *Konfessionalisierung im 16. Jahrhundert*, p. 79; R. Po-chia Hsia, *Social Discipline in the Reformation: Central Europe, 1550–1750* (London and New York, 1989), p. 155.

Chapter 3: The Thirty Years' War

1. Robert Bireley, *The Refashioning of Catholicism*, pp. 89–90. See also Robert Bireley, *The Jesuits and the Thirty Years War. Kings, Courts, and*

Confessors (Cambridge, 2003); Robert Bireley, *Maximilian von Bayern, Adam Contzen, S.J. und die Gegenreformation in Deutschland* (Göttingen, 1975); Robert Bireley, *Religion and Politics in the Age of the Counterreformation: Emperor Ferdinand II, William Lamormaini, S.J. and the Formation of Imperial Policy* (Chapel Hill, 1981).

2. Holborn, *A History of Modern Germany*, Vol. I, pp. 336–338; Bireley, *The Jesuits and the Thirty Years War*, esp. pp. 89–93.

3. Wolfgang Seibrich, *Gegenreformation als Restauration. Die restaurativen Bemühungen der alten Orden im deutschen Reich von 1580 bis 1648* (Münster, 1991).

4. Seibrich, *Gegenreformation als Restauration*, quote on p. 2, pp. 4–10; Bireley, *The Jesuits and the Thirty Years War*, chap. 4.

5. R. Reinhardt, *Reformation, Visitation, Inspiration.*

6. Forster, *Catholic Revival*, pp. 53–57.

7. Monastic restoration in Württemberg: Seibrich, *Gegenreformation als Restauration*, pp. 340–377.

8. Forster, *Counter-Reformation in the Villages*, pp. 158–161.

9. Seibrich, *Gegenreformation als Restauration*, p. 400.

10. Seibrich, *Gegenreformation als Restauration*, pp. 405–461.

11. Anton Schindling and Walter Ziegler, "Kurpfalz — Rheinische Pfalz und Oberpfalz" in *Territorien*, Vol. 5, pp. 8–49.

12. Schindling and Ziegler, "Kurpfalz – Rheinische Pfalz und Oberpfalz" in *Territorien*, Vol. 5, pp. 40–41.

13. Ziegler, "Bayern" in *Territorien*, Vol. 1, pp. 67–68.

14. Ziegler, "Bayern" in *Territorien*, Vol. 1, p. 68.

15. Evans, *The Making of the Habsburg Monarchy*, pp. 67–79.

16. Evans, *The Making of the Habsburg Monarchy*, pp. 68–69.

17. Evans, *The Making of the Habsburg Monarchy*, p. 70.

18. Ziegler, "Nieder- und Innerösterreich" in *Territorien*, Vol. 1, p. 131.

19. Hermann Rebel, *Peasant Classes. The Bureaucratization of Property and Family Relations under Early Modern Habsburg Absolutism, 1511–1636* (Princeton, 1983), esp. chap. 8; Ziegler, "Nieder- und Innerösterreich" in *Territorien*, p. 131; Evans, *The Making of the Habsburg Monarchy*, p. 71.

20. Evans, *The Making of the Habsburg Monarchy*, p. 71; Ziegler, "Nieder- und Innerösterreich" in *Territorien*, Vol. 1, pp. 130–131.

21. Ziegler, "Nieder- und Innerösterreich" in *Territorien*, Vol. 1, pp. 131–132.

22. Forster, *Counter-Reformation in the Villages*, chap. 5; Franz Maier, *Die bayerische Unterpfalz im Dreißigjährigen Krieg* (New York, 1990).

23. Forster, *Counter-Reformation in the Villages*, pp. 164–165; Anna Egler, *Die Spanier in der linksrheinishen Pfalz, 1620–1632* (Mainz, 1971).

24. Forster, *Counter-Reformation in the Villages*, p. 163.

25. Schindling and Ziegler, "Kurpfalz – Rheinische Pfalz und Oberpfalz" in *Territorien*, Vol. 5, p. 40; Friedhelm Jürgensmeier, "Kurmainz" in *Territorien*, Vol. 4, p. 93; Jürgensmeier, *Das Bistum Mainz*, (Frankfurt, 1988), pp. 213–214.

26. Dippold, *Konfessionalisierung am Obermain*, pp. 247–248; Günter Christ, "Bamberg" in *Territorien*, Vol. 4, pp. 160–163.

27. Dippold, *Konfessionalisierung am Obermain*, pp. 368–371.

28. Sicken, "Franken" in *Handbuch der bayerische Kirchengeschichte*, p. 262.

29. Christian Plath, *Konfessionskampf und fremde Besatzung. Stadt und Hochstift Hildesheim im Zeitalter der Gegenreformation und des Dreißigjährigen Krieges (ca. 1580–1660)* (Münster, 2005).

30. Sicken, "Franken" in Brandmüller, ed. *Handbuch der bayerischen Kirchengeschichte*, p. 260.

31. H.C. Erik Midelfort, *Witch Hunting in Southwestern Germany, 1562–1684* (Stanford, 1972); Wolfgang Behringer, *Witchcraft Persecutions in Bavaria. Religious Zealotry and Reason of State in Early Modern Europe* (Cambridge, 1987).

32. Midelfort, *Witch Hunting in Southwestern Germany*, pp. 138–139; Brian Levack, *The Witch-Hunt in Early Modern Europe*, pp. 116–117. Midelfort states that the connection between "Counter-Reformation" and witch-hunting in this case has not been conclusively proved.

33. Levack, *The Witch-Hunt in Early Modern Europe* (London and New York, 1985), p. 119; Joseph Klaits, *Servants of Satan. The Age of Witch Hunts* (Bloomington, 1985).

34. Lyndal Roper, *Witch Craze. Terror and Fantasy in Baroque Germany* (New Haven and London, 2004), p. 38.

35. Midelfort, *Witch Hunting in Southwestern Germany*, chap. 3, quote pp. 64–65.

36. Behringer, *Witchcraft Persecutions in Bavaria*, pp. 213–222.

37. Stuart Clark, *Thinking with Demons. The Idea of Witchcraft in Early Modern Europe* (Oxford, 1997), p. 508.

38. Clark, *Thinking with Demons*, p. 528.

39. Roper, *Witch Craze*, pp. 23–29.

40. Midelfort, *Witch Hunting in Southwestern Germany*, pp. 98–112.

41. Midelfort, *Witch Hunting in Southwestern Germany*, p. 86; Behringer, *Witchcraft Persecutions in Bavaria*, pp. 224–225.

42. Midelfort, *Witch Hunting in Southwestern Germany*, p. 105.
43. Midelfort, *Witch Hunting in Southwestern Germany*, p. 100.
44. Walter Ziegler, "Würzburg" in *Territorien*, Vol. 4, p. 121.
45. Behringer, *Witchcraft Persecutions in Bavaria*, pp. 224–229.
46. Walter Ziegler, "Würzburg" in *Territorien*, Vol. 4, p. 121; Günter Christ, "Bamberg" in *Territorien*, Vol. 4, pp. 161–162; Alois Schmid, "Eichstätt" in *Territorien*, Vol. 4, p. 177. The historians writing in this collection tend to downplay the witch hunts in their articles and generally uncouple them from Counter-Reformation, Tridentine reform, and confessionalization.
47. Dippold, *Konfessionalisierung am Obermain*, pp. 50–51.
48. Behringer, *Witchcraft Persecutions in Bavaria*, p. 226; Sicken, "Franken 1517–1648" in Brandmüller, ed. *Handbuch der bayerischen Kirchengeschichte*, pp. 253–255; Christ, "Bamberg" in *Territorien*, Vol. 4, p. 161.
49. Behringer, *Witchcraft Persecutions in Bavaria*, pp. 230–321.
50. Quotes from Behringer, *Witchcraft Persecutions in Bavaria*, p. 238.
51. Quote from Behringer, *Witchcraft Persecutions in Bavaria*, p. 285.
52. Roper, *Witch Craze*, pp. 1–6, 30–32, 222–246.
53. Bireley, *The Refashioning of Catholicism*, pp. 110–111.
54. Walter Pötzl, "Volksfrömmigkeit" in Brandmüller, ed. *Handbuch der bayerischen Kirchengeschichte*, pp. 895–901, esp. pp. 897–898.
55. Forster, *Catholic Revival*, p. 91.
56. Brückner, *Die Verehrung des Heiligen Blutes in Walldürn*, esp. pp. 59–63, 90.
57. Brückner, *Die Verehrung des Heiligen Blutes in Walldürn*, p. 68. The *Kirchenkasse* would reach 3000fl. by 1660.
58. Freitag, *Volks- und Elitenfrömmigkeit in der frühen Neuzeit*, pp. 239, 243.
59. Forster, *Catholic Revival*, pp. 90–91.
60. Brückner, *Die Verehrung des Heiligen Blutes in Walldürn*, esp. pp. 63–64.
61. Dünninger, *Maria siegt in Franken*, esp. p. 63.
62. Theodore Rabb, *The Struggle for Stability in Early Modern Europe* (New York, 1975), chap. 7, "International Relations and the Force of Religion." Quote, p. 82.
63. Holborn, *A History of Modern Germany. 1648–1840*, Vol. 1, p. 124.
64. Ernst W. Zeeden, *Die Entstehung der Konfessionen* (Munich and Vienna, 1965), Quoted in Etienne François, *Die unsichtbare Grenze*, p. 12.
65. Holborn, *A History of Modern Germany*, Vol. 1, pp. 16–19; Jürgensmeier, *Das Bistum Mainz*, pp. 220–227.
66. Holborn, *A History of Modern Germany*, Vol. 1, pp. 368–371.

67.   Martin Heckel, *Deutschland im Konfessionellen Zeitalter* (Göttingen, 1983), pp. 198–209. See also Kaspar von Greyerz, "Confession as a Social and Economic Factor" in Sheilagh Oglivie, ed. *Germany. A New Social and Economic History. Volume 2, 1630–1800* (London, 1996), pp. 318–319.

68.   Wolgast, *Hochstift und Reformation*, p. 345.

69.   Rudolf Vierhaus, *Deutschland im Zeitalter des Absolutismus* (Göttingen, 1978), esp. p. 18, where he uses the term *Selbstgenügsamkeit* (self-sufficiency or self-reliance); Rudolf Vierhaus, *Staaten und Stände. Vom westfälischen bis zum Hubertusburger Frieden* (Berlin, 1984), pp. 53–55. Turning inward can also be considered a sign of "backwardness" or a failure of "modernization." For a discussion of these problematic issues, see Peter Hersche, "Intendierte Rückständigkeit: zur Charakteristik des geistlichen Staates im alten Reich" in Schmidt, ed. *Stände und Gesellschaft im alten Reich* (Stuttgart, 1989).

Chapter 4: The German Church after 1650

1.   Gerhard Benecke, "The German Reichskirche" in William J. Callahan and David Higgs, eds. *Church and Society in Catholic Europe of the 18th Century* (Cambridge, 1979), p. 80. For comparison, secular princes governed 22.5 million subjects, imperial cities and secular lords 1 million each, imperial knights 0.5 million.

2.   The notion of the "incubator" comes from Mack Walker, *German Home Towns. Community, State, and General Estate* (Ithaca, 1971).

3.   Forster, *The Counter-Reformation in the Villages*, pp. 147–149. Von Sötern was also Prince-Bishop of Speyer.

4.   Hubert Jedin, "Die Reichskirche der Schönbornzeit" in *Kirche des Glaubens. Kirche der Geschichte*, Vol. I (Freiburg, 1966), pp. 455–468.

5.   Jürgensmeier, *Das Bistum Mainz*, pp. 220–223; Endres, "Franken 1648–1803" in Brandmüller, ed. *Handbuch der bayerischen Kirchengeschichte*, pp. 391–393.

6.   Alfred Schröcker, *Ein Schönborn im Reich. Studien zur Reichspolitik des Fürstbischofs Lothar Franz von Schönborn (1655–1729)* (Wiesbaden, 1978); Jürgensmeier, *Das Bistum Mainz*, pp. 233–234; Endres, "Franken 1648–1803" in Brandmüller, ed. *Handbuch der bayerischen Kirchengeschichte*, pp. 395–398.

7.   See James Allen Vann, *The Swabian Kreis. Institutional Growth in the Holy Roman Empire 1648–1715* (Brussels, 1975).

8. Alfred Schröcker, *Die Patronage des Lothar Franz von Schönborn (1655–1729). Sozialgeschichtliche Studie zum Beziehungsnetz in der Germania Sacra* (Wiesbaden, 1981); Peter Hersche, *Das deutsche Domkapitel im 17. und 18. Jahrhundert* Vol. II, Vergleichende sozialgeschichtliche Untersuchungen (Bern, 1984), p. 157.

9. Hersche, *Das deutsche Domkapitel*, esp. Vol. II.

10. The "knightly chapters" were those along the so-called *Pfaffengasse* (priests' alley): Bamberg, Würzburg, Mainz, Trier, Speyer, and Worms.

11. Hersche, *Das deutsche Domkapitel*, Vol. II, pp. 194–202.

12. Vann, *The Swabian Kreis*, esp. pp. 43–46. See also Konstantin Maier, *Die Diskussion um Kirche und Reform im schwäbischen Reichsprälatenkollegium zur Zeit der Aufklärung* (Wiesbaden, 1978).

13. Rudolf Vierhaus, *Deutschland im Zeitalter des Absolutismus (1648–1763)* (Göttingen, 1978), p. 18.

14. Manfred Becker-Huberti, *Die tridentinische Reform im Bistum Münster unter Fürstbishof Christoph Bernhard v. Galen 1650–1678. Ein Beitrag zur Geschichte der Katholischen Reform* (Münster, 1978); Rudolfine Freiin von Oer, "Münster" in *Territorien*, Vol. 3, pp. 127–128. Wolfgang Zimmermann, "Die 'siegreiche' Frömmigkeit des Hauses Habsburg" *Rottenburger Jahrbuch für Kirchengeschichte* 19 (2000): 157–175.

15. Becker-Huberti, *Die tridentinische Reform im Bistum Münster*, pp. 78–111.

16. Becker-Huberti, *Die tridentinische Reform im Bistum Münster*, pp. 125–142.

17. The only other bishop I can identify who conducted some visitations personally was Von Mespelbrunn in Würzburg in the 1570s.

18. Becker-Huberti, *Die tridentinische Reform im Bistum Münster*, pp. 57–67.

19. Becker-Huberti, *Die tridentinische Reform im Bistum Münster*, pp. 68–77.

20. Becker, *Konfessionalisierung in Kurköln*, pp. xiv–xv.

21. Becker, *Konfessionalisierung in Kurköln*, pp. 9–12, quote p. 12.

22. Becker, *Konfessionalisierung in Kurköln*, pp. 24–26, quote p. 25.

23. Becker, *Konfessionalisierung in Kurköln*, pp. 115–117; Peter Thaddäus Lang, "Reform im Wandel" in Lang and Zeeden, eds. *Kirche und Visitation*, pp. 145–146; Lang, "Die katholischen Kirchenvisitationen des 18. Jahrhunderts" *Römische Quartalschrift für christliche Altertumskunde und Kirchengeschichte* 83 (1988): 265–295.

24. Endres, "Franken 1648–1803" in Brandmüller, ed. *Handbuch der bayerischen Kirchengeschichte*, pp. 406–408, quote p. 408.

25. Endres, "Franken 1648–1803" in Brandmüller, ed. *Handbuch der bayerischen Kirchengeschichte*, pp. 409–414.

26. Endres, "Franken 1648–1803" in Brandmüller, ed. *Handbuch der bayerischen Kirchengeschichte*, pp. 417–423.

27. Wüst, "Schwaben 1648–1803" in Brandmüller, ed. *Handbuch der bayerischen Kirchengeschichte*, pp. 357–389.

28. Wüst, "Schwaben 1648–1803" in Brandmüller, ed. *Handbuch der bayerischen Kirchengeschichte*, p. 367.

29. Forster, *Catholic Revival*, pp. 210–217.

30. Schmid, "Altbayern 1648–1803" in Brandmüller, ed. *Handbuch der bayerischen Kirchengeschichte*, p. 301.

31. Schmid, "Altbayern 1648–1803" in Brandmüller, ed. *Handbuch der bayerischen Kirchengeschichte*, p. 302.

32. Schmid, "Altbayern 1648–1803" in Brandmüller, ed. *Handbuch der bayerischen Kirchengeschichte*, pp. 316–318.

33. Schmid, "Altbayern 1648–1803" in Brandmüller, ed. *Handbuch der bayerischen Kirchengeschichte*, pp. 318–327, esp. pp. 318–319.

34. Schmid, "Altbayern 1648–1803" in Brandmüller, ed. *Handbuch der bayerischen Kirchengeschichte*, pp. 305–311.

35. Schmid, "Altbayern 1648–1803" in Brandmüller, ed. *Handbuch der bayerischen Kirchengeschichte*, p. 310.

36. Louis Châtellier, *The Religion of the Poor. Rural Missions in Europe and the Formation of Modern Catholicism, c.1500–c.1800* (Cambridge, 1997), pp. 77–83.

37. Evans, *The Making of the Habsburg Monarchy* (Oxford, 1979), pp. 118–121; Charles Ingrao, *The Habsburg Monarchy, 1618–1815* (Cambridge, 1994) pp. 61–64.

38. Evans, *The Making of the Habsburg Monarchy*, pp. 124–126.

39. Robert Bireley, *The Counter-Reformation Prince. Anti-Machiavellianism or Catholic Statecraft in Early Modern Europe* (Chapel Hill and London, 1990), chap. 9, quote p. 232.

40. Anna Coreth, *Pietas Austriaca: österreichische Frömmigkeit im Barock* (Munich, 1982); Wolfgang Zimmermann, "Die 'siegreiche' Frömmigkeit des Hauses Habsburg" *Rottenburger Jahrbuch für Kirchengeschichte* 19 (2000): 157–175.

41. Zimmermann, "Die 'siegreiche' Frömmigkeit des Hauses Habsburg," pp. 166–169.

42. Bireley, *The Counter-Reformation Prince*, chap. 4.

43. Coreth, *Pietas Austriaca*, esp. chap. 3. See also Wolfgang Brückner, "Devotio und Patronage. Zum konkreten Rechtsdenken in

handgreiflichen Frömmigkeitsformen des Spätmittelalters und der frühen Neuzeit" in Klaus Schreiner, ed. *Laienfrömmigkeit im späten Mittelalter. Formen, Funktionen, politisch-soziale Zusammenhänge* (Munich, 1992), pp. 79–91.

44. Zimmermann, "Die 'siegreiche' Frömmigkeit des Hauses Habsburg," pp. 166–168.

45. Jean-Marie Valentin, *Les Jésuites et le théâtre (1554–1680). Contribution à l'histoire culturelle du monde catholique dans le Saint-Empire romain germanique* (Paris, 2001), chap. XIV.

46. Valentin, *Les Jésuites et le Théâtre*, pp. 668–671, quote p. 669.

47. Valentin, *Les Jésuites et le Théâtre*, p. 687. This idea is a major theme of Evans, *The Making of the Habsburg Monarchy*, esp. chaps 4, 5, 9–12.

48. Mack Walker, *The Salzburg Transaction. Expulsion and Redemption in Eighteenth-Century Germany* (Ithaca and London, 1992).

49. Wolfgang Zimmermann, "Der gute Hirte und der schlechte Mietling. Beobachtungen zum Konstanzer Klerus im konfessionellen Zeitalter" *Zeitschrift für die Geschichte des Oberrheins* 147 (1999): 319–337.

50. Luise Schorn-Schütte, "Priest, Preacher, Pastor: Research on Clerical Office in Early Modern Europe" *Central European History* 33 (2000): pp. 20–21. See also Werner Freitag, *Pfarrer, Kirche und ländliche Gemeinschaft*, esp. chaps 4 and 5 and Wietse de Boer, "Professionalization and Clerical Identity: Notes on the Early Modern Catholic Priest" in Wim Janse and Barbara Pitkin, eds. *The Formation of Clerical and Confessional Identities in Early Modern Europe* (Leiden, 2006), pp. 369–377.

51. Luise Schorn-Schütte, "The Christian Clergy in the Early Modern Holy Roman Empire: A Comparative Study" *Sixteenth Century Journal* 29 (1998): 719–721.

52. On Cologne: Becker, *Konfessionalisierung in Kurköln*, pp. 131–141. On concubinage: Forster, *Catholic Revival*, pp. 31–34; Andreas Holzem, *Religion und Lebensformen. Katholische Konfessionalisierung im Sendgericht des Fürstbistums Münster 1570–1800* (Paderborn, 2000), p. 204; Freitag, *Pfarrer, Kirche und ländliche Gemeinschaft*, pp. 211–213.

53. Freitag, *Pfarrer, Kirche und ländliche Gemeinschaft*, p. 211.

54. Holzem, *Religion und Lebensformen*, pp. 207–208.

55. Forster, *Catholic Revival*, pp. 175–176; Forster, *The Counter-Reformation in the Villages*, pp. 184–231; Freitag, *Pfarrer, Kirche und ländliche Gemeinschaft*, pp. 212–213; Luise Schorn-Schütte, "The Christian Clergy in the Early Modern Holy Roman Empire: A Comparative Study" *Sixteenth Century Journal* 29 (1998): 725–727.

56. Forster, *Catholic Revival*, pp. 202–203.
57. Cologne, Paderborn, Constance: Föllinger, "Zur Priesterausbildung in den Bistümern Köln, Paderborn und Konstanz nach dem Tridentinum," in Walter Brandmüller et al., eds. *Ecclesia Militans*, pp. 367–397. Trier: Raab, "Gegenreformation und katholische Reform im Erzbistum und Erzstift Trier (1567–1711)" *Römische Quartalschrift für christliche Altertumskunde und Kirchengeschichte* 84 (1989): 173–174. Augsburg: Wüst, "Schwaben 1648–1803" in Brandmüller, ed. *Handbuch der bayerischen Kirchengeschichte*, p. 364.
58. Schorn-Schütte, "The Christian Clergy in the Early Modern Holy Roman Empire: A Comparative Study" *Sixteenth Century Journal* 29 (1998): 724–725.
59. On Holzhauser, see *Catholic Encyclopedia* (1908 edition): http://www.newadvent.org/cathen/07439b.htm.
60. Dieter Weiß, "Franken 1648–1803" in Brandmüller, ed. *Handbuch der bayerischen Kirchengeschichte*, pp. 422–423.
61. See, for example, Zimmermann, "Der gute Hirte und der schlechte Mietling" *Zeitschrift für die Geschichte des Oberrheins* 147 (1999): 335–336.
62. Freitag, *Pfarrer, Kirche und ländliche Gemeinschaft*, pp. 187–190.
63. Freitag, *Pfarrer, Kirche und ländliche Gemeinschaft*, p. 189.
64. Raab, "Gegenreformation und katholische Reform im Erzbistum und Erzstift Trier (1567–1711)" *Römische Quartalschrift für christliche Altertumskunde und Kirchengeschichte* 84 (1989): 173–174.
65. Becker, *Konfessionalisierung in Kurköln*, pp. 82–87.
66. Châtellier, *Europe of the Devout*, pp. 69–70, 233–235. About one-half of the clergy were "country clerics and curés."
67. Châtellier, *Europe of the Devout*, pp. 82–83. Quotes all p. 83.
68. Renate Dürr, "Images of the Priesthood: An Analysis of Catholic Sermons from the Late Seventeenth Century" *Central European History* 33 (2000): 92.
69. Dürr, "Images of the Priesthood" *Central European History* 33 (2000): 93–94.
70. Zimmermann, "Der gute Hirte und der schlechte Mietling" *Zeitschrift für die Geschichte des Oberrheins* 147 (1999): 325–326. See also Freitag, *Pfarrer, Kirche und ländliche Gemeinschaft*, chap. 7.
71. Forster, *Catholic Revival*, pp. 185–186, with references.
72. Forster, *Counter-Reformation in the Villages*, p. 38; Peter Blickle, *Communal Reformation*; Conrad, *Reformation in der bäuerlichen Gesellschaft*.

73. Peter Blickle, "Warum blieb die Innerschweiz katholisch?" *Mitteilungen des historischen Vereins des Kantons Schwyz* 86 (1994): 29–38.

74. Forster, *Catholic Revival*, chaps 4 and 5.

75. Forster, *Catholic Revival*, pp. 199–206; Holzem, *Religion und Lebensformen*, pp. 199–202.

76. Renate Dürr, "Images of the Priesthood" *Central European History* 33 (2000): 91.

77. Freitag, *Pfarrer, Kirche und ländliche Gemeinschaft*, esp. chaps 4 and 5.

78. Forster, *Catholic Revival*, pp. 167–183; Forster, *The Counter-Reformation in the Villages*, pp. 194–199.

79. Forster, *Catholic Revival*, pp. 213–215.

80. Forster, *Catholic Revival*, chap. 6; Rudolf Reinhardt, *Die Beziehungen von Hochstift und Diözese Konstanz zu Habsburg-Österreich in der Neuzeit: Zugleich ein Beitrag zur archivalischen Erforschung des Problems "Kirche und Staat." Beiträge zur Geschichte der Reichskirche in der Neuzeit*, Vol. 2. (Wiesbaden, 1966).

81. Châtellier, *Tradition chrétienne*, pp. 231–243; Forster, *Catholic Revival*, pp. 220–228.

82. Holzem, *Religion und Lebensformen*, pp. 208–209.

83. Ulrich Pfister, "Pastors and Priests in the Early Modern Grisons: Organized Profession or Side Activity" *Central European History* 33 (2000): 41–65.

84. Rising incomes, see Forster, *Catholic Revival*; Holzem, *Religion und Lebensformen*; Freitag, *Pfarrer, Kirche und ländliche Gemeinschaft*. In general, see Schorn-Schütte, "Priest, Preacher, Pastor" *Central European History* 33 (2000): 21–23.

85. Forster, *Catholic Revival*, pp. 175–176.

86. Forster, *Catholic Revival*, pp. 44–47, 66, 170–178, 212. Also Forster, "The Elite and Popular Foundations of German Catholicism in the Age of Confessionalism: The Reichskirche" *Central European History* 26 (1994): 311–325; Francis Rapp, *Réformes et Reformation à Strasbourg*.

87. The Protestant clergy was also supported by the traditional benefice system, although the abolition of monasticism and the elimination of the episcopal structure in the Reformation had simplified it somewhat.

88. Forster, *Catholic Revival*, pp. 170–173. See also Forster, "Kirchenreform, katholische Konfessionalisierung und Dorfreligion um Kloster Salem, 1650–1750" *Rottenburger Jahrbuch für Kirchengeschichte* 16 (1997): 93–110.

89. Forster, *Catholic Revival*, pp. 165–167. This region was part of the Habsburg territory of *Vorderösterreich*, or Outer Austria.

90. Forster, *Catholic Revival*, pp. 159–162.

91. Forster, *Catholic Revival*, pp. 157–167.

92. Wolfgang Brückner, "Die Neuorganization von Frömmigkeit des Kirchenvolkes im nachtridentinischen Konfessionsstaat" *Jahrbuch für Volkskunde* N.F. 21 (1998): 9–10, quote p. 9.

93. Brückner, "Die Neuorganization von Frömmigkeit" *Jahrbuch für Volkskunde* N.F. 21 (1998): 9–10, quote p. 9.

94. Ernst Ludwig Grasmück, "Vom Presbyter zum Priester. Etappen der Entwicklung des neuzeitlichen Priesterbildes" in Paul Hoffmann, ed. *Priesterkirche* (Düsseldorf, 1987), pp. 126–127. On France, see especially Jean Delumeau, *Sin and Fear. The Emergence of Western Guilt Culture, 13th–18th Centuries* (New York, 1990) and John Bossy, *Christianity in the West, 1400–1700* (London, 1985).

95. Thomas DaCosta Kaufmann, *Court, Cloister, and City. The Art and Culture of Central Europe. 1450–1800* (Chicago, 1995), chap. 15; Henry-Russell Hitchcock, *Rococo Architecture in Southern Germany* (London, 1968); Hitchcock, *German Rococo. The Zimmermann Brothers* (London, 1968); Karsten Harries, *The Bavarian Rococo Church. Between Faith and Aesceticism*; R.J.W. Evans, "Kings and the Queen of the Arts" *The New York Review of Books*, Vol. 43, no. 9 (May 23, 1996), pp. 21–24.

96. Herrmann Tüchle, *Von der Reformation bis zur Säkularisation. Geschichte der katholischen Kirche im Raum des späteren Bistums Rottenburg-Stuttgart* (Ostfildern, 1981), pp. 248–249.

97. Peter Hersche, "Die südwestdeutschen Klosterterritorien am Ende des 18. Jahrhunderts. Versuch einer Bilanz" in Wolfgang Wüst, ed. *Geistliche Staaten in Oberdeutschland im Rahmen der Reichsverfassung. Kultur – Verfassung – Wirtschaft – Gesellschaft* (Epfendorf, 2002), p. 60.

98. Klaus Schreiner, "Mönchtum im Zeitalter des Barock. Der Beitrag der Klöster zur Kultur und Zivilisation Südwestdeutschlands im 17. und 18. Jahrhunderts" in Badisches Landesmuseum Karlruhe, ed., *Barock in Baden-Württemberg. Vom Ende des Dreißigjährigen Krieges bis zur Französischen Revolution*, Vol. 1, Katalog, Vol. 2, Aufsätze (Karlsruhe, 1981), p. 345.

99. Rainer A. Müller, "Kaisersäle in oberschwäbischen Reichsabteien. Wettenhausen, Kaisheim, Salem und Ottobeuren" in Wolfgang Wüst, ed. *Geistliche Staaten in Oberdeutschland*, pp. 305–327; Schreiner, "Mönchtum im Zeitalter des Barock," pp. 345–346.

100. Tüchle, *Von der Reformation bis zur Säkularisation*, p. 237.

101. Tüchle, *Von der Reformation bis zur Säkularisation*, p. 237.

102. Forster, *Catholic Revival*, pp. 95, 85–86, 230–233; Forster "Kirchenreform, katholische Konfessionalisierung und Dorfreligion um Kloster Salem, 1650–1750" *Rottenburger Jahrbuch für Kirchengeschichte* 16 (1997): 93–110.

103. Tüchle, *Von der Reformation bis zur Säkularisation*, pp. 243, 345–346.

104. Benno Hubensteiner, *Vom Geist des Barock. Kultur und Frömmigkeit im alten Bayern* (Munich, 1967), pp. 151–153.

105. Evans, *The Making of the Habsburg Monarchy*, p. 187.

106. Hsia, *Social Discipline in the Reformation*, p. 99; Schreiner, "Mönchtum im Zeitalter des Barock," pp. 346–347.

107. Schreiner, "Mönchtum im Zeitalter des Barock," p. 348.

108. Hubensteiner, *Vom Geist des Barock*, p. 158.

109. Derek Beales, *Prosperity and Plunder. European Catholic Monasteries in the Age of Revolution, 1650–1815* (Cambridge, 2003), pp. 46–47. Tüchle, *Von der Reformation bis zur Säkularisation*, pp. 226–230.

110. Hartmut Zückert, *Die sozialen Grundlagen der Barockkultur in Süddeutschland* (Stuttgart and New York, 1988).

111. Werner Freitag, *Volks und Elitenfrömmigkeit in der frühen Neuzeit* (Paderborn, 1991), pp. 215–216.

112. Ludwig Ohngemach, "Ehingen. Franziskaner" in Wolfgang Zimmermann and Nicole Priesching, eds. *Württembergisches Klosterbuch. Klöster, Stifte und Ordengemeinschaften von den Anfängen bis in die Gegenwart* (Ostfildern, 2003), pp. 217–218.

113. Andrea Polonyi, *Wenn mit Katakombenheiligen aus Rom neue Traditionen begründet werden* (St Ottilien, 1998), pp. 120–122.

114. Hubensteiner, *Vom Geist des Barock*, p. 157.

115. Tüchle, *Von der Reformation bis zur Säkularisation*, pp. 232–233.

116. Hersche, "Die südwestdeutschen Klosterterritorien am Ende des 18. Jahrhunderts," p. 58.

117. Alberich Siwek, *Die Zisterzienserabtei Salem. Der Orden, das Kloster, seine Äbte* (Sigmarigen, 1984), pp. 284–313.

118. Manfred Eder, "Die Zisterzienserinnen" in Friedhelm Jürgensmeier and Regina Elisabeth Schwerdtfeger, eds. *Orden und Klöster im Zeitalter von Reformation und katholischer Reform, 1500–1700*, Band I (Münster, 2005), pp. 119–120.

119. Anja Ostrowitzki, "Die Benediktinerinnnen" in Jürgensmeier and Schwerdtfeger, eds. *Orden und Klöster*, Band I, p. 65.

120. Ostrowitzki, "Die Benediktinerinnnen" in Jürgensmeier and Schwerdtfeger, eds. *Orden und Klöster*, Band I, p. 66.

121. Ulrike Strasser, "Cloistering Women's Past: Conflicting Accounts of Enclosure in a Seventeenth-Century Munich Nunnery" in Ulinka Rublack, ed. *Gender in Early Modern German History* (Cambridge, 2002), pp. 221–246; Ulrike Strasser, *State of Virginity. Gender, Religion, and Politics in an Early Modern Catholic State* (Ann Arbor, 2004).

122. Strasser, *State of Virginity*, chap. 5.

123. Strasser, *State of Virginity*, p. 172.

124. Anne Conrad, "Die Kölner Ursulagesellschaft und ihr 'weltgeistlicher Stand.' Eine weibliche Lebensform im Katholizismus der frühen Neuzeit" Wolfgang Reinhard and Heinz Schilling, eds. *Die katholische Konfessionalisierung* (Gütersloh, 1995), pp. 271–295. Anne Conrad, *Zwischen Kloster und Welt. Ursulinen und Jesuitinnen in der Katholischen Reformbewegung des 16./17. Jahrhunderts* (Mainz, 1991).

125. Conrad, "Die Kölner Ursulagesellschaft," pp. 288–289. Spiritual meal: *geistliches Abendmahl*. These kinds of female groups were not exceptional. See pp. 294–295.

126. GLAK 61/10498, 61/10501.

127. Bernhard Theil, "Buchau. Damenstift" in *Württembergisches Klosterbuch*, pp. 202–205; Bernhard Theil, "Das Damenstift Buchau am Federsee zwischen Kirche und Reich im Spätmittelalter und in der frühen Neuzeit" *Rottenburger Jahrbuch für Kirchengeschichte* 6 (1987): 155–167. The Swabian Cistercian houses of Heggbach, Gutenzell, Rottenmünster, and Baindt also achieved *Reichunmittelbar* (free Imperial) status: Tüchle, *Von der Reformation bis zur Säkularisation*, p. 235.

128. Thomas Weiland, "Kisslegg. Franziskaner-Terziarinnen" in *Württembergisches Klosterbuch*, pp. 306–307.

129. Winfried Assfalg, "Riedlingen. Franziskaner-Terziarinnen" in *Württembergisches Klosterbuch*, pp. 306–307.

130. Jörg Martin, "Munderkingen. Franziskaner-Terziarinnen" in *Württembergisches Klosterbuch*, pp. 356–358.

131. Ewald Gruber, "Saulgau. Franziskaner-Terziarinnen" in *Württembergisches Klosterbuch*, pp. 431–432.

132. Beales, *Prosperity and Plunder*, pp. 165–166.

133. There are few studies of the Jesuits in the post-Thirty Years' War period, compared to studies of the 1560–1620 period. Also, local and regional studies of this period rarely touch on the Jesuits.

134. Jeffrey Chipps Smith, *Sensuous Worship. Jesuit and the Art of the Early Catholic Reformation in Germany* (Princeton and Oxford, 2002), p. 103.

135. Hans Pfeifer, "Ellwangen. Jesuiten" in *Württembergisches Klosterbuch*, pp. 227–229.

136. Peter Rummel, "Jesuiten" in Brandmüller, ed. *Handbuch der bayerischen Kirchengeschichte*, pp. 843–845.

137. Dieter Manz, "Rottenburg. Jesuiten" in *Württembergisches Klosterbuch*, pp. 413–415.

138. Gerald Mager, "Rottweil. Jesuiten" in *Württembergisches Klosterbuch*, pp. 424–425. Dankwart Schmid, *Die Hauschronik der Jesuiten von Rottweil 1652–1773. Synopsis Historiae Domesticae Societatis Jesu Rottwilae* (Rottweil, 1989), esp. pp. 57–75.

139. Schmid, *Die Hauschronik der Jesuiten von Rottweil*, pp. 109–113.

140. Châtellier, *The Religion of the Poor*.

141. Forster, *The Counter-Reformation in the Villages*, p. 221.

142. Forster, *Catholic Revival*, pp. 223–226.

143. Châtellier, *The Religion of the Poor*; Rummel, "Jesuiten" in Brandmüller, ed. *Handbuch der bayerischen Kirchengeschichte*, pp. 853–854.

144. Hillard von Thiessen's book, although ostensibly a comparative study of two regions, is in fact a broad study and goes a long way toward correcting our lack of knowledge about the Capuchins in Germany. Hillard von Thiessen, *Die Kapuziner zwischen Konfessionalisierung und Alltagskultur. Vergleichende Fallstudie am Beispiel Freiburgs und Hildesheims, 1599–1750* (Freiburg im Breisgau, 2002).

145. Jendorff, *Reformatio Catholica*, p. 437. See also Forster, *Catholic Revival*, p. 226.

146. Hermann Schmid, "Bettel und Herrenklöster im Hochstift" in Kuhn et al., eds. *Die Bischöfe von Konstanz*, Vol. I, *Geschichte*, p. 232. See also "Capuchins" in *The Catholic Encyclopedia* (online) and the images in Matthias Ilg, "Der Kult des Kapuzinermärtyrers Fidelis von Sigmaringen als Ausdruck katholischer Kriegserfahrungen im dreissigjährigen Krieg" in Matthias Asche and Anton Schindling, eds. *Das Strafgericht Gottes. Kriegserfahrungen und Religion im Heiligen Römischen Reich Deutscher Nation im Zeitalter des Dreissigjährigen Krieges* (Münster, 2002), pp. 432–439.

147. Christian Plath, *Konfessionskampf und fremde Besatzung. Stadt und Hochstift Hildesheim im Zeitalter der Gegenreformation und des Dreißigjährigen Krieges (ca. 1580–1660)* (Münster, 2005), pp. 326–330.

148. Regina Pörtner, *The Counter-Reformation in Central Europe. Styria 1580–1630* (Oxford, 2001), pp. 233–238.

149. P. Beda Mayer, "Vorderösterreichische Kapuzinerprovinz" in *Der Franziskusorden. Die Kapuziner und Kapuzinerinnen in der Schweiz* [*Helvetia Sacra*, Section V, Vol. II, Part I] (Bern, 1974), p. 781.

150. Karl Hengst, ed. *Westfälisches Klosterbuch. Lexikon der von 1815 errichteten Stifte und Klöster von ihrer Gründung bis zur Aufhebung*, Teil 1 (Münster, 1992), pp. 203–206.

151. Ilg, "Der Kult des Kapuzinermärtyrers Fidelis von Sigmaringen" in Asche and Schindling, eds. *Das Strafgericht Gottes*, pp. 291–439.

152. Jendorff, *Reformatio Catholica*, pp. 440–441.

153. Forster, *Catholic Revival*, pp. 226–227.

154. Karl Hengst, ed. *Westfälisches Klosterbuch*, Teil 2, p. 100.

155. von Thiessen, *Die Kapuziner zwischen Konfessionalisierung und Alltagskultur*, pp. 145–154.

156. von Thiessen, *Die Kapuziner zwischen Konfessionalisierung und Alltagskultur*, pp. 162–166.

157. von Thiessen, *Die Kapuziner zwischen Konfessionalisierung und Alltagskultur*, pp. 226–251.

158. von Thiessen, *Die Kapuziner zwischen Konfessionalisierung und Alltagskultur*, pp. 35–36, 316–319, quote p. 473.

159. von Thiessen, *Die Kapuziner zwischen Konfessionalisierung und Alltagskultur*, pp. 411–449.

160. Lyndal Roper, "Witchcraft, Nostalgia, and the Rural Idyll in Eighteenth-Century Germany" *Past and Present* Supplement 1 (2006): 139–158.

161. Jendorff, *Reformatio Catholica*, pp. 442–443; Forster, *Catholic Revival*, pp. 227–228.

162. von Thiessen, *Die Kapuziner zwischen Konfessionalisierung und Alltagskultur*, pp. 69–79. The Capuchins faced similar opposition from the *Rat* in Münster when they came to that city in the 1610s. Karl Hengst, ed. *Westfälisches Klosterbuch*, Teil 2, p. 99.

163. Winfried Assfalg, "Riedlingen. Kapuziner" in *Württembergisches Klosterbuch*, pp. 399–400.

164. Winfried Hecht, "Rottweil. Kapuziner" in *Württembergisches Klosterbuch*, pp. 422–423.

Chapter 5: Baroque Catholicism

1. Brückner, "Die Neuorganisation von Frömmigkeit des Kirchenvolkes" *Jahrbuch für Volkskunde* N.F. 21 (1998): 7–32, esp.

p. 8; Wolfgang Brückner, "Zum Wandel der religiösen Kultur im 18. Jahrhundert. Einkreisungsversuche des 'Barockfrommen' zwischen Mittelalter und Massenmissionierung" in Ernst Hinrichs und Günter Wiegelmann, eds. *Sozialer und kultureller Wandel in der ländlichen Welt des 18. Jahrhunderts* (Wolfenbüttel, 1982), pp. 65–83.

2. Hartmut Lehmann, "Von der Erforschung der Säkularisierung zur Erforschung von Prozessen der Dechristianisierung und der Rechristianisierung im neuzeitlichen Europa" in Hartmut Lehmann, ed. *Säkularisierung, Dechristianisierung, Rechristianisierung im neuzeitlichen Europa* (Göttingen, 1997), p. 13.

3. Brückner, "Zum Wandel der religiösen Kultur im 18. Jahrhundert," p. 67. Alexander Jendorff argues some of these changes were already apparent before the Thirty Years' War: *Reformatio Catholica*, pp. 366–367.

4. Brückner, "Zum Wandel der religiösen Kultur im 18. Jahrhundert," p. 67; Forster, *Catholic Revival*, pp. 91–105; Rebekka Habermas, *Wallfahrt und Aufruhr: Zur Geschichte des Wunderglaubens in der frühen Neuzeit* (Frankfurt, 1991), chap. 3.

5. Forster, *Catholic Revival*, chap. 4.

6. Ludwig Veit and Ludwig Lenhart, *Kirche und Volksfrömmigkeit im Zeitalter des Barocks* (Freiburg, 1956), esp. chap. 1.

7. Veit and Lenhart, *Kirche und Volksfrömmigkeit*, chap. 2, quote p. 23.

8. Veit and Lenhart, *Kirche und Volksfrömmigkeit*, p. 33. *religiöse Schundware.*

9. Veit and Lenhart, *Kirche und Volksfrömmigkeit*, p. 35.

10. Brückner, "Die Neuorganisation von Frömmigkeit des Kirchenvolkes," p. 8.

11. Brückner, "Die Neuorganisation von Frömmigkeit," p. 8; Brückner, "Zum Wandel der religiösen Kultur im 18. Jahrhundert," p. 68.

12. Brückner, "Die Neuorganisation von Frömmigkeit," p. 9. See also Benno Hubensteiner, *Vom Geist des Barock. Kultur und Frömmigkeit im alten Bayern* (Munich, 1967), pp. 20–22.

13. Bireley, *The Refashioning of Catholicism*, p. 96.

14. See above Chapter 4.

15. Châtellier, *The Religion of the Poor*, pp. 80–82, 195–200; Forster, *Catholic Revival*, pp. 223–226.

16. Châtellier, *The Religion of the Poor*, p. 200.

17. Veit and Lenhart, *Kirche und Volksfrömmigkeit*, pp. 23–24.

18. Hermann Reifenberg, "Gottesdienstliches Leben" in Brandmüller, ed. *Handbuch der bayerischen Kirchengeschichte*, p. 617.

19. Forster, *Catholic Revival*, pp. 130–131; Reifenberg, "Gottesdienstliches Leben" in Brandmüller, ed. *Handbuch der bayerischen Kirchengeschichte*, p. 618. New rituals were published in Mainz (1671, 1695), Speyer (1719), Bamberg (1724/25), with further editions to about 1750.

20. Rev. H. J. Schroeder, *Canons and Decrees of the Council of Trent* (London, 1941), p. 151.

21. Becker, *Konfessionalisierung in Kurköln*, pp. 163–166; See also Veit and Lenhart, *Kirche und Volksfrömmigkeit*, p. 101.

22. Becker, *Konfessionalisierung in Kurköln*, p. 158; Joseph Jungmann, S. J. *The Mass of the Roman Rite: Its Origins and Development* (New York, 1961), pp. 141–151; John Bossy, "The Mass as a Social Institution, 1200–1700" *Past and Present* 100 (1983): 58–59; John Bossy, "The Counter-Reformation and the People of Catholic Europe" *Past and Present* 47 (1970): 68–69.

23. Hsia, *The World of Catholic Renewal*, p. 199.

24. Freitag, *Pfarrer, Kirche und ländliche Gemeinschaft*, p. 268.

25. Veit and Lenhart, *Kirche und Volksfrömmigkeit*, pp. 109–110. There are no systematic studies of this issue, but local studies indicate that frequent communion may have been more common on the borders between Catholic and Protestant regions, like Westphalia and Alsace, where if functioned as a *demonstratio Catholica*, and less common in solidly Catholic regions like the Rhineland.

26. John Bossy, "The Counter-Reformation and the People of Catholic Europe" *Past and Present* 47 (1970): 63–64.

27. Becker, *Konfessionalisierung in Kurköln*, pp. 57–60.

28. W. David Myers, *"Poor, Sinning Folk" Confession and Conscience in Counter-Reformation Germany* (Ithaca and London, 1996), pp. 133–143, quote p. 141.

29. Becker, *Konfessionalisierung in Kurköln*, pp. 169–170.

30. Veit and Lenhart, *Kirche und Volksfrömmigkeit*, pp. 113–115.

31. Veit and Lenhart, *Kirche und Volksfrömmigkeit*, p. 113.

32. Walter Pötzl, "Volksfrömmigkeit" in Brandmüller, ed. *Handbuch der bayerischen Kirchengeschichte*, pp. 954–956.

33. Brückner, "Die Neuorganisation von Frömmigkeit," p. 15.

34. Pötzl, "Volksfrömmigkeit" in Brandmüller, ed. *Handbuch der bayerischen Kirchengeschichte*, p. 956.

35. Freitag, *Pfarrer, Kirche und ländliche Gemeinschaft*, p. 270.

36. Bossy, "The Mass as a Social Institution, 1200–1700" *Past and Present* 100 (1983): 59.

37. Louis Châtellier, *Tradition chrétienne et renouveau catholique dans le cadre de l'ancien Diocèse de Strasbourg (1650–1770)* (Paris, 1981), pp. 441–446, 451–455.

38. Holzem, *Religion und Lebensformen*, pp. 250–255.

39. Becker, *Konfessionalisierung in Kurköln*, p. 52; See also Werner Freitag, "Tridentinische Pfarrer und die Kirche im Dorf. Ein Plädoyer für die Beibehaltung der etatistischen Perspektive" in Norbert Haag, Sabine Holtz, and Wolfgang Zimmermann, eds. *Ländliche Frömmigkeit. Konfessionskulturen und Lebenswelten, 1500–1850* (Stuttgart, 2002), p. 105.

40. Châtellier, *Tradition chrétienne et renouveau catholique*, pp. 440–446.

41. von Greyerz, *Religion und Kultur*, p. 75.

42. Brückner, "Die Neuorganisation von Frömmigkeit," pp. 21–22; Robert Scribner, "Ritual and Popular Religion in Catholic Germany at the Time of the Reformation" in *Popular Culture and Popular Movements in the Reformation* (London, 1987), p. 20.

43. Wolfgang Zimmermann, "Städtische Frömmigkeit und barocke Konfessionskultur in Konstanz" in *Christoph Daniel Schenck. 1633–1691* (Sigmaringen, 1996), pp. 36–38.

44. Evans, *The Making of the Habsburg Monarchy*, pp. 188–189.

45. Pötzl, "Volksfrömmigkeit" in Brandmüller, ed. *Handbuch der bayerischen Kirchengeschichte*, pp. 918–928; Andrea Polonyi, "Reliquientranslationen in oberschwäbische Benediktinerklöster als Ausdruck barocker Frömmigkeit" *Rottenburger Jahrbuch für Kirchengeschichte* 9 (1990): 77–84; Strasser, *State of Virginity*, pp. 136–148.

46. Polonyi, "Reliquientranslationen in oberschwäbische Benediktinerklöster," pp. 81–82.

47. Polonyi, "Reliquientranslationen in oberschwäbische Benediktinerklöster," p. 83.

48. Pötzl, "Volksfrömmigkeit" in Brandmüller, ed. *Handbuch der bayerischen Kirchengeschichte*, p. 919.

49. Polonyi, "Reliquientranslationen in oberschwäbische Benediktinerklöster," p. 83.

50. Scribner, "Ritual and Popular Religion in Catholic Germany at the Time of the Reformation," pp. 19–20.

51. Peter Hersche, "Wider 'Müssiggang' und 'Ausschweifung.' Feiertage und ihre Reduktion im katholischen Europa, namentlich im deutschsprachigen Raum zwischen 1750 und 1800" *Innsbrucker Historische Studien* 12/13 (1990): 99–101.

52.   Anna Coreth, *Pietas Austriaca*, translated by William Bowman and
      Anna Maria Leitgab (Bloomington, 2004), pp. 45–50.
53.   Forster, *Catholic Revival*, p. 113.
54.   Scribner, "Ritual and Popular Religion in Catholic Germany," p. 23;
      Pötzl, "Volksfrömmigkeit" in Brandmüller, ed. *Handbuch der bayer-
      ischen Kirchengeschichte*, pp. 954–956.
55.   Pötzl, "Volksfrömmigkeit" in Brandmüller, ed. *Handbuch der bayer-
      ischen Kirchengeschichte*, p. 954.
56.   Veit and Lenhart, *Kirche und Volksfrömmigkeit*, pp. 145–147.
57.   Becker, *Konfessionalisierung in Kurköln*, pp. 296–298.
58.   Veit and Lenhart, *Kirche und Volksfrömmigkeit*, pp. 174–175.
59.   Heinrich Schrörs, "Religiöse Gebräuche in der alten Erzdiözese
      Köln; ihre Ausartung und Bekämpfung im 17. und 18.
      Jahrhunderts" *Annalen des historischen Vereins für den Niederrhein* 82
      (1907): 158.
60.   Erzbischöfliches Archiv Freiburg (EAF) A1/742 (1788, 26 October).
61.   Forster, *Catholic Revival*, p. 115.
62.   Hermann Hörger, "Organizational Forms of Popular Piety in Rural
      Old Bavaria (Sixteenth to Nineteenth Centuries)" in Kaspar von
      Greyerz, ed. *Religion and Society in Early Modern Europe 1500–1800*
      (London, 1984), p. 213.
63.   Andreas Holzem, "Religiöse Erfahrung auf dem Dorf. Der soziale
      Rahmen religiöse Erlebens im Münsterland der Frühneuzeit" in
      Norbert Haag, Sabine Holtz, and Wolfgang Zimmermann, eds.
      Ländliche Frömmigkeit. Konfessionskultur und Lebenswelten 1500–1850
      (Stuttgart, 2002), pp. 181–205.
64.   Veit and Lenhart, *Kirche und Volksfrömmigkeit*, p. 23.
65.   Bossy, "The Counter-Reformation and the People of Catholic
      Europe" *Past and Present* 47 (1970): 57–58.
66.   Hans Krawarik, "Neue Methoden zur Erforschung konfessioneller
      Strukturen der Frühen Neuzeit" *Archiv für Kulturgeschichte* 70
      (1988): 377.
67.   Holzem, *Religion und Lebensformen*, pp. 424–426.
68.   Freitag, *Pfarrer, Kirche und ländliche Gemeinschaft*, p. 272.
69.   Becker, *Konfessionalisierung in Kurköln*, pp. 295–296.
70.   Holzem, *Religion und Lebensformen*, pp. 425–432.
71.   Holzem, *Religion und Lebensformen*, p. 427.
72.   Quoted in Holzem, *Religion und Lebensformen*, p. 428.
73.   Forster, *Catholic Revival*, pp. 108–109, 183–184, 199–206, 212.

74. See above, Chapter 2. Marriage literature, especially: Harrington, *Reordering Marriage and Society in Reformation Germany*; Strasser, *State of Virginity*, esp. chap. 1.

75. von Greyerz, *Religion und Kultur*, pp. 189–190.

76. Holzem, *Religion und Lebensformen*, p. 439.

77. Karant-Nunn, *Reformation of Ritual*, p. 9.

78. Reifenberg, "Gottesdienstliches Leben" in Brandmüller, ed. *Handbuch der bayerischen Kirchengeschichte*, pp. 631–632.

79. Becker, *Konfessionalisierung in Kurköln*, pp. 290–291.

80. Holzem, *Religion und Lebensformen*, pp. 341–359.

81. Peter Zschunke, *Konfession und Alltag in Oppenheim* (Wiesbaden, 1984), p. 103.

82. François, *Die unsichtbare Grenze*.

83. Peter Wallace, *Communities and Conflict in Early Modern Colmar: 1575–1730* (Atlantic Highlands NJ, 1995), chap. 7.

84. Forster, *Catholic Revival*, p. 108, Veit and Lenhart, *Kirche und Volksfrömmigkeit*, pp. 24–25.

85. Holzem, *Religion und Lebensformen*, pp. 434–435; Freitag, *Pfarrer, Kirche und ländliche Gemeinschaft*, p. 274.

86. Forster, *Catholic Revival*, pp. 109, 183–184, 204, 212.

87. Holzem, *Religion und Lebensformen*, pp. 436–438.

88. Reifenberg, "Gottesdienstliches Leben" in Brandmüller, ed. *Handbuch der bayerischen Kirchengeschichte*, p. 631.

89. Freitag, *Pfarrer, Kirche und ländliche Gemeinschaft*, p. 274.

90. Freitag, *Pfarrer, Kirche und ländliche Gemeinschaft*, p. 274, Holzem, *Religion und Lebensformen*, pp. 438–439.

91. Holzem, *Religion und Lebensformen*, p. 384.

92. Holzem, *Religion und Lebensformen*, p. 390. See also, Forster; *The Counter-Reformation in the Villages*, p. 115; Forster, *Catholic Revival*, p. 125.

93. Holzem, *Religion und Lebensformen*, pp. 390–397.

94. Holzem, "Religiöse Erfahrung auf dem Dorf," p. 195.

95. Becker, *Konfessionalisierung in Kurköln*, pp. 157–162. Becker argues that parish services may have gotten quite boring, as the faithful were expected to be passive observers (pp. 157–158).

96. Forster, *Catholic Revival*, p. 125.

97. Forster, *Catholic Revival*, pp. 157–167.

98. Forster, *Catholic Revival*, pp. 160–161.

99. Forster, *Catholic Revival*, pp. 133–146.

100. Forster, *Catholic Revival*, p. 143.

101. Louis Châtellier, *Europe of the Devout*, pp. 194–199, quote pp. 196–197.

102. Châtellier, *Europe of the Devout*, pp. 204–207, quote p. 205. Known as the *Todesangst Bruderschaften*, "fear of death brotherhoods."

103. Anna Coreth, *Liebe ohne Mass. Geschichte der Herz-Jesu-Verehrung in Österreich im 18. Jahrhundert* (Salterrae, 1994), pp. 47–52.

104. Coreth, *Liebe ohne Mass*, pp. 64–73.

105. Pötzl, "Volksfrömmigkeit" in Brandmüller, ed. *Handbuch der bayerischen Kirchengeschichte*, p. 932.

106. Becker, *Konfessionalisierung in Kurköln*, pp. 190–192.

107. Forster, *Catholic Revival*, pp. 138–139.

108. Pötzl, "Volksfrömmigkeit" in Brandmüller, ed. *Handbuch der bayerischen Kirchengeschichte*, p. 932.

109. Raab, "Gegenreformation und katholische Reform im Erzbistum und Erzstift Trier (1567–1711)" *Römische Quartalschrift* 81 (1989), p. 183.

110. Veit and Lenhart, *Kirche und Volksfrömmigkeit*, pp. 27–35, 204–208.

111. von Greyerz, *Religion und Kultur*, pp. 74–75.

112. Dieter Weiß, "Die Geistliche Regierung. Franken, 1648–1803" in Brandmüller, ed. *Handbuch der bayerischen Kirchengeschichte*, pp. 428–429.

113. Kaufmann, *Court, Cloister, and City*, p. 367.

114. Weiß, "Die Geistliche Regierung. Franken, 1648–1803" in Brandmüller, ed. *Handbuch der bayerischen Kirchengeschichte*, p. 434.

115. Volker Himmelein, "Das Zeitalter des Barock in Baden-Württemberg" in Himmelein et al., eds. *Barock in Baden-Württemberg* (Stuttgart, 1981), p. 12.

116. Kaufmann, *Court, Cloister, and City*, p. 371.

117. Forster, *Catholic Revival*, pp. 61–75; Brückner, "Die Neuorganisation von Frömmigkeit," pp. 18–20. These areas were "*Bildstocklandschaften.*"

118. Holzem, *Religion und Lebensformen*, pp. 237–260. Freitag, "Tridentinische Pfarrer und die Kirche im Dorf" in Norbert Haag, Sabine Holtz, and Wolfgang Zimmermann, eds. *Ländliche Frömmigkeit. Konfessionskulturen und Lebenswelten, 1500–1850* (Stuttgart, 2002), pp. 102–106.

119. Becker, *Konfessionalisierung in Kurköln*, pp. 36–76, esp. 37–38.

120. Holzem, "Religiöse Erfahrung aud dem Dorf," p. 195. See also Ursula Olschewski, "Der Einfluß der geistlichen Gemeinschaften auf Volksfrömmigkeit und religiöse Brauchtum" in Hengst, ed. *Westfälisches Klosterbuch*; pp. 403–434.

121. Freitag, *Volks- und Elitenfrömmigkeit*, p. 211.

122. Brückner, "Die Neuorganisation von Frömmigkeit," p. 14. In Franconia, going on procession to shrines was called *Wallen*; in Bavaria *Kirchfahrten*.
123. Brückner, "Die Neuorganisation von Frömmigkeit," pp. 13–15, quote p. 15.
124. Dünninger, *Maria siegt in Franken*, pp. 78–81.
125. Dünninger, *Maria siegt in Franken*, pp. 83–87.
126. Dünninger, *Maria siegt in Franken*, pp. 89–90.
127. See, for example, Brückner, *Die Verehrung des Heiligen Blutes in Walldürn*; Pötzl, "Volksfrömmigkeit" in Brandmüller, ed. *Handbuch der bayerischen Kirchengeschichte*, pp. 945–947.
128. Forster, *Catholic Revival*, pp. 91–105.
129. Châtellier, *Tradition chrétienne et renouveau catholique*, p. 446.
130. Pötzl, "Volksfrömmigkeit" in Brandmüller, ed. *Handbuch der bayerischen Kirchengeschichte*, p. 939.
131. Habermas, *Wallfahrt und Aufruhr*, pp. 77–90.
132. Forster, *Catholic Revival*, p. 94.
133. *Kurzkataloge der volkstümlichen Kult- und Andachtsstätten der Erzdiözese Freiburg und der Diözesen Limburg, Mainz, Rottenburg-Stuttgart und Speyer* (Würzburg, 1982).
134. Forster, *Catholic Revival*, p. 93, with further literature.
135. Forster, *Catholic Revival*, pp. 93, 95.
136. Pötzl, "Volksfrömmigkeit" in Brandmüller, ed. *Handbuch der bayerischen Kirchengeschichte*, pp. 935–939.
137. Pötzl, "Volksfrömmigkeit" in Brandmüller, ed. *Handbuch der bayerischen Kirchengeschichte*, p. 938.
138. Forster, *Catholic Revival*, p. 117.
139. Becker, *Konfessionalisierung in Kurköln*, pp. 199–225, quote p. 222.
140. Werner Freitag's study focuses on only six shrines in the Bishopric of Münster: Freitag, *Volks- und Elitenfrömmigkeit*. Andreas Holzem's enormous study of Catholicism in Münster hardly discusses pilgrimage and procession: Holzem, *Religion und Lebensformen*. On shrines in Germany more generally, see Lionel Rothkrug, "Popular Religion and Holy Shrines. Their Influence on the Origins of the German Reformation and their Role in German Cultural Development" in *Religion and the People, 800–1700*, James Obelkevich, ed. (Chapel Hill, 1979).
141. Veit and Lenhart, *Kirche und Volksfrömmigkeit*, p. 63.
142. Freitag, *Volks- und Elitenfrömmigkeit*, p. 211; Pötzl, "Volksfrömmigkeit" in Brandmüller, ed. *Handbuch der bayerischen Kirchengeschichte*, p. 941.
143. Forster, *Catholic Revival*, pp. 96–97.

144. Forster, *Catholic Revival*, pp. 97–102.

145. Habermas, *Wallfahrt und Aufruhr*, pp. 46–66.

146. Juliane Roh, *Ich hab wunderbare Hilf erlangt. Votivbilder* (Munich, 1957), pp. 20–21; see also pp. 34–35.

147. Roh, *Ich hab wunderbare Hilf erlangt*, pp. 26–27.

148. Brückner, *Die Verehrung des Heiligen Blutes in Walldürn*, pp. 98–108.

149. Brückner, *Die Verehrung des Heiligen Blutes in Walldürn*, p. 102; Pötzl, "Volksfrömmigkeit" in Brandmüller, ed. *Handbuch der bayerischen Kirchengeschichte*, p. 946.

150. Pötzl, "Volksfrömmigkeit" in Brandmüller, ed. *Handbuch der bayerischen Kirchengeschichte*, p. 936; Forster, *Catholic Revival*, pp. 97–102.

151. Brückner, *Die Verehrung des Heiligen Blutes in Walldürn*, p. 98.

152. Becker, *Konfessionalisierung in Kurköln*, p. 220; Pötzl, "Volksfrömmigkeit" in Brandmüller, ed. *Handbuch der bayerischen Kirchengeschichte*, p. 935.

153. Habermas, *Wallfahrt und Aufruhr* and Kristiane Schmalfeldt, "Sub tuum praesidium confugimus. Unser Leibe Frau in der Tanne zu Triberg" *Freiburger Diözesan Archiv* 108 (1988): 1–302 are two good examples.

154. Habermas, *Wallfahrt und Aufruhr*, p. 29.

155. Habermas, *Wallfahrt und Aufruhr*, pp. 35–44.

156. Habermas, *Wallfahrt und Aufruhr*, pp. 34–35, 44.

157. Brückner, *Die Verehrung des Heiligen Blutes in Walldürn*, Dünninger, *Maria siegt in Franken*.

158. Forster, *Catholic Revival*, pp. 97–102.

159. Freitag, *Volks- und Elitenfrömmigkeit*, esp. pp. 218–230.

160. Forster, *The Counter-Reformation in the Villages*, pp. 120–129.

161. Strasser, *State of Virginity*, pp. 132–135, quote p. 135.

162. Wilfried Enderle, *Konfessionsbildung und Ratsregiment in der katholischen Reichsstadt Überlingen (1500–1618)* (Stuttgart, 1990), esp. pp. 377–384. Forster, *Catholic Revival*, pp. 52–53.

163. On the communal church: Blickle, *The Revolution of 1525*; Blickle, *Communal Reformation*; Blickle, ed. *Zugänge zur bäuerlichen Reformation*; Conrad, *Reformation in der bäuerlichen Gesellschaft*; Scribner, "Communalism" *Historical Journal* 37, no. 1 (1994): 199–207; Fuhrmann, *Kirche und Dorf*; Forster, *Counter-Reformation in the Villages*, esp. chap. 1. On communes and communalism more generally, Heide Wunder, *Die bäuerliche Gemeinde in Deutschland* and Robert Scribner, "Communities and the Nature of Power" in Robert Scribner, ed. *Germany: A New Social and Economic History*, Vol. 1, pp. 1450–1600.

164. Forster, *Catholic Revival*, esp. chap. 5. See also Jendorff, *Reformatio Catholica*, pp. 327–329.
165. Forster, *Catholic Revival*, p. 189.
166. For the Swiss region of Graubünden (Grisons, Grey Leagues), see Immacolata Saulle Hippenmeyer, *Nachbarschaft, Pfarrei und Gemeinde in Graubünden 1400–1600* (Desertina, 1997).
167. Freitag, *Pfarrer, Kirche und ländliche Gemeinschaft*, chap. 8.
168. Freitag, *Pfarrer, Kirche und ländliche Gemeinschaft*, p. 309.
169. Châtellier, *Tradition chrétienne et renouveau catholique*, pp. 455–460.
170. von Greyerz, *Religion und Kultur*, pp. 190–203.
171. von Greyerz, *Religion und Kultur*, p. 199. [*dass religiöse Erfahrung in der Frühen Neuzeit ganz wesentlich durch die Prioritäten des Alltagsleben hindurchgefiltert wurde*].
172. Hörger, *Kirche, Dorfreligion und bäuerliche Gesellschaft*.
173. Holzem, *Religion und Lebensformen*, p. 439.
174. Richard van Dülmen, *Kultur und Alltag in der frühen Neuzeit. Dritter III. Religion, Magie, Aufklärung. 16–18. Jahrhundert* (Munich, 1994).
175. Much of the below is based on my earlier effort at this analysis: Marc R. Forster, "With and Without Confessionalization. Varieties of Early Modern German Catholicism" *Journal of Early Modern History* 1, 4 (1998): 340–343. I also attempted to characterize regional differences within Southwest Germany: Forster, *Catholic Revival*, pp. 233–240.
176. Ursula Olschewski, "Der Einfluß der geistlichen Gemeinschaften auf Volksfrömmigkeit und religiöse Brauchtum" in Hengst, ed. *Westfälisches Klosterbuch*, pp. 403–434.
177. See Rothkrug, summarized in: "Popular Religion and Holy Shrines" in Obelkevich, ed. *Religion and the People, 800–1700* (Chapel Hill, 1979). William Christian, *Local Religion in Sixteenth Century Spain* makes a similar point about Spain.

Chapter 6: German Catholicism in the Late Eighteenth Century

1. Peter Burke, *Popular Culture in Early Modern Europe* (New York, 1978).
2. Châtellier, *Religion of the Poor*, p. 147.
3. Beales, *Prosperity and Plunder*, pp. 80–81.
4. Forster, *Catholic Revival*, pp. 172–173.
5. Beales, *Prosperity and Plunder*, pp. 36–37, 68; Châtellier, *Religion of the Poor*, pp. 211–214; T.C.W. Blanning, "The Enlightenment in Catholic Germany" in Roy Porter and Mikulaus Teich, eds. *The*

242 NOTES

Enlightenment in National Context (Cambridge, 1981), pp. 119, 121;
James Van Horn Melton, "From Image to Word: Cultural Reform
and the Rise of Literate Culture in Eighteenth-Century Austria"
Journal of Modern History 58 (1986): 112–115.

6.   Châtellier, *Religion of the Poor*, p. 213. Quote from Muratori's *Della regolata divozione dei Cristiani* (1768).

7.   Derek Beales, *Joseph II. In the Shadow of Maria Theresa, 1741–1780* (Cambridge, 1987), p. 474.

8.   *Catholic Encyclopedia*, 1912 edition (online); Philipp Schäfer, "Theologische Wissenschaft" in Brandmüller, ed. *Handbuch der bayerischen Kirchengeschichte*, pp. 520–521.

9.   Châtellier, *Religion of the Poor*, pp. 214–215.

10.   Schäfer, "Theologische Wissenschaft" in Brandmüller, ed. *Handbuch der bayerischen Kirchengeschichte*, pp. 521, 528–529.

11.   Châtellier, *Religion of the Poor*, p. 215.

12.   Peter G. Tropper, "Pastorale Erneuerungsbestrebungen des süddeutsch-österreichischen Episcopats im 18. Jahrhundert. Hirtenbriefe als Quellen der Kirchenreform" in Erwin Gatz et al., eds. *Der Episcopat des Hl. Römischen Reichs 1648–1803* (Rome, Freiburg, Vienna, 1988) (*Römische Quartalschrift für Alterskunde und Kirchengeschichte*, 83, 1988), p. 304.

13.   Melton, "From Image to Word" *Journal of Modern History* 58 (1986): 114.

14.   Harm Kleuting, "Einleitung: Aufklärung und Katholizismus in Deutschland des 18. Jahrhunderts" in Harm Klueting, ed. *Katholische Aufklärung – Aufklärung im katholischen Deutschland* (Hamburg, 1993), pp. 10–12.

15.   Blanning, "The Enlightenment in Catholic Germany" in Porter and Teich, eds. *The Enlightenment in National Context*, p. 120.

16.   Forster, *Catholic Revival*, pp. 97–102.

17.   Beales, *Prosperity and Plunder*, pp. 162–163. See also Charles Ingrao, *The Habsburg Monarchy 1618–1815* (Cambridge, 1994), pp. 166–168.

18.   Schmid, "Altbayern" in Brandmüller, ed. *Handbuch der bayerischen Kirchengeschichte*, pp. 328–329; Weiß, "Franken 2648–1803: Die geistliche Regierung" in Brandmüller, ed. *Handbuch der bayerischen Kirchengeschichte*, pp. 444–445.

19.   Winifried Müller, "Der Jesuitenorden und die Aufklärung in süddeutschen-österreichischen Raum" in Harm Klueting, ed. *Katholische Aufklärung – Aufklärung im katholischen Deutschland* (Hamburg, 1993), pp. 225–244. There is some irony in this since the Jesuits had

favored a more internalized, individual Catholicism in the late six-teenth century.

20. Michael Printy, "Perfect Societies: German States and the Roman Catholic Revolution, 1648–1806" Dissertation, University of California, Berkeley, 2002; Blanning, "The Enlightenment in Catholic Germany" in Porter and Teich, eds. *The Enlightenment in National Context*, pp. 119–120.

21. Marc Forster, "Febronianism" *Dictionary of Early Modern History*.

22. Harm Kleuting, "Einleitung: Aufklärung und Katholizismus in Deutschland des 18. Jahrhunderts" in Klueting, ed. *Katholische Aufklärung – Aufklärung im katholischen Deutschland*, pp. 17–18.

23. Kleuting, "Einleitung: Aufklärung und Katholizismus in Deutschland des 18. Jahrhunderts" in Klueting, ed. *Katholische Aufklärung – Aufklärung im katholischen Deutschland*, pp. 19–20.

24. Paul Münch, *Lebensformen in der frühen Neuzeit* (Berlin, 1998), p. 363.

25. Peter Hersche, "Wider 'Müssigang' und 'Ausschweifung.' Feiertage und ihre Reduktion im katholischen Europa, namentlich im deutschsprachigen Raum zwischen 1750 und 1800" *Innsbrucker Historische Studien* 12/13 (1990): 107.

26. Quoted in Paul Münch, *Lebensformen in der frühen Neuzeit* (Berlin, 1998), pp. 363–364.

27. Münch, *Lebensformen in der frühen Neuzeit* (Berlin, 1998), pp. 366–368, quote p. 366.

28. Hersche, "Wider 'Müssigang' und 'Ausschweifung'" *Innsbrucker Historische Studien* 12/13 (1990): 100–102, 106–107.

29. Hersche, "Wider 'Müssigang' und 'Ausschweifung'" *Innsbrucker Historische Studien* 12/13 (1990): 108–109; H. C. Erik Midelfort, *Exorcism and Enlightenment. Johann Joseph Gassner and the Demons of Eighteenth Century Germany* (New Haven and London, 2005), p. 42.

30. There is a massive amount of work on Joseph II. See Beales, *Joseph II*.

31. Beales, *Prosperity and Plunder*, chap. 6.

32. Beales, *Prosperity and Plunder*, pp. 192–204.

33. Forster, *Catholic Revival*; Eva Kimminich, *Religiöse Volksbräuche im Räderwerk der Obrigkeiten. Ein Beitrag zu Auswirkung aufklärerischer Reformprogramme am Oberrhein und in Vorarlberg* (Frankfurt am Main, 1989).

34. Hersche, "Wider 'Müssigang' und 'Ausschweifung.'" *Innsbrucker Historische Studien* 12/13 (1990), pp. 117–118.

35. Eva Kimminich, *Religiöse Volksbräuche*, pp. 128–129.

36. Hersche, "Wider 'Müssigang' und 'Ausschweifung.'" *Innsbrucker Historische Studien* 12/13 (1990), pp. 118–121.

37. Quoted in Münch, *Lebensformen in der frühen Neuzeit* (Berlin, 1998), p. 365. Another version in Peter Hersche, "'Lutherisch Werden' – Reconfessionalisierung als paradoxe Folge aufgeklärter Religionspolitik" in Gerhard Ammerer and Hanns Haas eds. *Ambivalenzen der Aufklärung. Festschrift für Ernst Wangemann* (Munich, 1997), pp. 155–156.

38. Quoted in Hersche, "'Lutherisch werden'" in Ammerer and Haas eds. *Ambivalenzen der Aufklärung* (Munich, 1997), p. 155.

39. Hersche, "Lutherisch Werden" in Ammerer and Haas eds. *Ambivalenzen der Aufklärung* (Munich, 1997), pp. 157–159.

40. Kimminich, *Religiöse Volksbräuche*, pp. 21–22.

41. Forster, *Catholic Revival.*

42. Hersche, "Lutherisch Werden" in Ammerer and Haas eds. *Ambivalenzen der Aufklärung* (Munich, 1997), pp. 163–164.

43. Rudolf Schlögl, "Rationalisierung als Entsinnlichung religiöser Praxis? Zur sozialen und medialen Form von Religion in der Neuzeit" in Peter Blickle and Rudolf Schlögl, eds. *Die Säkularisation im Prozess der Säkularisierung Europas* (Epfendorf, 2005), p. 51.

44. Andreas Holzem, "Säkularisation in Oberschwaben. Ein Problemgeschichtlicher Abriss" in Blickle and Schlögl, eds. *Die Säkularisation im Prozess der Säkularisierung Europas*; 261–315, esp. pp. 267–268.

45. Beales, *Prosperity and Plunder*, p. 301.

46. Blanning, "The Enlightenment in Catholic Germany" in Porter and Teich, eds. *The Enlightenment in National Context*, pp. 122–126.

47. Rudolf Schlögl, *Glaube und Religion in der Säkularisierung. Die katholische Stadt – Köln, Aachen, Münster – 1700–1840* (Munich, 1995).

48. Schlögl, *Glaube und Religion in der Säkularisierung*, p. 281.

49. Schlögl, *Glaube und Religion in der Säkularisierung*, p. 333.

50. Schlögl, *Glaube und Religion in der Säkularisierung*, p. 335.

51. Michael Pammer, *Glaubensabfall und wahre Andacht. Barock Religiosität, Reformkatholizismus und Laizismus in Oberösterreich, 1700–1820* (Munich, 1994).

52. Pammer, *Glaubensabfall und wahre Andacht*, pp. 24–25.

53. Pammer, *Glaubensabfall und wahre Andacht*, pp. 263, 277–279.

54. Holzem, "Säkularisation in Oberschwaben" in Blickle and Schlögl, eds. *Die Säkularisation im Prozess der Säkularisierung Europas*, p. 281.

55. Holzem, "Säkularisation in Oberschwaben" in Blickle and Schlögl, eds. *Die Säkularisation im Prozess der Säkularisierung Europas*, p. 262.

56. Holzem, "Säkularisation in Oberschwaben" in Blickle and Schlögl, eds. *Die Säkularisation im Prozess der Säkularisierung Europas*, p. 268.

Conclusion

1. See Margaret Lavinia Anderson, "The Limits of Secularization: on the Problem of the Catholic Revival in Nineteenth-Century Germany" *Historical Journal* 38 (1995): 647–670; David Blackbourn, *Class, Religion and Local Politics in Wilhelmine Germany. The Centre Party in Württemberg before 1914* (New Haven, 1980); David Blackbourn, *Marpingen, Apparitions of the Virgin Mary in Nineteenth-Century Germany* (New York, 1994); Helmut Walser Smith, "Religion and Conflict: Protestants, Catholics, and Anti-Semitism in the State of Baden in the Era of Wilhelm II" *Central European History*, 27, 3 (1994): 288–314.

2. See Thomas A. Brady, Jr. "Confessionalization – The Career of a Concept" in John M. Headley, Hans J. Hillderbrand, and Anthony J. Papalas, eds. *Confessionalization in Europe, 1555–1700. Essays in Honor and Memory of Bodo Nischan* (Aldershot, 2004), esp. pp. 19–20.

Bibliography

Bast, Robert James, *Honor your Fathers. Catechisms and the Emergence of a Patriarchal Ideology in Germany, 1400–1600*, Leiden, Boston, Cologne: Brill, 1997.

Beales, Derek, *Prosperity and Plunder. European Catholic Monasteries in the Age of Revolution, 1650–1815*, Cambridge University Press, 2003.

Behringer, Wolfgang, *Witchcraft Persecutions in Bavaria. Religious Zealotry and Reason of State in Early Modern Europe*, Cambridge University Press, 1987.

Bireley, Robert, *The Refashioning of Catholicism, 1450–1700. A Reassessment of the Counter-Reformation*, Washington: Catholic University Press, 1999.

Bireley, Robert, *The Jesuits and the Thirty Years War. Kings, Courts, and Confessors*, Cambridge University Press, 2003.

Blickle, Peter, *The Revolution of 1525. The German Peasants' War in New Perspective*, Baltimore: Johns Hopkins University Press, 1981.

Blickle, Peter, *Communal Reformation: The Quest for Salvation in Sixteenth-Century Germany*, New Jersey: Humanities Press, 1992.

Bossy, John, "The Counter-Reformation and the People of Catholic Europe" *Past and Present* 47 (1970): 51–70.

Bossy, John, *Christianity in the West, 1400–1700*, Oxford University Press, 1985.

Bossy, John, *Peace in the Post-Reformation*, Cambridge University Press, 1998.

Brandmüller, Walter (ed.), *Handbuch der bayerischen Kirchengeschichte*, Vol. II, *Von der Glaubenspaltung bis zur Säkularisation*, St. Ottilien: EOS Verlag, 1993.

Châtellier, Louis, *Europe of the Devout. The Catholic Reformation and the Formation of a New Society*, Cambridge University Press, 1989.

Châtellier, Louis, *The Religion of the Poor. Rural Missions in Europe and the Formation of Modern Catholicism, c.1500–c.1800*, Cambridge University Press, 1997.

Coreth, Anna, *Pietas Austriaca: österreichische Frömmigkeit im Barock*, Munich: Oldenbourg, 1982.

Delumeau, Jean, *Catholicism between Luther and Voltaire: A New View of the Counter-Reformation*, London: Burns and Oates, 1977.

Evans, R. J. W., *The Making of the Habsburg Monarchy, 1500–1700*, Oxford University Press, 1979.

Forster, Marc R., *The Counter-Reformation in the Villages. Religion and Reform in the Bishopric of Speyer, 1560–1720*, Ithaca and London: Cornell University Press, 1992.

Forster, Marc R., "With and Without Confessionalization: Varieties of Early Modern German Catholicism" *Journal of Early Modern History* 1, 4 (1998); 315–343.

Forster, Marc R., *Catholic Revival in the Age of the Baroque. Religious Identity in Southwest Germany, 1550–1750*, Cambridge University Press, 2001.

François, Étienne, *Die unsichtbare Grenze. Protestanten und Katholiken in Augsburg, 1648–1806*, Sigmaringen: Thorbecke, 1991.

Harries, Karsten, *The Bavarian Rococco Church. Between Faith and Aesceticism*, New Haven: Yale University Press, 1983.

Harrington, Joel, *Reordering Marriage and Society in Reformation Germany*, Cambridge University Press, 1995.

Harrington, Joel F. and Smith, Helmut Walser, "Confessionalization, Community, and State Building in Germany, 1555–1870" *The Journal of Modern History* 69 (1997): 77–101.

Holzem, Andreas, *Religion und Lebensformen. Katholische Konfessionalisierung im Sendgericht des Fürstbistums Münster 1570–1800*, Paderborn: Ferdinand Schöningh, 2000.

Hsia, R. Po-Chia, *Society and Religion in Münster: 1535–1618*, New Haven: Yale University Press, 1984.

Hsia, R. Po-Chia, *Social Discipline in the Reformation: Central Europe 1550–1750*, London and New York: Routledge, 1989.

Hsia, R. Po-chia, *The World of Catholic Renewal. 1540–1770*, Cambridge University Press, 1998.

Karant-Nunn, Susan, *The Reformation of Ritual. An Interpretation of Early Modern Germany*, London and New York: Routledge, 1997.

Kaufmann, Thomas DaCosta, *Court, Cloister, and City. The Art and Culture of Central Europe. 1450–1800*, University of Chicago Press, 1995.

Leonard, Amy, *Nails in the Wall. Catholic Nuns in Reformation Germany*, Chicago: University of Chicago Press, 2005.

Luebke, David M., *His Majesty's Rebels. Communities, Factions, and Rural Revolt in the Black Forest, 1725–1745*, Ithaca and London: Cornell University Press, 1997.

Midelfort, H. C. Erik, *Witch Hunting in Southwestern Germany, 1562–1684*, Stanford University Press, 1972.

Midelfort, H. C. Erik, *Exorcism and Enlightenment. Johann Joseph Gassner and the Demons of Eighteenth Century Germany*, New Haven and London: Yale University Press, 2005.

Myers, W. David, *"Poor, Sinning Folk" Confession and Conscience in Counter-Reformation Germany*, Ithaca and London: Cornell University Press, 1996.

O'Malley, John, *The First Jesuits*, Cambridge, MA and London: Harvard University Press, 1993.

O'Malley, John, *Trent and All That. Renaming Catholicism in the Early Modern Era*, Cambridge, MA and London: Harvard University Press, 2000.

Patrouch, Joseph F., *A Negotiated Settlement. The Counter-Reformation in Upper Austria under the Habsburgs*, Boston, Leiden, Cologne: Brill, 2000.

Pörtner, Regina, *The Counter-Reformation in Central Europe. Styria 1580–1630*, Oxford University Press, 2001.

Reinhard, Wolfgang "Gegenreformation als Modernisierung? Prolegomena zu einer Theorie des konfessionellen Zeitalters" *Archiv für Reformationsgeschichte* 68 (1977): 226–252.

Reinhard, Wolfgang and Schilling, Heinz (eds), *Die katholische Konfessionalisierung*, Heidelberg: Gütersloher Verlagshaus, 1995.

Roper, Lyndal, *Witch Craze. Terror and Fantasy in Baroque Germany*, New Haven and London: Yale University Press, 2004.

Rothkrug, Lionel, "Popular Religion and Holy Shrines. Their Influence on the Origins of the German Reformation and their Role in German Cultural Development" in *Religion and the People, 800–1700*, James Obelkevich (ed.), Chapel Hill: University of North Carolina Press, 1979.

Sabean, David, *Power in the Blood. Popular Culture and Village Discourse in Early Modern Germany*, Cambridge University Press, 1984.

Schilling, Heinz, "Confessionalization in the Empire: Religious and Societal Change in Germany between 1555 and 1620" in *Religion, Political Culture and the Emergence of Early Modern Society. Essays in German and Dutch History*, Leiden: Brill, 1992; 205–245.

Schindling, Anton and Ziegler, Walter (eds), *Die Territorien des Reichs im Zeitalter der Reformation und Konfessionalisierung. Land und Konfession*, Vols 1–7, Münster: Aschendorff, 1989–1999.

Schmidt, Heinrich Richard, *Konfessionalisierung im 16. Jahrhundert*, Munich: R. Oldenbourg Verlag, 1992.

Schorn-Schütte, Luise, "Priest, Preacher, Pastor: Research on Clerical Office in Early Modern Europe" *Central European History* 33 (2000).

Scribner, Robert W., "Why was there no Reformation in Cologne?" *Bulletin of the Institute of Historical Research* 49 (1976).

Scribner, Robert W., *For the Sake of Simple Folk*, Cambridge University Press, 1981.

Scribner, Robert W., "Ritual and Popular Religion in Catholic Germany at the Time of the Reformation" *Popular Culture and Popular Movements in the Reformation*, London: Hambledon Press, 1987.

Scribner, Robert W., "Communalism: Universal Category or Ideological Construct? A Debate in the Historiography of Early Modern Germany and Switzerland" *Historical Journal* 37, 1 (1994): 199–207.

Smith, Jeffrey Chipps, *Sensuous Worship. Jesuits and the Art of the Early Counter-Reformation in Germany*, Princeton University Press, 2002.

Soergel, Philip, *Wondrous in His Saints. Counter-Reformation Propaganda in Bavaria*, Berkeley: University of California Press, 1993.

Strasser, Ulrike, *State of Virginity. Gender, Religion, and Politics in an Early Modern Catholic State*, Ann Arbor: University of Michigan Press, 2004.

Walker, Mack, *German Home Towns: Community, State, and General Estate, 1648–1871*, Ithaca: Cornell University Press, 1971.

Walker, Mack, *The Salzburg Transaction. Expulsion and Redemption in Eighteenth-Century Germany*, Ithaca and London: Cornell University Press, 1992.

Wilson, Peter, *From Reich to Revolution: German History, 1558–1806*, London: Palgrave, 2004.

Index